International Business

■ GLOBAL MANAGER SERIES ■

International Business

A Manager's Guide to Strategy in the Age of Globalism

Carl A Nelson

INTERNATIONAL THOMSON BUSINESS PRESS
I(T)P® An International Thomson Publishing Company

London • Bonn • Johannesburg • Madrid • Melbourne • Mexico City • New York • Paris
Singapore • Tokyo • Toronto • Albany, NY • Belmont, CA • Cincinnati, OH • Detroit, MI

International Business

I(T)P®   A division of International Thomson Publishing Inc.
The ITP logo is a trademark under licence

British Library Cataloguing-in-Publication Data
A catalogue record for this book is available from the British Library

First edition published 1999

Typeset by J&L Composition Ltd, Filey, North Yorkshire
Printed in the UK by TJ International, Padstow, Cornwall

ISBN 1–86152–315–7

International Thomson Business Press
Berkshire House
168–173 High Holborn
London WC1V 7AA
UK

http://www.itbp.com

DEDICATION

To

Dr. Fred Dow, Ph.D., Professor Emeritus
International Business,
Dr. David Feldman, Ph.D., former Dean of Business,
and
Dr. Dorothy Harris, Ph.D., former Associate Dean of Business,
all of United States International University.
They were the lights who illuminated my way into this field.

Contents

APPENDICES   **253**

Foreword

Periodically someone comes up with a new and innovative approach to understanding the real world. In this case Carl Nelson, for the first time, shows how international business is linked to economic development. Alas, the global business manager awaits the key elements needed to formulate a strategy to take advantage of the opportunities offered by governments!

This book covers the critical material needed to understand how the global business system works. Nelson astutely shows the reader all the business methods by which wealth is exchanged across borders and explains how modern businesses organize for world-class competition. His treatment of impediments to world trade is also uncommon. A discussion of culture is included with the discussion of competing theories and public policies all of which are a basis for world disharmony.

Most interesting is Nelson's introduction of the concept of Artificial Comparative Advantage which allows the global manager to visualize the trade-development linkage and from that to grasp the tools which nations use to control their own destiny. More than 200 countries are all vying to ensure national growth at competitive rates. Carl Nelson shows the steps for structuring harmonious mechanisms within the global context.

I recommend this book to readers across the business communities who want a better understanding about how modern international business really works and the way it will be in the twenty-first Century and the age of globalism.

Michael McManus, Ph.D.
President
The International School of Management
San Diego, California

Preface

Close your eyes. Now allow your mind to have a picture of earth as it was at the beginning of humankind. Can you see the water that covers more than 70 percent of the surface? Do you see the waves splashing upon the shores that surround several large barren islands we now call continents and thousands of smaller ones. Now visualize, over the millenniums, the proliferation and migration of people spreading across the land until today almost every dry mile is inhabited. As the people dispersed they divided the islands into countries and said, "this is my nation to govern." But the ground upon which those people settled was unequally endowed—some had diamonds, some oil, some had nothing except sand, but all had people. For centuries those people struggled to make do with their natural endowments—their leaders chased every new thought process and theory hoping to find the enlightened mechanism that would quickly improve their people's lot. On some of the islands the people's welfare improved, while on others they remain even today abject poor and despicably miserable.

As near term as the seventeenth century most humanity viewed life as short and brutish—and they expected it to remain so. However, during the latter half of the twentieth century the governments of some of those nations that were under-endowed of natural resources (land), human capital (labor), financial capital, management (know-how) and technology discovered a system by which endowments could be artificially enhanced. International trade provided a means to grow economically and their people began to enjoy significantly longer, healthier and more enjoyable lives. They did this by applying a sixth endowment factor we now call "intelligence" (refined data or information). By importing absent endowments and exchanging wealth in the form of products and services with people in other nations who needed them, they ratcheted up national economic performance and improved the general human condition.

This book is about what we know today about how international business works in the "age of globalism." How it serves as the purveyor of wealth across borders, and how that knowledge can help build our own business strategy. But it is also about how cross-border trade is linked to economic development.

Some people in business say "what's economic development have to do with me—why should I care about national growth and international relations?" True, it is not the purpose of private businesses to be involved directly in national economic development. In its origin, free enterprise was just that—provide a product or service in the hope of making a profit. But it turns out that although the profit motive remains unchanged and trade remains generally random, trade flows can be and often are influenced by governments which offer incentives to private businesses to artificially change their country's comparative advantage.

There was a time when international relations was just about "power"—separated in thought from commerce. Now it is about economics which begets power and any business person who develops a strategy to take his or her company into the global arena better understand how enterprise works in relation to governments.

We know now that international business has become an evolving system that serves to change national development by importing absent endowments and exporting the wealth (goods and services) from which those endowments spring. We know cross-border commerce has become the engine of national economic growth and the unquestioned first choice for private sector business expansion. On the top floors of business Brazil, Germany, or Japan voices can be heard, "Go where the people need our products. Go global!"

Now, picture in your mind a spider's web of interconnected businesses overlaying the national boundaries on earth. Do you see network economies, strategic alliances, satellite communications, and cyberspace with capital moving with the speed of light? But also visualize another web of "supra-national" organizations overlaying the spider's web, the purpose of which is to support and encourage the growth of international business but also to establish a harmonized set of rules by which the web can grow fairly. Can you see how complex the layers of webs are? And how complex it is to manage a global business within such a system?

International Business: A Manager's Guide to Strategy in the Age of Globalism is intended to assuage the complexity by "telling it the way it really is." Only then can you develop your strategy to compete. The book is different because it describes international business as a system explaining its parts in relationship to governments in such a way that business people can formulate their global strategy. In it you will find a serving of theory interspersed with practical and antidotal information. Because the book has a distinctly different approach it will not be without controversy as it takes on many of the historical theories of why we trade across borders and offers new approaches heretofore never fully explained. It discusses the tools with which you as a manager must become familiar in order to navigate through the complex layers of international business webs.

If you want to know what globalism is all about this book is for you. Business managers, students, and those who seek careers in international relations and government will find it useful. But it is also for those who just want to know the way international business really works.

As author, I would like who ever reads this book to take away more than notions of how to grow global markets, increase business profits and improve earnings. It is private sector business that initiates international trade; international trade is free enterprise; and free enterprise leads to greater global welfare. It wasn't that long ago that merchants were the least esteemed of any class. However, interdependence has brought them new respect. The modern global business paradigm crosses national borders where we find some companies with greater power even than nations. Therefore, as the next generation of business leaders, you must constantly ask yourself, "What's the purpose of my enterprise? Is it short-term stock valuation? Immediate returns on capital invested? Or is it long-term enterprise survival for the social good?"

Acknowledgments

I am deeply indebted to the following persons who took time to read and critique the draft manuscript: Tino Bartholome, Titus Begmann, Mike Boeling-Messing, Falko Diener, Marc Feuerstein, Oliver Fischer, Aviva Gandelmann, Bettina Kellermann, Nina Alexandra Knebes, Jost Benedikt Koerfer, Phillip Lubos, Jan-Hendrick Maag, Claudia Nanninga, Pia Naumann, Oliver Riedle, Jan Roettgermann, Dirk Ruenz, Ralph Schomburg, Marc Schramm, Maja Sophia Schulte, Marc Stolte, Patrick Strumpf, Thomas Termeer, Eick-Hendrlk von Ramin, Dirk Zimmermann, Steven E. Young, Dan Konnerth, Kirk Anthony Delmas, Jose D. Bustos, David G. Kotrady, J.M. Jorgensen, John Bradley, Ted Kozlow, Ernesto Acosta, Bob Lucin, Paul Straud, Jim Melvin, Rick Whipple, Stuart Siegel, Elizabeth M. (Goldman) Cushinsky, Editors: Julian Thomas, So-Shan Au, Lisa J. Williams and Marketing Manager, Jacqui Baldwin. My thanks also to McGraw-Hill and the UN for their permission to reproduce material from their publications.

About the author

Carl Nelson has more than 40 years of global experience in government and private business. This experience includes having lived and worked for two years in Japan, one year in South Vietnam, and being intimately knowledgeable about the Western Pacific and the Indian Ocean area. His early career took him to Northern European and Mediterranean nations. His experience also includes third-world economic development under the Agency for International Development (USAID) and Mexican *maquiladora* operations. As a specialist in international economics and trade, Carl is listed in Who's Who in California and Who's Who in the World.

Dr. Carl A. Nelson, a former Captain in the United States Navy, is professor of international business at the School of International Management (ISM), San Diego where he teaches graduate level courses. He previously taught at United States International University (USIU), University of Redlands, and Webster University and served on the faculties of the U.S. Military Academy at West Point and the U.S. Naval Academy at Annapolis, Maryland.

Dr. Nelson is also president of Global Business Systems (GBS), an international business consulting and training company. He specializes in presenting seminars and workshops on the basics and advanced business applications of global trade. He has given these seminars to Asian, American, Mexican, and Russian business persons.

His international experience is complemented by his academic training. He earned his Doctorate in Business Administration (D.B.A.), Finance, (emphasis on international finance and trade) from the United States International University in San Diego, California. He was recognized by USIU with its 1989 outstanding alumni award. Dr. Nelson is also a graduate of the Naval War College (C&S) at Newport, R.I., holds a Master of Science degree in Management (Economics/Systems Analysis) from the Naval Post Graduate School in Monterey, California, and a Bachelor of Science degree (Engineering) from the U.S. Naval Academy at Annapolis, Maryland.

PART ONE

Setting the scene for the twenty-first century

Introduction

> More businessmen in all countries should seize the opportunities of the market—it is the entrepreneur who must initiate production and trade that leads to greater welfare.
>
> *Jan Pen (Former Professor of Economics and Director of Economic Policy The Netherlands.)*

Today, the nations of earth are interdependent. It is not a condition that will happen in the future. Some call it "Space Ship Earth," the "Global Village," or the "World Economy"—no matter what it's called the "age of globalism" is here and is a condition which will continue to dominate world economics into the twenty-first century and beyond.

As a result of this modern phenomena, the opportunities for world trade expansion have never been greater. Children in Pakistan wear Levis, the Chinese have satellite television, and American housewives stretch their budgets by purchasing less expensive goods imported from overseas. Businesses from all over the world have crossed national borders and invaded global markets.

Background

Think about it, before and during the first half of the twentieth-century, say from 1900–1945, with few exceptions, businesses anywhere in the world were only local or at most regional. Beginning sharply after World War II businesses followed the expansion of the highway systems of their respective countries and began to develop markets across their nation. However about 25 years after World War II, say about 1965, the balances of international trade, particularly among the newly industrialized nations, grew sharply and they remain vibrant today. New nation-states sprang into life during the 1989–1991 Eastern European political revolutions ready to join the evolving global business system. At the same time economic revolutions created trade blocs for a "new Europe" and a changing North American business structure. The globalism invasion was underway!

The future is not uncertain. Let there be no doubt about that. Just as the genie of democracy is out of the bottle, so are the genies of globalism and interdependence, and they cannot be put back. The global movement is irreversible and international business has become the last commercial frontier to conquer before interspacial trade.

Globalism and interdependence means that the worldwide policies of businesses and nations tend towards more openness in economic co-operation, collaboration, and coordination. The leaders of the many global businesses which have emerged understand that the freer system has brought incredible growth of international trade and investment. The global movement has also caused governments to realize that the "new economic age" will bring even more interdependence of businesses and national economies, and that the greatest gains come not from conflict but from a harmonious system.

Today no citizenry can focus only on their own enterprise or economy because all nations benefit from the interdependence of global finance, trade, and the supporting supranational organizations. An understanding of global business as a system is a requisite to building a strategy— those who don't are seriously handicapped and most probably will not be able to cope.

As a result there is a growing interest from executives and managers, as well as students who plan to enter a business career or work for governments and supranational organizations, in activities that relate to the international system. Enrollments in courses that explain global business are up because people wish to be able to interpret global economic events in terms of their own complex business strategies.

For 40 years my work took me to the Pacific Rim. I lived in Japan for two years and often visited the "Four Tigers." I observed how a mixture of planning, free enterprise, and exporting changed those nations. In the past, economic growth theory advocated "pushing" the development of the domestic market, but the "new economic growth model" that I observed worked in reverse. By making things and selling those things wherever in the world people could afford them, foreign currency was brought back to improve the welfare of the domestic population. International trade "pulled" newly industrialized countries (NIC) such as Taiwan, South Korea, and Singapore into the mainstream of economic growth.

From this export-oriented mechanism came growing similarities of world cultures and that portends greater harmony and even less chance of war. It would seem, then, that greater interdependence of nations is good for business and humankind.

Today, too many managers worldwide fail to understand the importance of the international business bridge. Too many can't seem to visualize it as a system that is evolving and continually maturing.

International business cannot be understood in isolation. It must also include its relationship to government and economic development.

Those who teach economics and those who practice business have differing points of view. The first attempts to come to grips with the more theoretical micro and macro aspects of economics. They study numbers and attempt to make sense of the real world. Business, on the other hand, lives in a real world of profits and losses. Their job is to distinguish the elements of the successful enterprise where there are ups and downs and winners and loosers—a zero sum game. In their environment there is no money for some but for others there is always money, even where there appears to be none.

The subject of this book is business, not economics. Key words include: global business, international business, transnational commerce, international trade, and profits and losses. In practice these words connote a bridge between the domestic markets of one nation and the domestic markets of another. This book seeks to explain that bridging system as an evolving worldwide process and the essential element to the development of an international business strategy.

Concept

The concept of *International Business: A Manager's Guide to Strategy in the Age of Globalism* is to explain to managers, in a universal way, how the international business system works so that business strategy can be formulated. Strategy is about predicting the future and setting about to put in place activities based on what is expected to occur. Only by understanding the global business system can managers project changes and make adjustments.

Theme

Global business is fraught with conflict, confusion, and competition at national borders, yet its growth is dynamic, pervasive, and the struggle for harmony is continuous.

Approach

The approach is to show the holistic system and its parts that overlay nation-state boundaries and permit wealth to be exchanged across those borders and to understand the various processes at work to improve cross-border business. From this study the global manager is better prepared to formulate the firm's strategy.

International Business: A Manager's Guide to Strategy in the Age of Globalism presents all the material found in traditional international business books but does not follow the traditional treatment which compartmentalizes the subject into "trade and investment" in an undefined environment. Rather, this book deals with the subject strategically in terms of how businesses interact with governments that attempt to use laws to manipulate business for their own nation-state's economic self-interest. In other words this book seeks to show global business in its relative position among governments and supranational organizations in their quest to develop economically. It treats the subject in terms of how enterprises and governments interact for their own economic self-interest yet attempt to harmonize barrier disputes.

Audience

This book is for a universal audience. It differs from others in that it is aimed at a variety of readers who seek to better understand what is happening as we enter the twenty-first century. These are executives and managers as well as students of business, economics, government, and international relations who need a basic understanding of global business as an adjunct to their growth.

International Business: A Manager's Guide to Strategy in the Age of Globalism is for all forward-thinking people interested in international trade: entrepreneurs, managers and decision makers. But, the book is particularly useful for those small and medium-sized manufacturing and service companies who are ready for new international challenges.

Scope

The book covers all aspects of modern international business including the melting of the U.S.S.R. into the free world market and the expansion of regional economic integrations such as EC-92 and NAFTA.

What is different about this book?

International Business: A Manager's Guide to Strategy in the Age of Globalism is significantly different from any other international business book because, for the first time, it shows how trade is tied to economic development with its linkages to government. Early economic trade theorists did not consider economic development, but this book shows in a practical way that the two are inseparable.

Special features

- for a universal audience;
- has a global setting;
- explains international business as a system;
- connects the subject to strategic planning;
- reviews the context of the global business system;
- shows how international trade is linked to economic development;

- explains, as a learning device, the framework called artificial comparative advantage (ACA) which is used to understand the interaction of governments to business in the global business system;
- explains the means of economic exchange across national borders in terms of the enterprise versus government;
- reveals the many aspects of the global harmonization process;
- includes discussion of economic integrations such as EU, APEC, and NAFTA;
- discusses the public policy issues with which managers must be concerned;
- reviews the primary means by which trade and investment are exchanged among nations;
- shows the importance of understanding culture and behavior;
- puts into context the supranational organizations that provide the glue for the global business system.

How this book is organized

It is impossible to study all aspects of the international business system at the same time. Therefore, the book is organized into four major parts as they relate to the bridging of international economic wealth across borders and the concomitant growth development that results. Even though treated separately, each part is interdependent of the others and the intent of the book is for the reader to visualize the synergy of a whole system.

Part One, "Setting the Scene for the Twenty-first Century," explains the evolving global business system in the context of the confusion and competition it faces at borders as well as the harmonious system intended to overcome that dilemma. It also introduces the various mechanisms by which global wealth is exchanged. All this is accomplished in four chapters: Chapter One discusses global business as a system and offers important definitions; Chapter Two reviews for the reader the different methods by which economic wealth is exchanged across national borders; Chapter Three offers methods to organize the global firm, and Chapter Four shows the reader modern worldwide sourcing.

Part Two, "Disharmony at the Borders" discusses the origin of border friction. Chapter Five gives a snap-shot of the implications of diverse cultural behavior. Chapter Six narrates early conflicting trade beliefs in terms of "classical" theories. Chapter Seven is about competing economic development theories. Chapter Eight reviews the opposing public policy issues facing global businesses.

Part Three, "Competition at the Borders," relates the exchange of wealth (products and services) across borders in terms of the give and take of government incentives and barriers intended to artificially stimulate the growth of their economies. Chapter Nine links trade to development and offers a new paradigm called artificial comparative advantage (ACA). Chapter Ten explains the various schemes nations used to induce trade and investment. Chapter Eleven deals with the distortions caused by trade barriers.

Part Four, "In Search of Harmony," outlines the system of supra-national organizations that function to negotiate fair trade, investment policies and laws among nations, including the various forms of economic integration and cooperation. Chapter Twelve explains the World Monetary System and its subsystems. Chapter Thirteen describes the elements of trade harmonization, and Chapter Fourteen examines regional economic integration as part of the harmonization process.

Global business: an evolving system

International trade is, by definition, trade with foreigners.

*Jan Pen (Former Professor of Economics and
Director of Economic Policy, The Netherlands.)*

Part One consists of four chapters, which when tied together explain the major elements of the evolving global business system. The business manager of today is faced with confusion and competition as well as attempts to bring harmony and has several mechanisms at his or her disposal to exchange wealth across borders. In this part we discuss each of these elements as follows:

■ Chapter 1 The Evolving System
■ Chapter 2 The Means of Wealth Exchange
■ Chapter 3 Organizing For World-Class Business
■ Chapter 4 Sourcing Globally

The theme of this book is that, in the age of globalism, cross-border business (trade and investment) is an evolving system which is fraught with both confusion, conflict and competition at national borders. Nevertheless, its growth in the twenty-first century will be dynamic, pervasive, and the struggle for harmony continuous. The concept of the book is that global strategy cannot be formulated unless the global business system is understood.

This *global business system* is the support system that overarches nation-states and their national economies and harmonizes business methods, rules, and processes that permit greater flows of wealth across borders. Because national borders do not always coincide with economic borders this system is a growing movement toward a linkage of the economies.

To formulate a business strategy that keeps your firm in global competition the system must be understood.

Why?

Because doing business in more than one country is complex. Cross-border business is about interaction with foreigners. They belong to another nation, speak strange languages, use different currencies, socialize differently, and their politics, laws and governments differ. New trade and investment rules are negotiated at increasing pace, causing global businesses to change strategies rapidly. Nation-states continue to spring to life or disappear almost daily. Some grow rapidly while others stagnate. Supranational organizations such as the World Trade Organization, the World Bank, and the International Monetary Fund are involved and add to the complexity. Therefore, international business cannot be studied in isolation—it must be understood in its relationship with the world political system.

Despite this complexity and diversity, economic transfer is taking place at increasingly greater volumes and is given credit for the flourishment of world economic development. The term commonly used to describe this growth phenomena is globalism.

Globalism

Globalism has many meanings. First, it is used in the sense of a movement or a trend, something in motion. Some say "the world is getting smaller." Another use of the term has to do with businesses that view their market in a global context as opposed to a national or domestic sense. Finally, there is its use as it relates to commonalty or standardization of production practices, products, and services across many different countries.

Interdependence

Interdependence is the notion that individual businesses, products, and national economies are no longer independent in their operations but are reliant to some extent on the commingling of the economies, business and products of other nations. Because there are no autarkies all nations benefit from interdependence.

Difference between globalism and interdependence

Globalism does not equate to interdependence because the latter implies a pervasive commingling that transcends control by political forces but also implies a need for greater cooperation and collaboration. Globalism in itself may simply be the act of independently extending business operations across as many borders as possible.

Background: growth of global business

As a matter of understatement, what began when ancient gatherers on the continent of Africa exchanged their excess with neighboring foragers has greatly expanded. Over time the evolutionary process swelled as early humans formed tribes and sent adventurers beyond their forests, their land borders, and finally their shores. Eventually the Pharaohs of Egypt sent camel caravans tramping the continent and Persians sent buyers to China. Then the likes of Vasco de Gama, Columbus and Magellan began crossing oceans. In the period 1500–1800 Western Europe established empires and colonies to support their international trade reach and, before we realized, 5000 years of international trade history was behind us.

Figure 1.1 shows roughly the growth of gross global product (GGP) and international trade over time. The curve of gross global trade (GGT) was essentially flat until the late 1800s when the development of Clipper Ships changed the slope. The curve sprang to life about the turn of the twentieth century and took a dynamic upward bend as the technology revolution heated up. Steam-powered ships with range were followed by the innovation of international radio. The invention of the Otto and

Figure 1.1 Technology and growth over time

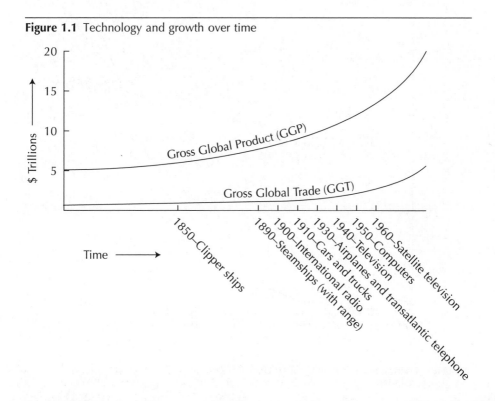

Diesel cycles brought trucks, then airplanes. Then came television, computers and satellites and the boom was here.

The explosion

The most revolutionary stage of earth's history occurred during the period from 1945 to the present when we put to better use technology and began freeing markets.

But the real explosion of international trade didn't begin until about 1965, twenty years after World War II. Like spring, all over the globe economies awakened from a sleep caused by the ravages of death and destruction. The boom came after production capability had been restored and when people wanted more of everything. Figure 1.2 shows the growth of world exports in U.S. dollars since about 1950 and highlights the dynamic increase of the most recent twenty years. The curve would be even more dramatic except the data does not include the

Figure 1.2 Growth of world exports

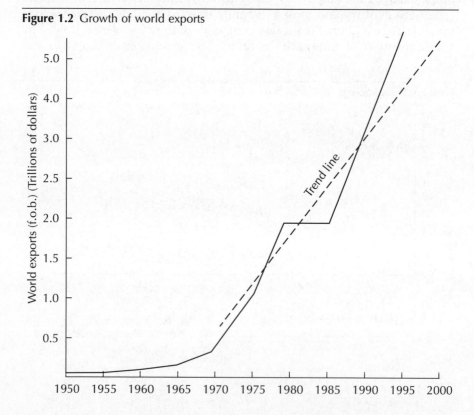

Source: Constructed by the author from United Nations annual reports 1983 through 1989 and International Monetary Fund statistics 1948 through 1989. Not adjusted for real dollars.

financial flows of foreign direct investment (FDI) nor trade among the non-market countries. Even though there have been regional economic set-backs, like the American recession of the early 1980s, and the Asian problem of the late 1990s which cause flat periods, the overall trend-line is dynamically upward.

The United Nations uses several currency conversion rates to measure gross global product (GGP) (a discussion of the alternative currency conversion rates is offered in Appendix C). Figure 1.3 shows the growth of GGP as it expanded at a sixfold rate during the twenty-year period 1970 through 1989 (expressed in U.S. dollars). Despite population growth, world percapita rates are expanding at essentially the same pace as GGP.

Figure 1.4 is an extrapolation and extension of Figure 1.3. It shows that gross world product could be as much as $100 trillion by the middle of the twenty-first century, much of which is attributed to the growth of global trade. If this forecast comes true earth will have experienced the greatest wealth expansion in the history of humankind.

The world has now experienced 50 years of freeing trade during which time world output has expanded sixfold and world trade has expanded fourteenfold. In 1950, only seven percent of world output

Figure 1.3 Growth of gross global product 1970–1989

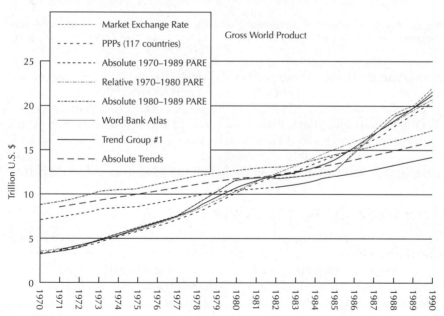

Source: Trends in international distribution of gross world product, Special Issue National Accounts Statistics, Series X No. 18, Department for Economic and Social Information and Policy Analysis, Statistical Division, United Nations, New York, 1993. Reproduced with permission.

Figure 1.4 Growth of gross global product

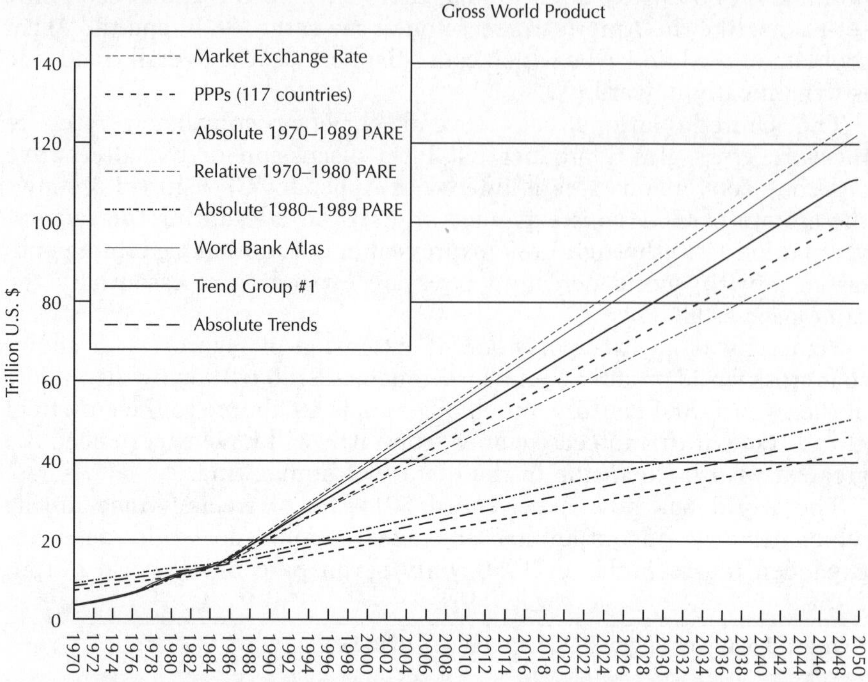

Gross World Product

Source: Trends in international distribution of gross world product, Special Issue National Accounts Statistics, Series X No. 18, Department for Economic and Social Information and Policy Analysis, Statistical Division, United Nations, New York, 1993. Reproduced with permission.

was attributed to international trade. Today that figure is 23 percent and the OECD predicts it could approach 50 percent by 2020.

But, the real evidence of wealth is the growth of the world's middle class. People in Asia and South America as well as parts of Eastern Europe are experiencing changes in their lives never before expected. They now have the wealth to be credible consumers of the things most people want— cars, homes, modern household goods and the education of their children.

Free trade the wealth driver

Free trade is a theoretical concept that assumes international trade should be guided by the "invisible hand" of the market unhampered by government measures such as tariffs or non-tariff barriers. Often attributed to Adam Smith, an eighteenth-century economist, this utopian idea implies no regulation by governments. Those who espouse it believe that market forces by themselves determine the outcome of business success. Most practical business managers view the term "free trade" simply as a goal.

Realistic thinkers understand that pure *laissez-faire* cross-border business activity is unattainable. They see the objective of trade liberalization is to achieve "freer trade" because it is generally recognized among trade policy officials that some restrictions on trade are likely to remain in effect for the foreseeable future.

Fair trade, on the other hand, has two definitions. The first is the concept that all nations should operate under the same set of international trade and investment rules, i.e. a common commercial code. The second definition occurs when one nation unilaterally imposes or threatens reciprocal action on the businesses of another nation which have caused a distortion of the international trade and investment markets with whom the first nation could not get agreement. The unilateral implications of "fair trade" actions are protectionist and are often claimed to be taken only to "level the playing field."

Wealth is exchanged among nations by several mechanisms (discussed at length in Chapter Two) but the strongest mechanism has been the growing number of individual global businesses.

The global business

For the purposes of this book the definition of business is: "Make and/or sell goods or services for profit in a global context." The organizations that adhere to this definition are called *global businesses*.

The global business is one that has a worldwide point of view and makes no distinction between domestic and international business. In practical terms it may favor one market region over another, but that is probably a result of early growth—emerging from the imprint of its founding country or more probably because of some tax or investment advantage. A global viewpoint eventually invades every business decision that effects the bottom line. Leaders are selected for the organization because of their international experience and their espoused agreement with this viewpoint. Products and raw materials are marketed and sourced on a worldwide basis and staff have global responsibilities.

Kenichi Ohmae (1990) and others have offered that for companies to grow in the global market they must adopt the concept of *equidistant economic denationalization*, that is, their operations become country neutral in terms of headquarters, personnel, production, and sales. Figure 1.5 demonstrates this concept of equidistant thinking.

Complexity at the borders

Global business does not exist freely across borders. As shown in Figure 1.6, private businesses experience complexity at the borders of other

Figure 1.5 Equidistant global strategic vision

Figure 1.6 Complexity at the border

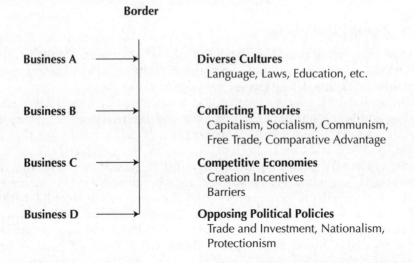

countries in the form of cultural differences, conflicting trade theories, competing development theories, and opposing political policies.

The concept that charity begins at home is alive and well. A nation's economy is under the care of economic physicians called politicians and they determine what happens as things and people cross political borders. The health of a national economy comes into conflict with that of the overlaying global business system when the welfare of those within a nation are at issue.

Some use the term "economic development" only in the sense of the struggle of those nations that are less developed in terms of relative personal living standards. But, development is the primary concern of every national government and is the summation of those complex factors of infrastructure, human health and education, as well as capital which permits people to achieve a higher living standard.

Economic growth is the way economic development is measured. It tends to be measured in terms of nation-states, but can be measured in terms of global growth. Growth is typically measured as a percentage of improvement of gross domestic product over historical norms, but is being measured more and more as gross global product including the benefits of cross-border trade.

The emotions of *nationalism* conflict with business profits at the borders of nation-states. In order to influence the economic destiny of their state, governments develop interstate controls that give and take away as conditions change.

Interstate controls are the laws, regulations, procedures, and practices between nations or economic unions of nations that inhibit or stimulate "free trade." Some controls are *barriers* which cause significant distortions to free trade while, at the same time, others are stimulants in the form of *incentives*, thus, controls may be visualized as having a part in driving economic growth.

All sovereign nations, to some extent control the flow of goods, thought, services, funds, freedom of movement, etc. across their borders. Not all barriers are bad; not all stimulants are good. For instance public health conditions in one nation may dictate certain barriers to free trade that may differ from another.

Barriers as used in this book are the laws, rules, and business practices imposed at and within the borders of one nation to *restrict* the success of businesses of another nation. Their intent is sometimes innocent, but more often are designed to keep global businesses out in order to protect domestic businesses.

Protectionism is the deliberate use or encouragement of barrier restrictions on imports to enable inefficient domestic producers to compete successfully with foreign producers.

For purposes of explanation, incentives are the various laws and rules, exceptions to laws and rules, and financial "carrots" offered by governments to stimulate or create global business and trade. These schemes are designed to encourage foreign businesses to operate in a given country for purposes of economic development and growth.

Visualizing the single harmonizing system

To provide harmonious support for global businesses a system of supranational and supra-regional organizations has evolved. Granted, a world government as such does not exist, and the system is mainly a set of gentlemen's agreements. Nevertheless, it does function and is operational in a relatively efficient way. One way to visualize the single system is shown pictorially in Figure 1.7. It shows supra-national and supra-regional organizations, and bilateral arrangements as umbrellas overarching a box containing a web of private global businesses such as multinational corporations and private trading companies.

All nations have interstate controls; however, the laws, regulations, procedures and practices vary among the states often making it difficult

Figure 1.7 Global harmonization system

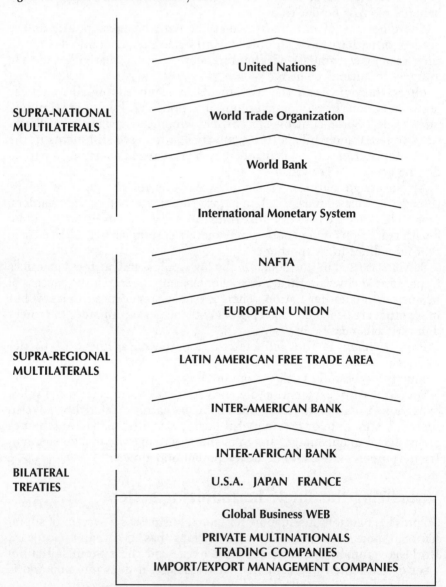

for businesses to operate on a global basis. Interstate controls cause conflict when they restrain free trade and investment to the extent that there are major distortions. This can lead toward protectionism, depression, and war.

Harmonization is the process of defining in peaceful, cooperative negotiations a common set of rules and procedures so that international trade and investment can be progressive and without conflict.

Many people believe the key to peace is contented people—they don't fight. Therefore, the notion of supra-national organizations offers opportunities for harmonization. As an example there have been inspirations by intellectuals to establish strong global supra-national organizations to administer the harmonization process. Some, like the League of Nations, have failed. Others, like the United Nations and the World Trade Organization (formerly the General Agreement on Tariffs and Trade (GATT)), still exist under the hope that sovereign nations might see fit to make them work.

The harmonization support system, a supra-national/regional environment that transcends every nation's political and social limits and its thrust toward harmony is continuous and evolving. This system which overlays nation–state boundaries and permits cross-border trade and investment to take place is also synergistic, that is, the whole is greater that its parts. Not all nations are full-fledged members—some are only partial members and a few continue to stay on an inward, protectionist course. Nevertheless, each year, the global business system becomes more formalized and trusted and all nations benefit from the system.

There are about 200 sovereign nations in the world (including the former Soviet members). Of those, about 132 are members of the World Trade Organization (WTO), about 170 are members of the United Nations, and 160 are members of the World Bank and the International Monetary Fund (IMF). In addition to these large supra-national support organizations, there are an untold number of smaller regional alliances, treaties, and unions both public and private that draw the interchange of global business into a more cooperative and coordinated sphere.

We do know there are no autarkies; therefore, whether official members or not, all nations benefit from the interdependence of global trade and the supporting organizations.

Summary

During the course of the last half of the twentieth century international trade has become the engine of world development. Private sector enterprises known as "global businesses" have been the dominant mechanism for the exchange of this global wealth, and to do so they must develop strategies to extend their business through the web of complexity brought about by differing national cultures and political systems. As a result of the dynamic growth of global trade a system has evolved which attempts to harmonize the rules of inter-state business, thus fostering even more international trade. This system includes the several supra-national organizations such as the WTO, United Nations and others.

Caution!

Business is inherently competitive and, even with level playing fields, there will always be winners and losers.

The next chapter reviews the different methods by which global wealth is exchanged across borders.

CHAPTER TWO

Means of wealth exchange

To maintain a leadership position in any one developed country a business . . . increasingly has to attain and hold leadership positions in all developed countries world-wide. It has to be able to do research, to design, to develop, to engineer and to manufacture in any part of the developed world, and to export from any developed country to any other. It has to go transnational.

Peter F. Drucker (Clarke Professor of Social Sciences at the Claremont Graduate School.)

Of course, there cannot be a global business system and trade cannot make a contribution to the economic growth of nations unless there is a means for the wealth of one nation, in terms of product, services, and financial flows, to be exchanged across national borders.

Modern wealth exchange

Wealth exchange is the result of enterprises (public and private) within one country making a good or service and transferring that good or service to enterprises within other countries for currency or counter-trade. We also mean the physical movement or transferral of the factors of endowment from one country to another. Figure 2.1 reminds us that those factors—land (natural resources in the form of raw materials), labor (human capital), financial capital, know-how (management), technology, and intelligence—are *fully mobile* in the modern world.

This chapter deals with the exchange process in two parts:

1 the business vehicles for making and selling goods or services;
2 the modern logistics methods used to physically move the goods.

Background

It was not that long ago that merchants obtained capital to invest in new voyages by giving notes, and using profits from successful voyages to supply the interest and pay off the loans. In this way, or by buying a

Figure 2.1 Factors of endowment

- LAND   (RAW MATERIALS)

- LABOR   (HUMAN CAPITAL)

- CAPITAL   (FINANCIAL)

- KNOW-HOW   (MANAGEMENT)

- TECHNOLOGY

- INTELLIGENCE

THEN CAME FACTOR MOBILITY

fractional interest in a particular ship for a specific voyage, a village cooperated to exchange their goods with those from another land by investing in the enterprises of the very ships they helped to build.

Success of a trading voyage in those days depended principally upon the captains of the ships who expedited exchange (commerce) in addition to being master of the vessel. A day or two prior to the sailing a letter would be given to the captain, which would have been phrased in broad terms, leaving him ample room for maneuver. The instructions sometimes expressed no more than pious hopes of what might be achieved in the course of the voyage. Concern for the ability to finance a new adventure, to preserve the safety of the one underway, or to stave off a sudden crisis became a part of the trading frame of mind and dominated mercantile thinking well into the nineteenth century. According to the code, the merchant's word was his bond.

Means of wealth exchange

Today the means of exchanging goods, services, and investment has become very sophisticated with many routinized processes that are well understood across the globe. The dominant portion of the economic transfer across national and economic borders is the result of private business transactions using practical methods perfected during hundreds of years of experience.

Wealth transfer across borders is a random process conducted for profit. It is virtually impossible to precisely measure and analyze the exchange because of the volume of the spider's web of activity and the fact that enterprises change their means to take advantage of trade creation opportunities or to counter barriers.

Individuals, through portfolio investment, account for a larger and larger portion of wealth transfer; however, multinational corporations

(MNC) or global businesses (GB) from almost every nation are still the dominant vehicle. Other major vehicles are trading intermediaries, the largest of which, like the Japanese *sogo shosha*, are multi-billion dollar enterprises. Banks provide a service to private savers as well as firms and therefore are in themselves a vehicle for economic transfer. Public and private investors use the services of global stock markets and thus contribute to the economic transfer system.

"Multinational corporation" is a term used to explain a giant company of an industrialized nation with multi-country affiliates which may or not formulate their own business strategy. By broadest definition, these are large enterprises with production facilities in at least two countries. For some they were the colonial style companies of the 1960s and 1970s perceived to have raped and pillaged Third World countries of their resources and remitted shameful profits to their home bases in industrialized nations.

Global businesses, on the other hand, differ from the MNC in that the GBs are no longer locked into the definition that explains them as giant companies born in an industrialized nation. More often they are smaller firms from developed and less-developed countries alike that have learned from the MNCs. They are thrusting towards globalness and have tailored an incremental strategy, country-by-country adopting whatever tactics best suits that company.

The wealth exchange bridge

Wealth exchange can be pictured as if it were a bridge across borders (land, sea, or air) that has three levels, each level increasingly more complex than the one below. The transaction level can be viewed as the mechanics of everyday cross-border operations. The next highest level, and therefore more complex, is the tactics level, i.e. the organizational means whereby exchange takes place. The third and highest, and most complex, level are the strategies and policies that overlay and govern the lower two levels of the bridge.

As shown in Figure 2.2, the bridge levels are bounded at national borders by interstate controls: "incentives" and "barriers" which stimulate trade at the same time as they diminish it.

Transaction level of wealth exchange

The first level includes those elements of exchange at the basic level of cross-border management which lead to the actual transaction:

■ the product;
■ making contacts in foreign countries;
■ conducting market research;

Figure 2.2 Wealth exchange bridge

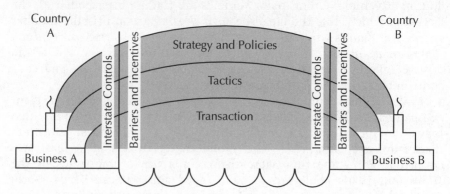

- pricing;
- market planning and execution;
- negotiations;
- property rights;
- communications;
- travel;
- transaction finance;
- risk avoidance/management;
- physical distribution;
- documentation;
- understanding national export/import rules, country-by-country.

Tactical level of wealth exchange

The methods of cross-border entry into another country can be viewed as the tactics of global trade and investment. They are:

- export;
- import;
- the use of intermediaries such as trading companies and export management companies (EMC);
- form associations;
- start a firm (wholly owned);
- acquire a firm (wholly owned);
- merger;
- joint venture;
- franchise;
- market subsidiary;
- licensing;
- direct mail;

- production sharing;
- multilevel marketing;
- influencing trade by being a change agent;
- transformation of goods.

Strategy and policy level of wealth exchange

Governments attempt to artificially steer and guide the development of nations. Political motives vary, but in general the intent is to ensure that whatever wealth accrues within the borders is distributed according to the needs and preferences of the people of the sovereign lands. In practice the preferences of people in countries vary greatly.

Some country markets are freer than others and regulation of international trade varies. None adhere to pure *laissez-faire* trade policies. Most governments manipulate the market in major ways.

It is not unusual that nations formulate complex growth development strategies which include regulation of interstate trade; therefore, as expressed earlier, global trade is inseparably linked to economic development. The primary influence of country strategy and policy is usually a combination of theories, that is, whatever works for a given nation. One of three country strategic approaches are generally taken:

- *Inward looking*: protectionist, independent of the global economic system.
- *Outward looking*: free traders, competition welcoming, integral part of the global economic system.
- *Mixture* of inward/outward.

Global businesses adjust their strategies and policies to take best advantage of changing government maneuvers. Table 2.1 shows how businesses match strategies with country strategies.

Country risk

Of course, in addition to consideration of the country strategic approaches, business strategy must also consider *country risk*. Country risk most often conveys a negative connotation related to major political

Table 2.1 Matching business strategy to country strategy/policy

Country strategy/policy	Company strategy
Inward looking	Outsider
Outward looking	Insider
Mixture	Risk sharing/learning

events such as coups and wars; however, it is perceived by private business and governments alike in more complex terms than just politics. Analysis of country risk is a calculation of the impact of the following factors on wealth exchange:

- *Political stability*: war, revolution, coups, etc.
- *Economic or financial*: balance of payments, high inflation, repayment of loans.
- *Labor conditions*: strikes, militant workers.
- *Legal*: changing laws, taxes, tariff, quotas, permits, currency convertibility.
- *Terrorism*.

There is a long list of methodologies used to analyze country risk. They are measured either quantitatively ("hard", "objective"), qualitatively ("soft", "subjective"), or mixed data to assess, forecast, and manage the risk of doing business in certain countries. Typically these studies focus on government actions.

Soft data is based on expert advice of the "old hands" who know what is going on in a given nation.

Hard data (dominated by the banking industry) is the result of quantifying data in indices and using econometric models, computer models and statistical appraisals to ranking countries. In reality, country risk is about the relationship of the mix of the above factors to the economy and it greatly influences wealth exchange by global businesses.

Extrapolating exchange tactics

Obviously country risk is a major element to developing the appropriate exchange tactic for a given nation, but just as many enterprise decisions are based on economic development schemes presented by governments.

By closely monitoring and analyzing changing government strategic approaches modern enterprises attempt to proactively anticipate government strategy/policy changes, identify profitable ventures, and thereby satisfy owner expectations. As it expands its international reach, the strategic decision of global businesses (GB) to enter a country requires an examination of the laws and regulations and the underlying concepts generally professed by local government strategy/policy makers. By extrapolation, enterprises decide whether to do business in a given country at all and, if so, design wealth transfer tactics that accommodate those strategies. In other words, enterprise managers monitor for changes in the political thinking of the rulers of nations, then tailor exchange strategies and tactics, country by country.

Matching tactics to country strategies

Corporate wealth exchange strategies and tactics vary according to country strategies and risk. In other words, if a nation's strategy or risk factors change, wealth transfer must be appropriate and match that strategy with applicable tactics. Table 2.2 shows how these tactics relate to country strategy/policy and risk factors. Many of these tactics may be used for more than one purpose.

Outsider tactics

Outsider tactics are those which keep wealth exchange of one company at arm's length from those of another nation because that country's strategic approach is inward looking, protectionist and independent of the global economic system. Outsider tactics include: exporting (international marketing), importing, forming associations, using intermediaries, licensing, and direct mail.

Exporting (international marketing)

Most nations support exporting as a strategy because when home products are exported jobs stay at home, foreign currency is induced, and it has a positive effect on the nation's balance of payments.

Exporting is the process of selling a product or service from a manufacturing base in one country to customers in another country. This tactic is most successful when:

■ the home currency (exchange rate) is weak against the importing country's currency;
■ the product life cycle can be extended;
■ the importing country has low tariff barriers;
■ consumers are inclined to buy goods from foreign countries;

Table 2.2 Matching major enterprise tactics to national strategy/policy and risk

Insider	Risk sharing/learning	Outsider
Start a firm	Marketing subsidiary	Exporting
Acquire a firm	Production sharing	Importing
Merger	Partnering	Associations
Joint venture		Intermediaries
Franchise		License
		Direct mail
		Transformation

- there is encouragement to import by a foreign government;
- there is high country risk;
- diversification of financial risk across a broader market is important.

Importing (global sourcing)

Today, people care little about where a product is made, only that there is a need, it is good quality, the right price, and stable production. Therefore economic exchange includes a mix of foreign and domestic content. Most modern sourcing programs are complex in that they involve make or buy and just-in-time decisions (discussed more fully in Chapter Four). Success using this tactic requires consideration of lower costs of production or higher quality inputs than can be obtained in the domestic market.

Form associations

A useful concept for wealth exchange is the formation of associations for export. In the United States, the law is titled the Export Trading Company Act of 1982. It is extremely flexible and permits, with agreement of the government, the formation of very creative organizations or associations to compete in cross-border trade. Many countries have similar laws. By joining with banks and other firms, smaller companies share costs, knowledge, and other capabilities to achieve economies of scale in order to gain an international foothold. The law provides a wide range of methods to circumvent anti-trust laws. Other countries have similar laws. The largest of associations are the Japanese *Keiretsu* system that include giant groups of firms such as Mitsubishi, Mitsui, and Sumitomo which are multi-billion dollar enterprises.

Advantages of forming associations

Associations afford several advantages for economic transfer, all of which come by way of joint export activities.

- *Barriers*. Firms can end-run non-tariff trade barriers by sharing costs of difficult foreign government labeling, packaging and quality requirements.
- *Bidding*. By teaming-up, firms can respond to foreign orders which might exceed the capacity or capability of any single firm.
- *Capital*. Greater funds in the form of equity can be brought to export activities by bank participation.
- *Economies of scale*. Joint venture agreements between domestic companies to compete internationally bring increased efficiency.

■ *Market research.* Firms that join together share the costs of foreign market research, and travel.
■ *Market entry and development.* Firms with complementary products can achieve cost reductions for advertising, trade shows, missions and other joint activities.
■ *Shipping.* Carriers will negotiate lower discounts and longer rate contracts because joint arrangements can provide needed volume and scheduling guarantees.

Using intermediaries

The use of intermediaries offers several advantages and any examination of the process of establishing a cross-border wealth exchange includes the possibility of using an intermediary. They often offer the quickest way to get started with minimum outlay of capital. Equally as important is the ability of the exporter to observe and learn about how to do business in another country before committing to an insider strategy.

Intermediaries come in several forms: general trading companies; export trading companies; import/export management companies; and even "piggybacking" with a large multinational firm.

Advantages of using an intermediary

The primary reasons for using intermediaries are:

■ They conserve financial resources (out-of-pocket cash flow) that would otherwise be consumed during the years that your firm took to develop its own international marketing department.
■ Export sales come quicker because intermediaries already have agents, distributors and customers in place.
■ Firms learn by observing the professionals in order to eventually develop their own international department.
■ Intermediaries save time by concentrating their effort on overseas sales, thus allowing the firm to concentrate on the domestic market.

Licensing

A licensing agreement offers the exporter the fastest entry into another country without the logistical headaches of the production pressures of exporting. Long-run profits and control are exchanged for royalties. It at once reduces risk, circumvents import restrictions and protects intellectual property rights.

Licensing is not only the fastest means of getting into a foreign market, it is also a means of establishing a foothold with little capital outlay. It provides valuable advantages for a small or medium-sized company to gain market entry, most notable is the ability to gain some local knowledge before committing to its own operations. It also offers a shield against political risk, in that by dealing through a local firm expropriation or other political measures are forestalled or minimized. From the foreign government's point of view licensing is often a preferred arrangement because it brings opportunities for technology transfer.

Direct mail

Using the postal systems or the Internet to market products is growing internationally. Of course the method is no better than the technology of the nations involved. The method is sensitive to being able to target a specific market for a specific product that lends itself to this methodology. It is generally an outsider's marketing method.

Transformation of goods

By transformation we mean using such mechanisms as bonded warehouses, free (trade) zones or free trade areas to change the content of goods in order to take advantage of preferential tariffs (discussed more fully in Chapter Eleven).

Insider tactics

Insider tactics are those which match with the insider strategy of gaining a local position in a national economy which welcomes foreign competition and country risk is low. Insider tactics include: starting a firm, acquiring a firm, mergers, partnering (joint ventures), and franchising.

Start a firm

Investment in a start-up in another country is expensive, but this tactic benefits control of the enterprise. Not every country will allow foreign ownership. In those that will, the entering argument is intelligence. Without knowledge, return on the investment will become extensive in terms of time and promotional costs.

Acquisition

The advantage of acquisitioning an already established firm should be obvious—it already has local knowledge recognition. Success is keyed to thorough research related to financial soundness and suitability as an extension of the firm's mission.

Merger

Mergers, like start-ups and acquisitions, bring the same advantages, but can have the same pitfalls as an acquisition. Even more dangerous is the difficulty of accommodating missions across borders and implanting the foreign firm's strategy.

Partnering (joint venture)

"Partnering" is the forming of strategic alliances or joint ventures to increase long-term stability and leverage. Control is the key word in the joint venture. Parties must be "singing the same tune" and from the same "sheet of music." This method of entering foreign markets has swept the world in recent years.

Franchising

Franchising is an inexpensive way to become an insider in another country. Not every product lends itself to franchising, but those that do often develop strong relationships and excellent management by competent owners.

Franchises produce new business opportunities, new jobs, and new entrepreneurs because they allow people with limited capital and experience to succeed in their own enterprise. In the United States, statistics show that about 95 percent of all franchises are still in business after five years compared to less than 20 percent of independently owned businesses.

Some say that franchising was the business phenomena of the twentieth century and because of the success of such giants as McDonald's, Kentucky Fried Chicken, and Dunkin' Donuts franchising will become the expansion method of the twenty-first century. In any case the process can be complicated and requires sound advice.

Risk sharing/learning

Caution is the watch-word when entering countries that have confused or mixed strategic approaches or where country risk is moderate to high. In those cases wealth exchange through risk sharing buys time to learn their business methods and culture. Risk sharing/learning includes using marketing subsidiaries and production sharing.

Marketing subsidiaries

Marketing subsidiaries are either wholly owned or joint ventures organized to support direct exporting, by providing timely information about tactical entry and sales effort. Short of taking a complete insider position, the marketing subsidiary represents a physical presence and, therefore, a greater commitment than arm's length exporting. Most marketing subsidiaries are centrally located in the target country and are a prelude to taking a more permanent insider position.

Production sharing

Some nations have surpluses of one factor of endowment or another. The United States has a surplus of technology, know-how, and intelligence, while Mexico and other lesser developed nations have a surplus of labor or raw materials. To stimulate economic development, all nations formulate schemes to take advantage of their surpluses. Singapore and Mexico (maquiladora program) are among the most aggressive in the development of schemes to showcase the added value of less expensive labor costs. The concept of production sharing is a viable tactical concept to be considered by any business that has a product with high labor content.

Developing business with non-market and new-market countries

Perestroika (restructuring) and glasnost (openness) have brought surprising market opportunities. Needless to say restructuring from Marxism to capitalism will not happen overnight. During the shake-out period many companies are carefully assessing methods of developing this eventual consumer explosion. Production sharing and joint venturing are the dominant tactics.

Minor tactics

Minor tactics, as opposed to the major ones of outsider, insider, and risk sharing/learning, are those that are peripheral to the spine of most country's major strategic approaches. They are the tactics of change and influencing change. They may lead to long-term profits, but are designed to carefully probe without major resource commitment.

Influence the government

This tactic may be the most useful in terms of reducing interstate controls which often satisfy special interest manufacturers at the expense of the competitive process and consumers. It includes using lobbyists and public relations firms to influence lawmakers. Understanding a country's method of seeking remedies to unfair barriers to trade is another element managers have at their disposal to try to "level the playing field."

Forfaiting and countertrade: special financing techniques

Forfaiting and *countertrade* are special techniques used to take advantage of trade creation opportunities in those countries where capital and foreign exchange are in short supply.

A bank enters into a forfaiting when it buys a debt instrument from an exporter at a discount. The benefit is cash flow for the exporter.

Countertrade is an umbrella term for the range of exchanges of goods without using currency as the medium (see Chapter Twelve for a fuller explanation).

Pulling it together

Table 2.3 summarizes the various entry tactics that are matched to a company strategy to satisfy wealth exchange. Figure 2.3 shows that a company may vary its tactics country-by-country depending on each country's strategic approach and country risk.

Physical distribution: logistics and transportation

This is an area of international business too often overlooked, nevertheless, the importance of logistics is of the highest rank. Why? Because technological advancements in transportation platforms and

Table 2.3 Matching tactics to strategy

Company strategy	Entry tactics
Prerequisite	Understand the culture.
No growth	Business stays at home market or postpones economic transfer.
Outsider	Export, import, association, intermediary, licensing, direct mail.
Insider	Start a firm, acquire a firm, joint venture, merger, franchise.
Risk sharer/learner	Market subsidiary, production sharing, joint venture.
Influence governments	Fight unfair trade by being a change agent.

Figure 2.3 Matching strategies

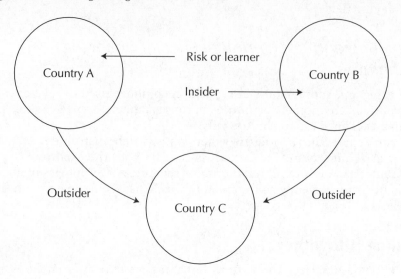

communications places logistics at the top of the list of reasons why global trade is growing so rapidly.

Distribution, sometimes also referred to as logistics, includes transportation and is the means by which goods are physically moved from the manufacturer in one country to a manufacturer or customer in another. This section of the chapter discusses three vital aspects which you should have an appreciation: shipping, intermodalism, and transportation communications.

Shipping

Arranging land, ocean, and air shipping of international cargo can be done directly by the importer or exporter. Inland transportation is handled much the same as a domestic transaction, except that certain export marks must be added to the standard information shown on a domestic bill of lading. Instructions to the inland carrier to notify the ocean or air carrier should also be included.

Water transportation

About 90 percent, by gross tonnage, of all goods transported internationally continues to travel by water.

There are three types of ocean service: conference lines, independent lines, and tramp vessels. An *ocean conference* is an association of ocean carriers that have joined together to establish common rates and shipping conditions. Conferences have two rates: the regular tariff and a lower, contract rate. You can obtain the contract rate if you sign a contract to use conference vessels exclusively during the contract period. *Independent lines* accept bookings from all shippers contingent on the availability of space and are often less expensive than conference rates. An independent usually quotes rates about 10 percent lower than a conference carrier in situations where the two are in competition. *Tramp vessels* usually carry only bulk cargoes and do not follow an established schedule; rather they operate on charters.

Regardless of the type of carrier you use, the carrier will issue a booking contract, which reserves space rented on a specific ship. Unless you cancel in advance, you may be required to pay even if your cargo doesn't make the sailing. To rent space on a ship you must be insured with ocean marine insurance. An insurance broker or your freight forwarder can arrange this for you.

Air transportation

Air freight continues to grow as a popular and competitive method for international cargoes. In fact, on a unit cost dollar volume basis it competes on an equal footing with water transportation.

Growth has been facilitated by innovation in the cargo industry. Air carriers have excellent capacity, use very efficient loading and unloading equipment and handle standardized containers. The advantages are:

- *Speed of delivery* which gets perishable cargoes to the place of destination in prime condition;
- *Response* to unpredictable product demands;
- *Rapid movement* of repair parts.

Air freight moves under a general cargo rate or a commodity rate. A special unit load rate is available when using approved air shipping containers.

Land transportation

Worldwide transportation over land has become less regulated and, therefore, more competitive and efficient. Importers and exporters look primarily to land transportation to move their goods to the nearest port of departure or as one leg of a sea, land, or air combination, often referred to as intermodalism.

The European Union is planning to establish "rail-cargo" freeways across Europe that would allow freight shipments to bypass most customs inspections and link to major sea ports. For instance, by the year 2000 it should be possible to ship by rail on a "cargo freeway" all the way from Scandinavia to a southern Italy port without border delays.

Intermodalism

Intermodalism is the movement of international shipments via container using a mix of transportation methods and is the system of the future. The concept makes use of the most efficient and cost effective methods to move goods. Intermodalism is an umbrella term that refers to any use of more than one form of transportation in moving goods from origin to destination. It's benefits are manifold:

- enhances on-time performance;
- provides better control to markets and sales channels;
- expands operating scope;
- controls shipments across transportation modes;
- clarifies railroads and motor carriers relationships.

Containerization

Containerization is a relatively new method of packaging and protecting goods for long-distance shipping. Standard-sized containers are provided by carriers. For open ocean shipping the standard pieces of equipment are the 20-foot, 40-foot, and the 45-foot container. The maximum weight of any container of whatever cube is about 44,000 pounds, to permit hauling on public roads.

Load centering

This concept stimulated the sophistication of today's intermodal world. As ships grew to hold more containers they became more expensive to operate. One way to reduce costs was to hold down the number of port calls. In order to fill the ships at fewer ports, the cargo has to be funneled into these load centers. The simplification and organization of movements of cargo has become the "fair haired" child of transportation specialists. An entirely new set of terms have developed around the concept.

A *micro-bridge* is the routing of a container to or from anywhere in the United States to or from any port. A *minibridge* moves a container that originates or terminates in a U.S. port other than the one where it enters or leaves the country. A *land-bridge* off-loads a container at any

U.S. port, ships it cross-country by rail, then reloads aboard a vessel for final movement to a foreign destination. *RO/RO* refers to the *roll on/ roll off* capability of containerized cargo, which is the foundation of intermodalism.

An example of intermodalism might be a container of goods originating in Europe but destined for Japan. It could be rolled on to a truck that rolls it on to a ship destined for the USA. On arrival it is rolled off the ship onto a truck or train in Newport News, Virginia (RO/RO), where it would be joined other containers trucked in from Florida, (minibridge) also destined for Japan. The containers would then be moved across the United States (land-bridge) then rolled off the train or truck and onto a ship in Long Beach, California which would complete the movement to Tokyo. Figure 2.4 illustrates the intermodal concept.

> A commercial cargo port near the city of Poti in Georgia on the eastern end of the Black Sea is bringing new life to the old Silk Road that historically linked Asia with the Mediterranean. The new Silk Road will include road and rail corridors tied to maritime routes and valuable oil pipe lines.

Transportation communications

Satellite communications and computerization have transformed control of logistics into a modern phenomena. Goods packaged in Germany can be tracked as they progress geographically and intermodally across oceans and land masses. Today, paperless documentation is a matter of reality in global logistics. Video "teleconferencing" eliminates the need for decision makers to come together physically, while "cyberspace" allows such matters as contract negotiations to take place in real time.

Figure 2.4 The intermodal concept

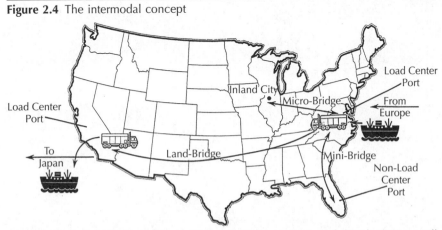

Source: Nelson, C. (1996) *Import/Export: How to Get Started in International Trade*, McGraw-Hill. Reproduced with the permission of the McGraw-Hill Companies.

Summary

Never before have the fruits of human labor been available across the globe in such quantity and quality. Businesses apply the best tactics and strategies to exchange their products with each nation where they do business. By taking advantage of the best mix of the factors of endowment we produce in one county, add content and value in another, and sell the products in another. The result is the exchange of wealth and consumer satisfaction. Global logistics and intermodalism is the backbone of globalism. Without it, the globalism movement would not survive.

The next chapter offers various methods to organize the global firm.

■ CHAPTER THREE ■

Organizing for world-class business

Our products now are known
in every zone,
Our reputation sparkles like a
gem,
We've fought our way thru
And new fields we're sure to conquer too,
For the ever onward IBM
(IBM company song)

This chapter is about organizing manufacturing and service firms to support the best operational transactional, tactical, and strategic choices that suit the firm's global business growth.

What's really happening?

Some managers of firms which could be competitive in the global arena are not yet aware of what's happening in the rest of the world. Here are the facts:

■ Modern manufacturing companies, small, medium-sized, and large, have adjusted to the realities of global competition. Marketplaces are full of consumer products from other nations, the best quality for the least expense the better. Women, who do most of the world's household marketing, no longer inspect where a product was made. They respond to "pocketbook" economics.

■ Modern service companies are adjusting to the realities of a world of global competition. Service industries like McDonald's are everywhere, fulfilling the wants and desires of people in the consumer marketplace worldwide.

■ Many service companies, like architects and construction firms, have overseas operations and compete for contracts all over the world.

■ Modern marketers fly around the world meeting distributors and developing networks of other contacts. They attend major trade shows and strategically target advertising programs.

■ Capital equipment and raw materials purchasers are searching for the best value—worldwide.

■ Manufacturer's buyers no longer source only within the boundaries of their own country for component parts. Technology is changing rapidly, so much so that many firms believe they are better-off forming multi-year strategic alliances with companies that are experts at staying with the "state-of-the-art" in their industrial specialty.

■ A growing number of companies have overseas manufacturing and assembly operations and source raw materials and components from all over the world.

■ Globalization is not something that will happen in the future, it has happened. Decision makers now visualize the marketplace in multi-national terms.

■ To maintain "world-class" products, manufacturers keep their R&D people continually searching for the latest technologies worldwide.

■ International growth almost always takes longer. Owners know they must have a realistic time horizon and plenty of patience, but they can ultimately expect a good return on capital invested.

■ Based on a company's financial condition and other decision factors, top managers form committees to consider a wide range of international business options including exporting, importing, going with a trading company, production sharing, co-investing, and various global marketing strategies.

■ Firms then reorganize their company and personnel to manage the options selected.

> Even Stanley Tools of New Britain, Connecticut, an old line Yankee company that in the past has been as American as apple pie, has adopted the strategy of putting their factories in Europe and the Far East to be nearer their foreign markets.

What we make

As a result of the way we are, life is changing, and the things we make are changing. Shortly after the middle of this century, most countries of the world began manufacturing different things than yesteryear. It is called the "high-tech post-industrial era." Smokestack industries have been replaced by the "clean industries"—incubators of new technology and firms that are users of high-tech to develop world-class products.

World-class

Consumers want that which is considered to be "world-class." That is, the things with the level of quality that people in other countries are enjoying. In other words, because of television and the Internet, the world market, instead of the domestic market, is determining what consumers want to buy. World-class is often a perception that a product is the best of the best. That perception is sometimes influenced by good advertising, often using world-class people for promotion purposes. Michael Jordan, the exceptional American world-class professional basketball player, represents a line of sports equipment intended to convey that that company's recreational products are therefore world-class.

Quality standards

Even standards have become world-class. The Japanese led the way to higher levels of quality when they adopted Dr W. Edwards Deming's concepts of statistical quality control. People want quality products so most manufacturers worldwide have joined the International Standards Organization (ISO) in Geneva which has established global guideposts. Companies that wish to be certified must follow rigid instructions and be examined by a team of independent auditors. In order to sell into world markets ISO certification is practically a must.

An example is the electronics industry. The American Electronics Association characterizes electronics as 70 percent small business. Yet electronics is now America's largest manufacturing industry. It is three times larger than the auto industry, ten times the steel industry, and accounts for six percent of America's national product. And the competition to develop world-class products is vibrant.

Product sectors

Products can generally be characterized in four broad sectors. Those quadrants, as identified in Figure 3.1 are:

- Quadrant #1: High-volume commodities such as grains.
- Quadrant #2: High-volume, highly differentiated products such as automobiles, computers, and TV sets.
- Quadrant #3: Low-volume commodities.
- Quadrant #4: Low-volume, highly differentiated products and services.

How we trade

Major international trading companies typically trade in Quadrant 1, the sector of high volume commodities where profit is great.

Figure 3.1 Product sectors

	Commodities	Differentiated Products (Technical systems)
High Volume Textiles, Raw Materials	QUADRANT 1 Typical trading company	QUADRANT 2 Large firms do it themselves
Low Volume	QUADRANT 3 Too expensive to do alone therefore use associations	QUADRANT 4 Small & medium-sized manufacturing and service companies What U.S.A. wants to sell

The General Motors, Sonys, and IBMs of the world are in Quadrant 2—they need little help to compete globally.

Those that trade in Quadrant 3 often form associations, simply because profit margins are small, and economies of scale are essential.

Quadrant four

The lower right quadrant in the Figure 3.1, the low-volume, highly differentiated (technical) product and services area is where the world needs to facilitate wealth exchange. But it is almost as difficult to operate in Quadrant 4 as it is in quadrant 3 because of the complexity and expense.

It is in Quadrant 4 that 90 percent of manufacturing and service firms are offering their products.

Quadrant 4 companies are the hundreds of thousands of small (from five to 250 employees) and medium-sized (between 250 and 1000 employees) firms worldwide that are struggling to participate in the global market.

Quadrant 4 is also the sector where there have been the greatest changes. It is the quadrant of innovation—where high-tech products are spawned. It is also the quadrant where thousands of smaller firms are competing for international trade.

The origin of content phenomena

To maintain a nation's standard of living yet be able to move ahead into the future and compete at the leading edge, the low- and mid-tech customer gap must be filled. Consumers need many less expensive, but world-class products. These products generally come from two places: companies that have substituted automation for labor, and companies that import low cost parts from countries that have high productivity and lower wage rates.

People's attitudes about product content have changed. Once upon a time "Made in the U.S.A." meant good old American know-how and quality, unsurpassed in the world. At another time, "Made in Japan" meant cheap, low-quality copies. Then came the "origin of content phenomena." In the 1970s and 1980s products with labels "Made in Hong Kong," "Made in Japan", "Made in Germany", or "Assembled in Singapore," began penetrating world markets and the origin of content took on less and less importance to the consumer. The reality of today is that few products have the pure content of one nation. Product content is more often a mixture of labor, raw materials, capital, and know-how, whatever it takes to provide a world-class product at best price for the consumer who cares little about how or where it was made. What does count is global name identification: Kodak, Fuji, Mercedes, IBM, etc.

Most businessmen and economists believe that to retain purity of national content at the expense of competition is protectionism and economic suicide. They believe content is a business decision not a political decision—what is good for the consumer is good for business.

It's a misconception that the only successful international businesses have their own branch offices and plants in foreign countries. Certainly many do, but the vast majority of importers and exporters are just successful domestic manufacturers or service companies.

Many smaller firms are not waiting. When asked about the benefits of international trade, the President of a small electronics outfit said to the effect: "For most companies, expanding the firm's market area to include the entire globe can only benefit our overall sales picture." Some foreign markets will not be as rich or as promising as others. But the potential for even modest sales gains outweighs the associated costs or risks. An increase in volume usually means rising profits as well as an opportunity to utilize excess production capacity. For some products it can often extend the life cycle that was otherwise on the decline.

Despite perceived stones in their path, many Quadrant 4 firms have overcome the obstacles.

Does a firm have to sell 90–100 percent to foreign countries? Of course not. A company may begin international trade by importing less expensive components, but eventually this leads to export opportunities. A firm that exports 15–50 percent of total sales has an aggressive program. On the other hand a company that is selling totally overseas is probably missing many sales right in their own domestic market.

It is important to recognize in today's interdependent business setting that marketing is a global activity and domestic marketing by itself has less meaning. Aggressive international companies are not deterred by lack of cash flow or inability to form their own foreign department. They search for alternative business arrangements.

Tactical planning and policy determines how the business fits into the marketplace. Every enterprise should consider a mix of business tools and organize to maximize profit on a global scale.

The future of international business for the small and medium-sized manufacturer and service company is essentially no different than for any firm in any country in the world. As the global economy becomes more knowledge intensive and the sunrise (high technology) industries emerge at even faster rates, businesspersons will find the search for markets even more diverse. Regardless of the size of the firm, getting to the markets of a world that has growing interdependence will require economies of scale and knowledge-centered arrangements that can bring together the most sophisticated international business techniques.

The strategic committee

A strategic committee should assess the firm's international competencies and recommend to top management the best method to enter the global market place. Once formed, this group should be chartered as a standing committee of the firm to examine the organization on an annual basis.

Strategic boundaries

The earliest task of the strategic committee is to examine the firm's strategic boundaries. The boundaries of the business are defined by what the firm does, i.e. what its products are and what others do for it. In other words, what the firm makes, what it buys and how it sells.

Vertical adjustments to your strategic boundaries are the "what and where," "make or buy" decisions that relate to the expansion or contraction of single functions or product lines. Horizontal adjustment relates to changes of strategic boundaries through the expansion or contraction of multiple functions or diversification into new industries.

Forward integration is a vertical adjustment synonymous with market power, that is, going on the offensive to increase sales volume. This can be accomplished, for instance, by opening your own retail stores, or beginning a direct-mail operation. Another means to forward integrate might be to export your products or establish an overseas subsidiary in order to be nearer your foreign markets.

Backward integration is the defensive strategy of reducing costs and protecting the firm against exploitation from powerful sources of raw materials and product by searching for new, less costly sources or producing the component yourself.

Figure 3.2 visualizes business decisions left and right of center. Those to the left are decisions related to reducing production costs, and those to the right as those having to do with expanding markets. The term integration means the consideration of what you do and what others do for you and those decisions are made based on quality, price, delivery, and reliability.

Growth

When international sales volume becomes a significant component of total company business the firm will, no doubt, have already formed a separate export department using one of the ways described later. During this growth period the firm should carefully watch cost and selling patterns. An export department is primarily a sales department and if a major part of business originates from one country or a specific area of the world, the firm should consider forming an overseas subsidiary. This subsidiary could be for manufacturing, marketing (export), sourcing (import), for distribution, or it could be a combination assembly and/or manufacturing operation.

Expansion may be in many countries on many continents with many products and each of the insider, outsider, and risk/learner options discussed in Chapter Two should be considered. After those decisions are made the firm will have several organizational options available, depending on selling patterns, sales growth and significant legal or tax advantages recommended by lawyers, accountants and strategists. In selecting the proper organization for the firm the critical elements are:

1 Avoid duplication, i.e. divisions or departments doing the same function.
2 Avoid suboptimization, that is treating international business as a separate segment of corporate business thus preventing their optimal use in the best interest of the total organization.

Figure 3.2 Strategic boundaries

<<<< Backwards integration ◄──────► Foreward integration >>>>

Production sharing	Make	Manufacture components	Wholesales	Distributors	Export
or	or	or	or	or	or
Build at home	Import	Assemble	Retailers	Sales reps.	Build fac.

Intelligence: the prerequisite

The prerequisite for any successful international business venture is *intelligence*. Before the firm's international effort can move forward it must invest in market research, either by the firm's own personnel or with the assistance of an organization specializing in that field. From this search for broader markets will come a strategic approach.

Personnel

The most important aspect of the growth of the firm's international operations effort will be the selection of the right people to carry out the plan. The dominant personal characteristic of these employees will be the ability to work on a team in a multicultural environment.

The start-up organization

Expansion of the international department will be a function of capitalization. As a minimum the organization should have an export manager, a sales person and administrative support.

Expand from domestic base

The firm can develop from within by expanding the duties of a few personnel who show an interest in things international. Usually one or more members of the firm's domestic marketing organization have the inclination and ambition to begin forming the new department. Slowly, over time, allow those personnel to become the international department. The key to success is finding a leader personality who is capable of developing a plan, being responsible for training the staff and generally functioning as the international manager. Often a firm will bring in an outside consultant at this point, one who is a seasoned manager and who has had experience with start-ups. Other duties related to export marketing, finance and traffic are spread among the various domestic departments and integrated with their normal activities.

Advantages

Personnel who already know the firm's products, organization, and key employees in other departments bring advantages in terms of initial stability to the development of a new department. There is a built-in level of trust that is never there initially when outsiders are hired for a new function. In reality this method of developing from within brings with it some cost savings in the short run. Often only the job descriptions of "old hands" are enriched, not their salaries.

Disadvantages

The flip side to this method of growing from a base of employees from within is that the present staff will have their time diluted and the development of the new department will often take a "back seat" to their normal duties. Two things can suffer: (1) the current job, with the inevitability of errors, omissions, and delays that a new exporter can ill afford; and (2) the timely start-up of the new department. For the same reasons, when an outside consultant is hired, that person sometimes has a difficult time getting the attention of the current staff due to their overload condition.

Recruit a staff and form a separate department

The second option is the recruitment of a staff that is already trained and has developed a track record at other companies. In this case the firm would create a separate export department by hiring several key employees to concentrate on the development of export business. The first to be hired would, of course, be the export manager who, with the firm's support, would hire the remainder of the staff using the schedule developed in the strategic plan as modified by the actual growth pattern of world sales activity.

Advantages

By having a separate export department in charge from the beginning, management can get better data and a feel for the development process. Recruited personnel often have established contacts and relationships with support organizations. The company's image will be enhanced and employee morale within the department should not become a problem.

Disadvantages

Top management of the company must be cautious of new management for international operations that bring with them approaches that are too optimistic, interjecting utopian sales projections based on their experiences with other established firms. This method will require a period of familiarization for new employees to learn how the company operates and about your products.

The modern approach to global business seeks synergism (the whole is greater than the parts). Just as international marketing (exporting) must be integrated with the firm's total marketing strategy, so must international sourcing (importing) be integrated with total purchasing and manufacturing strategies. Integration will again require the firm to re-define the boundaries of its business.

Organization models

There are several ways to organize your firm to accommodate changes as it grows in the international arena. While there is no rigid pattern, most global companies are organized geographically, functionally or by product line.

The changing organization

It is essential that you remember that there is no best organizational method—no standard model. Each global business must design the organization that works best for its product line and global application. A good example is WebTV, a company headquartered in "Silicone Valley" near San Francisco, California. WebTV developed a product that permits an Internet connection through the household television. It licenses their invention to major manufacturers such as Philips and Sony. Their organization is their own creation. It carves out functions to match their company's purposes. Figure 3.3 shows the WebTV organization structure.

Start-ups

The first organization will either be split off from the domestic marketing or purchasing departments or organized as a new entity. The beginning effort is generally focused on one or two high priority target countries. Figure 3.4 shows how this organization might look.

Figure 3.3 WebTV organization

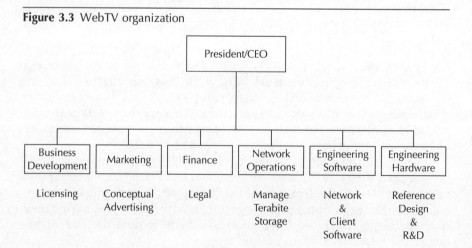

Figure 3.4 Start-up organization

Organizing geographically

You may find early on that the firm is serving several countries in a region that are close to one another yet far from the home base. This is the typical beginning of restructuring the organization by geographical area.

By organizing a headquarters or a "marketing subsidiary" in the region there is a common base for management and it becomes easier to communicate, thus optimizing marketing know-how. Figure 3.5 is an example of such a structure.

Flat geographic

The main draw back of this geographic organization is the tendency to dilute the global view point. Over time regions begin to take on domestic view points and there is the danger of suboptimization. To overcome this tendency, a strong coordination management style must be put in place.

One top manager overcomes this tendency by keeping a close rein from the corporate headquarters. His organization is flat and tight. He has four subordinate managers in the home office with him, each has a region in which the company does business through sales representatives. The representatives, in each of the 50 countries where it does business, are natives of that country, familiar with the people, businesses and government, and has "pop" (responsiveness) which translates to bigger sales as a result of using representatives. His flat organization looks like Figure 3.6.

Figure 3.5 Geographical organization

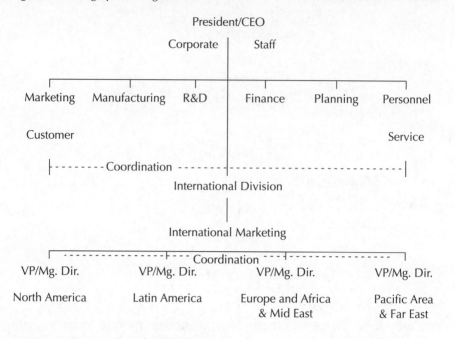

Figure 3.6 Flat geographic organization

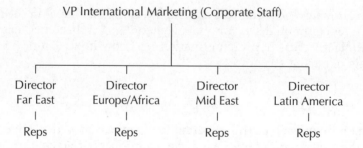

Functional organization

A functional organization lends itself to a firm that has very homogeneous lines of products and line executives have global responsibilities. Figure 3.7 is typical of a functional organization.

Organizing by product

Another means of organization is along the lines of Figure 3.8, in which each line product has its own international sales organization. This is a

Figure 3.7 Functional organization

Figure 3.8 Organizing by product

world company approach where product groups are responsible for global marketing and sourcing. This method is typical for firms with several unrelated product lines for which their marketing tasks vary more by product than by region.

The integrated international organization

Figure 3.9 shows an organization structure for an integrated manufacturing system. It shows that the worldwide sourcing manager (WWSM) is at the same level within the organization as the line purchasing managers. He or she is a principal assistant to the purchasing director who is responsible for developing policy and procedures and providing a vision for line purchasers who are closely linked to the worldwide marketing manager (WWMM) and marketing counterparts in the integrated organization.

Organize for tax benefits

There are no tax incentives for importing, but most countries offer tax advantages to firms that export. For example, the United States tax code offers what amounts to about a 15 percent exclusion of the taxable income earned on international sales to the firm that organizes an off-shore office through which it passes its export documentation. Called a foreign sales corporation (FSC), this subsidiary organization

Figure 3.9 Integrated international organization

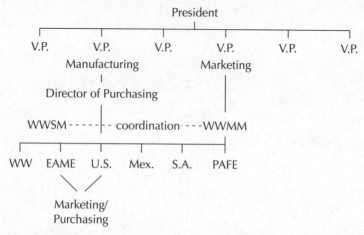

Note: WW (Worldwide); EAME (Europe, Africa, Middle East); U.S. (United States); Mex. (Mexico); S.A. (South America);PAFE (Pacific Area, Far East)

must maintain a summary of its permanent books of accounts at the foreign office, and have at least one director resident outside the United States. Some 23 foreign countries, those which have an agreement to exchange tax information with the United States, and all U.S. possessions like the Virgin Islands, Guam, and Saipan have already established offices capable of providing direct support as your foreign sales corporation.

Needless to say, you should consult an accountant who specializes in international taxes to assist you to understand your country's equivalent tax scheme and set up whichever organization is applicable and to best advantage for your firm.

Summary

To compete today, firms must adapt to the new way or take to the highway of second-class world citizenship. To produce world-class products at the most competitive costs, global businesses are marketing and sourcing wherever in the world it makes good business sense. And to do that organizations must be creative—there is no best model.

The next chapter explains modern worldwide sourcing.

CHAPTER FOUR

Sourcing globally

Imports can be consumed, and consumption is the most conspicuous end of economic activity.

Jan Pen (Former Professor of Economics and Director of Economic Policy, The Netherlands.)

Outsourcing of components, products and raw materials is done routinely in most of today's businesses. However, things have happened in the past several decades which have increased the complexity of sourcing decisions and in turn affected the development of a manufacturing strategy.

New sourcing strategies for global markets

Until recently manufacturing integration concerned make or buy decisions only in the domestic market. However, during the twenty-year period from about 1965 through 1985 firms, worldwide, introduced a growing line-up of improved products. Now the list of world-class competitors includes manufacturers on every continent and the window for buying decisions has widened.

Purchasing has often been regarded as an operative necessity to ensure the supply to meet quality and punctuality of delivery. Due to globalization competition on the world markets has increased. Nowadays companies have to realize that purchasing has more potential then just making certain that the company is supplied with the right goods, at the right time, with the right quality. Businesses seek to improve their competitiveness through worldwide integration of their purchasing activities.

Competitive world-class manufacturers are spread across the world resulting, during the last decades, in an increase in complexity. A factor which has added to this complexity is the "origin of content phenomena." Whether it be consumer or capital goods, today's purchasers are discriminating and fickle. Today's consumers care little whether a product is "Made in . . ." Germany, Japan, or in the USA. Today they care about having a high quality product, high value and in some cases a well-known brand name. As a consequence of this the importance of purchasing and sourcing has grown. To compete on the world markets, companies must face the fact that they have to purchase efficiently and therefore will be required to be supplied globally as well as domestically.

Furthermore, technology is advancing—products are becoming more complex and development costs are increasing. Due to competition in world markets product life-cycles have become shorter and prices are falling. As a consequence, the tasks of the purchasing department have expanded and today, in order to produce more complex goods for a lower price, they include strategic functions such as sourcing globally and creating lean but efficient supplier networks.

To compete in the global marketplace with world-class products, Quadrant 4 manufacturing firms will, sooner rather than later, be required to consider a mix of foreign and domestic content.

In this context even the Ministry of International Trade and Industry (MITI) in Japan states that Japanese industry gains its competitive advantage from the cooperative relationships with the suppliers and the lean structure of the supplier network.

Nowadays modern strategic sourcing concepts are set up all over the world in order to use the potentials of the world markets and to create more efficient supplier networks.

This has created more complex sourcing decisions which affect the manufacturing process. Worldwide purchasing has become a big player requiring new approaches and redefinition of business boundaries. A firm no longer has the luxury of limiting make or buy decisions only to its domestic country, because good, unemotional business sense requires consideration of international alternatives such as:

1 importing raw materials and component parts;
2 manufacturing off-shore;
3 assembling off-shore.

Each of these alternatives are discussed in detail in later chapters. Chapter 10, for instance, explains the great under-tapped, off-shore manufacturing and assembly capacity, particularly along America's southern border in Mexico.

A representative example for a global sourcing concept is the current E-Class of Mercedes-Benz. The suppliers for the new middle-class model I are situated throughout the entire world. Thirty-eight percent of the suppliers are based in Germany, but 40 percent are based in rest of Europe and 22 percent are spread all over the world.

Another example is the component network of the Ford Escort. While that automobile is assembled in Germany and the United Kingdom, the suppliers are based in the Netherlands, Sweden, Belgium, United Kingdom, France, Canada, United States, Spain, Italy, Switzerland, Japan, Austria, Denmark, Norway and Germany.

Figure 4.1 shows the global manufacturing process of a Ford Escort made in Europe.

The decision

The decision to enter the world of global sourcing holds two major obstacles for top management. The first is attitudinal—it may require cultural adjustment. A kick-off must be announced, showing commitment by management that foreigners will now be in the purchasing loop. This brings a new requirement to research and study other countries, and learn about their people.

The second important barrier has to do with method. The "direct method" wherein the firm decides to do it itself, or the "indirect method" in which a trading intermediary does the purchasing. The wise company considers a mix of methods. For instance, some components or materials are better suited to be handled by the firm. For others,

Figure 4.1 Global manufacturing: the component network for Ford Escort in Europe

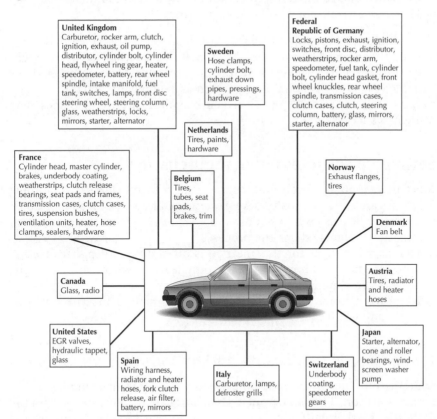

United Kingdom
Carburetor, rocker arm, clutch, ignition, exhaust, oil pump, distributor, cylinder bolt, cylinder head, flywheel ring gear, heater, speedometer, battery, rear wheel spindle, intake manifold, fuel tank, switches, lamps, front disc steering wheel, steering column, glass, weatherstrips, locks, mirrors, starter, alternator

Sweden
Hose clamps, cylinder bolt, exhaust down pipes, pressings, hardware

Federal Republic of Germany
Locks, pistons, exhaust, ignition, switches, front disc, distributor, weatherstrips, rocker arm, speedometer, fuel tank, cylinder bolt, cylinder head gasket, front wheel knuckles, rear wheel spindle, transmission cases, clutch cases, clutch, steering column, battery, glass, mirrors, starter, alternator

Netherlands
Tires, paints, hardware

France
Cylinder head, master cylinder, brakes, underbody coating, weatherstrips, clutch release bearings, seat pads and frames, transmission cases, clutch cases, tires, suspension bushes, ventilation units, heater, hose clamps, sealers, hardware

Belgium
Tires, tubes, seat pads, brakes, trim

Norway
Exhaust flanges, tires

Denmark
Fan belt

Canada
Glass, radio

Austria
Tires, radiator and heater hoses

United States
EGR valves, hydraulic tappet, glass

Spain
Wiring harness, radiator and heater hoses, fork clutch release, air filter, battery, mirrors

Italy
Carburetor, lamps, defroster grills

Switzerland
Underbody coating, speedometer gears

Japan
Starter, alternator, cone and roller bearings, windscreen washer pump

the firm might be better off to go through an import management company (IMC) that specializes in your needs. The decision depends on the company and its products, its size and competitors. The trend for many start-ups is total outsourcing.

Due to the dynamic globalization process national economies have grown more and more interdependent and new potential markets have emerged. Global sourcing describes a trend to open up international sources of supply and to use the potentials of these world markets. A global sourcing strategy offers the possibility to profit from the world-wide competition and to use possible cost or technology advantages of foreign suppliers. The reasons for the global sourcing trend can be summarized as follows:

- Wage differences between industrialized nations and less developed countries.
- Cost advantages of less developed countries in service and other infrastructural prices.
- Improved possibilities for know-how transfer and information exchange due to modern telecommunication developments.
- Decrease of transportation costs and times.

It is important to understand that the decision to source globally may not simply be based on the cost advantages that a foreign supplier might have. Other factors have to be taken into consideration to make a suitable decision. National factors such as technical standards, legislation as well as cultural, political and economical circumstances may influence success.

Setting up for international purchasing

Most international purchasing begins after a firm's domestic sourcing processes are well established. An experienced buyer, with some foreign connection, learns of a less costly opportunity, or has an interest in international travel, starts the process.

The learning curve for this method is often quite steep, because the new-to-international buyer must not only learn how to search globally, but also learn the ins-and-outs of importing as well.

To speed entrance into worldwide sourcing, many firms hire someone who already has importing experience.

Purchasing is purchasing and importing is importing

Sourcing only becomes importing when you buy from a company in a foreign location. The same principals of purchasing that work within the domestic market will not always work in the broader international scope. The complications are searching and advertising, then handling the transactional aspects of importing.

Tariff treatment

Familiarity with the harmonized tariff schedule is important when considering the best tactical advantages of international sourcing.

General Systems of Preferences (GSP)

In order to stimulate their economic development, the United Nations, through their General Systems of Preferences (GSP), has designated certain countries, territories and associations of countries as "recipients" of special tariff preferences from the most developed nations. Some 84 independent nations are eligible under these tariff schedules.

Twenty-eight non-independent and three associations of countries are also eligible. In order to qualify for duty-free entries under this program, it must be established that the sum of the direct cost of processing operations performed in the country, plus the materials produced in the country are more than 35 percent of the appraised value of the product at the time of its entry into the developed nation.

Needless to say, country of origin markings are required as an element of proof.

Country of origin markings

Every article of foreign origin entering a country must be legibly marked with the English name of the country of origin, unless an exception from marking is provided for in the law. Basically, the law requires that the "ultimate purchaser" or last person in the recipient country who receives the article in the form in which it was imported, be informed as to where the article was made.

In the case of production sharing (explained later), the parent company of the overseas organization is the ultimate consumer of the imported articles and requests a waiver from the marking requirements. Waivers are granted when the imported article is substantially transformed into a new and different product in the developed country, wherein the imported article is not sold or offered for sale in its imported condition either over the counter or as a replacement part.

The integrated manufacturing system

The complexities of today requires relationships with companies, foreign and domestic to work as a team to optimize modern manufacturing concepts.

Just-in-time (JIT)

The fundamental idea of just-in-time (JIT) sourcing is that the suppliers produce and deliver according to the demand of the customer in order to minimize the stock. It is the aim of JIT to reduce the goods in stock and to lower the costs of stock, because large inventories can be regarded as nonproductive assets that cause opportunity costs.

The JIT concept has been developed and first implemented by Toyota. The process synchronizes the delivery of goods with the demand of the customer. The goods and materials arrive at exactly the time they are needed. This can be regarded as an ideal condition because the use of all involved resources is minimized. But although the JIT strategy provides great potentials for cost-savings it is not always easy to implement. The logistical coordination of the different suppliers and individual goods may cause high organizational efforts. Toyota for example has to coordinate the quality, the quantity and the correct time of delivery for several thousands of supplied components per each car.

Modern businesses attempt to avoid large inventories and their associated warehousing costs. They represent lost revenue because they are assets sitting on a shelf not earning even the lowest of market interest rates. Of course, some inventory must be carried, but most companies limit that to no more on the shelf than the minimum required to meet predetermined statistical fill levels.

Most manufacturers have instructed the managers of their purchasing department to move toward JIT. The term means just what it says— components and materials needed in the production process arrive precisely at the time the production line needs the item, thus limiting the required inventories and reducing the concomitant costs of production. Underlying the JIT philosophy is the elimination of waste, with waste being defined as anything which adds only cost to a product, and not value.

Value analysis (VA)

Value analysis drives the JIT process, because by definition only an activity that physically changes a product such as machining, plating, assembly, etc. adds value—activities such as moving something to and fro, counting, or storing adds only cost, not value.

In the production process of capital equipment, as well as highly differentiated consumer products, parts can generally be separated into two categories. The first, typically called the "trivial many" (not categorized this way to downgrade their importance but rather to expose their costs) are those parts which often account for only about 20 percent of the total product cost. The other category is often referred to as the "vital few" because they are the primary cost drivers of the final product. They are called the "vital few" because they often only amount to 20 percent of the total items, yet can account for as much as 80 percent of the cost. Identified as the "significant cost drivers", it is the "vital few" that receive the concentrated effort through a multi-functional commodity management approach.

Because value-adding operations comprise only a minuscule portion of the entire operation (some have calculated less than one percent) JIT has become one of the most important innovations to reduce costs.

As it turns out, JIT has its own set of problems such as quality control, reliability of sources, and cash-flow performance. These are significant barriers to overcome for the domestic buyer and can seem insurmountable when sourcing internationally. Nevertheless, many firms have established sound relationships with overseas firms, often at significant cost savings.

Modular sourcing

This strategy is especially well established in the automotive industry throughout the world and the importance is growing steadily. It allows the manufacturers to reduce the number of suppliers and goods that are purchased at the same time. This purchasing tool puts components together that before were purchased separately from different suppliers in order to create modules that can be purchased from one single supplier. An example might be the instrument panel of a car. Modular sourcing is a purchasing strategy that enables companies to lower production and purchasing complexity. Modular sourcing offers an improved efficiency and increases the level of competitiveness.

The high level of effort involved with the set up of modular sourcing the concept requires supplier—manufacturer relationships which are in general long term and cooperative.

Due to this new form of supply cost reductions can be combined with improved quality because manufacturers profit from the know-how and the innovativeness of the supplier.

Single sourcing

Companies with a single sourcing policy are supplied by only one supplier per item. The aim of single sourcing is to cut down the purchasing costs as well as the logistical efforts. Multiple sourcing has become less meaningful in practice and the importance of the single sourcing strategy has grown mainly because multiple sourcing concepts are closely connected with complex supplier networks which involve high costs for coordination and transactions. Today businesses tend to reduce the number of suppliers by focusing on a small number of reliable firms with which they create a lean but effective supplier network. This fact reflects the trend towards long-term and cooperative supplier relationships. Manufacturers intensify the relationship by trying to achieve synergy through the use of specific know-how suppliers, both of whom profit from this kind of vertical cooperation.

Focusing on a single supplier can be a double-edged sword, due to the lack of competition between the different suppliers and the low degree of supply assurance. On the other hand, single sourcing offers considerable potentials to reduce administration costs and to diminish capacities in the purchasing department. Furthermore, tooling costs or other investments in the supply relationship have to be paid only once instead of twice or more times.

Dual sourcing

A possible compromise might be the use of a dual sourcing strategy because in contrast to the single sourcing, dual sourcing assigns two different and independent suppliers for each supplied good. The dual sourcing strategy still permits implementation of a small and efficient supplier network but keeps administration and purchasing expenditures at an acceptable low level. Dual sourcing uses the potential of the single-sourcing strategy, reduces risks of concentration on one supplier, and guarantees competition between the suppliers, thus providing a higher level of supply assurance.

Strategic sourcing

To achieve the optimum integrated system, many firms have established an office, often a single person, whose task it is to step away from the day-to-day "rat race" of purchasing and look at the total procurement picture. The title commonly used for this position is worldwide purchasing manager (WWPM).

By virtue of his or her separation from the typical headaches of day-to-day buying, the WWPM can take a proactive approach to sourcing instead of being reactive. This same person can include JIT and VA philosophies as part of this new approach to sourcing, and they can even be included at the product design stage. Those that have taken this step have learned one thing. It pays off handsomely in savings through the reduction of costs for primary "cost drivers."

In the past most purchasers have used the traditional simplistic buying criteria of price, quality, delivery and service for all items, and only searched the domestic market. "Strategic sourcing" is the technique of starting with the "now situation" for the firm's product. It consists of investigating JIT, VA, pricing, supply assurance, adequacy of quality, and a host of services as these criteria relate to the total cost of the product, isolating the significant cost drivers, then searching the world for the right suppliers of those cost drivers.

The commodity management approach

The strategist does not focus on the "trivial many," instead he or she focuses on the "vital few."

When using this sourcing technique, it is important to remember to establish market driven target costs on a "landed basis" so as to be able to compare "apples with apples." This is vital when comparing foreign sources with domestic sources. What may seem a good deal from an overseas supplier may prove to be too expensive when transportation, tariffs, and coordination headaches are included in the calculation of landed cost.

Solar Turbines Inc. of Southern California, a subsidiary of Caterpillar, has experienced, in the words of Frank Rugnetta, Manager of Worldwide Sourcing, "mind-boggling success" using the commodity management approach. There has been as much as 80 percent reduction for some items and routinely 30–40–50 percent reductions in costs for most of their major cost drivers.

Commodity management team (CMT)

To analyze the "vital few," the worldwide sourcing manager typically forms and chairs a commodity management team (CMT) made up from key players from design, quality assurance, manufacturing, finance, marketing, and any others needed to satisfy the requirement. Through a facilitation process on the part of the worldwide sourcing manager, the CMT develops marketing, technical, quality and commercial objectives for every major cost driver in the production process in terms of cost, state of the art requirements, quality, supply assurance, product development, financial, managerial, and stability criteria.

The outcome of CMT meetings is the development of a market driven target cost (landed) and with well-developed criteria for each of the vital few.

The strategic team then assists in setting up a prioritization for the vital few so that the worldwide sourcing manager can then state purchasing objectives in such a way as to derive a strategic "master purchasing plan" The purpose of this plan is to reduce costs, yet maximize the "macro business decision," i.e. in some instances purchasing must subordinate its goals to achieve what is best for the company.

The analytical method used by the CMT for the sorting, choosing, and prioritization is often one similar to the Jepner-Treigo decision-analysis process. This and other similar methods force the CMT to make rather simple decisions of "must haves" and "wants". These techniques force line managers to assign priorities (usually on a scale of 1 to 10) to the vital few, component by component, in such a way that a ranking can be determined. This kind of decision analysis should not be avoided under the false perception that it requires sophisticated computers. It can be done by Quadrant 4 firms with fairly simple manual number manipulations.

The request for proposal

The traditional steps of purchasing are:

1 issue the invitation for bid (IFB) or request for proposal (RFP) which defines specifications;
2 wait for responses;
3 analyze, then accept the lowest price of responsible bidders.

Now, using the CMT method, the approach is reversed. Members of the line purchasing organization make individual IFB or RFP releases against the "master plan" which defines for the bidders precisely what the target price of each "vital few" component must be in order for them to compete. In other words the sourcer tells the sourcee what his price must be and explains the objectives that must be met for that price.

One such offering by Solar Turbines, Inc. resulted in 40 bids which were then reduced by an elimination process to a short list of six. Although the RFP was advertised internationally, the final winner was not a foreign company (Japanese and German firms did bid). A U.S. manufacturer won the bid and ultimately entered into a long-term strategic alliance with Solar to provide the items in question on a just-in-time (JIT) basis. This meant that the winner became a "partner" in Solar's production process and was given proprietary information so that their own production system could be integrated with that of Solar.

Advantages

Lower ultimate costs is the most obvious advantage to using the CMT method, but more important is increased efficiency, reduction of suppliers, synchronous flow, and improved transportation costs.

Disadvantages

The worldwide purchasing approach requires a continual internal dialog of the overall business concept and how specific commodities can best contribute to the overall business objectives. As a result, there is a time cost due to the need for increased and continuous training of purchasing and manufacturing personnel.

Search capability

Don't be misled. It is not just the "vital few" that are sourced worldwide. The "trivial many" have excellent potential for foreign sources, but these are generally left to the operational buyer. This means, just as it did for international marketing, that the prerequisite for international sourcing success is intelligence. Modern firms should invest in research, either by their own personnel or with the assistance of a firm that specializes in the collection of international data. Purchasing personnel need information in order to satisfy the just-in-time (JIT) requirements of providing the required amount, at the required time, at the lowest ultimate cost, and at the highest quality.

To meet this critical need many, larger firms have organized special divisions dedicated to supporting purchasing's needs for such information as worldwide labor costs, raw materials, floating exchange rate information, and tax and tariff implications of overseas sourcing. Smaller firms rely on a cooperative approach where information gathered by overseas marketing personnel is shared.

Benefiting from production sharing

Competing in the global age of interdependence requires taking the output of production and vaulting that product into the international market place. But if price isn't competitive and quality isn't world-class, nothing happens.

Many Quadrant 4 companies have products that are no longer at the cutting edge of technology. Facing flat domestic sales, they are interested in expanding overseas but, to sustain their competitiveness, cost adjustments are required.

If your product fits this montage, you would do well to analyze your plant processes and consider a different mix of the factors of production, capital, materials, know-how, and labor.

Most, if not all, of the countries that offer production sharing are classified as developing or least-developed nations. Because the advantages for these countries are jobs, technology transfer, economic development, and foreign exchange income, attracting production-sharing opportunities has become very competitive. The most obvious benefit to companies is the surplus of labor that translates into relatively low wage rates. Not all countries offer less expensive labor for production sharing. Some countries offer technology, brain power and productivity.

Who are the labor exporters?

Some say production sharing is the fastest growing industry in the world today (see Chapter Ten for a fuller explanation). Mexico, closest to the vast United States domestic market, is the fastest growing of these off-shore production-sharing areas. Mexico also has the greatest market share followed by Singapore, Taiwan, China and Malaysia. Compared with other off-shore centers, the distances from Mexico to most market-places in the United States are shortest. On the other hand, Asian, West African, and Central American locations often provide advantages when the target market is Asia, Europe, or South America.

Even the countries of the former Soviet Union are moving into the production-sharing business. Free economic zones have been authorized for areas ranging from Armenia and Estonia to the Port of Nakhodka in the Soviet Far East. The foreign investment incentives for these zones include: duty-free export and import; a reduction in tax and lease payment discounts; labor policies governed by the local zones; and application for free market prices. Fifty percent of the production and assembly would be ordered by the state at state prices, the remainder at market prices.

Who are the technology exporters?

Nations that have invested heavily into research and development, such as the United States, Japan and many European nations, are sources of technology sharing in production systems. Because it is highly mobile, transfer is eagerly sought by less-developed nations to complement their lower wage rates.

Who are the brain-power exporters?

Similarly, countries that have invested in higher education frequently have a pool of experts who enter the production-sharing mix. These highly mobile people often complement the technology input.

Who are the productivity exporters?

As it turns out, less expensive labor is not always the best production-sharing option. For higher technology production, those nations who have a higher educated and trainable work force bring to the workplace higher productivity in terms of output per hour.

Strategic sourcing in practice

In 1994, because the American market for the their car was the second largest in the world, BMW set up a manufacturing plant in Spartanburg,

South Carolina. Due to the importance of this market, BMW decided to take an "insider" position and transfer the production of the current BMW Z3 Roadster to the United States. This was intended to improve local competitiveness and give BMW increased representation. This strategy proved so successful that since September 1995, the entire world production of the BMW Z3 has been manufactured in South Carolina.

BMW's purchasing policy was futuristic and combined every one of the above sourcing concepts. By integrating suppliers very early in the development process and focusing on a small, carefully selected number, BMW and their selected suppliers established a long-term cooperative relationship. BMW demanded that suppliers be absolutely reliable with regard to the quality, punctuality and ability to provide a just-in-time delivery. BMW set up a modular sourcing strategy in combination with global- and single-sourcing concepts.

For the interior of the new Z3, BMW intended to focus on one single supplier, achieve synergy effects, reduce redundancies and increase the productivity. After a selection process in which suppliers from all over the world were taken into consideration, BMW formed a strategic alliance with the French supplier Sommer Alibert Lignotock (SAL). SAL is a leading supplier of interior plastic parts, has 14,000 employees and a turnover of about $3 billion.

SAL had to set up its own production site directly beside the BMW plant in South Carolina. This required a big financial risk—an investment of $13 million—and required SAL to be highly involved into the success of the Z3. On the other hand, BMW granted SAL single-supplier status as long as the Z3 is produced. This gave SAL the security necessary for monetary investment and commitment to the planning process. BMW even gave their permission for a small number of qualified SAL employees to take part in the development process of the Z3.

Both companies developed, in vertical cooperation, an interior module. They put all plastic components and parts of the interior together to complete a plastic interior module or system. This module consisted of several small and large parts and components such as the whole instrument panel, the console, door-panels, all kinds of facings and many more items.

BMW and SAL are regarded as pioneers because this modular supply concept is unique and a comparable interior module system cannot be found worldwide.

Both parties benefited from the new cooperative supply relationship. Profiting from the know-how and the specific development competence of the supplier, BMW reduced redundancies, transaction costs and achieved total development costs that are considerably below those of a more traditional sourcing concept. BMW even managed to combine this cost decrease with an improvement of the quality and a shortening of the strategically important "time to market."

SAL enlarged its percentage of components contributed to the BMW Z3, improved its influence on the development process and managed to increase the level of dependency by becoming a single supplier. In addition SAL gained a competitive edge with this reference model and stated its position in the world market as an advanced and reliable supplier.

Although there were some start-up problems, BMW successfully implemented the new sourcing strategy and gained a competitive advantage. Success has been proved by the fact that research and development costs were reduced considerably and the time needed for development decreased.

Summary

Worldwide sourcing has become the "smart" side of international business. No nation has a patent on workers, technology, or brain power nor do they have a right to say that their workers or products are better than another. Companies of each country survey the world for the best mix to import for their world-class production efforts. Modern firms are using integrated manufacturing systems that analyze value and use just-in-time techniques, complemented by production-sharing practices that are tailored to their profit needs.

Globalization has changed the world markets—businesses and consumers have internationalized. There is a high level of competition, advancing technology, and higher development costs. Shorter product life-cycles force companies to purchase more efficiently. Due to this, the tasks of purchasing are expanding and becoming more strategic. Modern strategic sourcing concepts use the potential of world markets to create more efficient supplier networks.

Modular sourcing allows the manufacturer to reduce the number of suppliers and purchased goods at the same time. It puts components together to create modules which can be bought from a single supplier. Modular sourcing enables manufacturers to lessen the complexity of production and purchasing.

Companies with a single-sourcing policy are supplied by only one supplier per item. The aim of single sourcing is to cut down purchasing costs as well as the logistical efforts. The manufacturers reduce the number of suppliers because they cannot afford large and cost-intensive supplier networks.

The fundamental idea of just-in-time is that suppliers produce and deliver according to the demand of the customer, in order to minimize inventories. Just-in-time strategy tends to reduce costs of stock—large inventories are regarded as nonproductive assets.

The next chapter is the first of Part Two, which discusses the seeds of border friction. Chapter Five gives a snapshot of the implications of culture and behavior.

PART TWO

Disharmony at the borders

Mastering diverse cultures

Fear and suspicion are obstacles to clear thinking, especially on matters where foreigners are concerned.

Jan Pen (Former Professor of Economics and Director of Economic Policy, The Netherlands.)

Part Two consists of four chapters which, when tied together, explain why there can be disharmony at the borders, thus adding to the complexity of cross-border business. People within national borders are often prisoners of historical thought processes, which drive their attitudes. In this part we discuss each of the underlying problems that a global business manager might face:

■ Chapter Five: Diverse Cultures
■ Chapter Six: Early Trade Theories
■ Chapter Seven: Opposing Development Theories
■ Chapter Eight: Conflicting Public Policies

Diverse cultures

Setting aside conflicting trade and development theories which influence competitive economic policies for later discussion, the initial collision one experiences when conducting cross-border business is contrasting cultures.

This chapter contains excerpts from my book *Protocol For Profit: A Manager's Guide To Competing Worldwide*, the first in the Global Manager Series. You may wish to read that book for a fuller discussion of culture and its implications for global business. In it you will learn about the connection between culture and protocol, the eight common elements of international business protocol, culturally related travel tips, negotiating tips, and the tips and traps of country conditions and protocols, country by country.

What is at issue here?

We need to understand and deal with diverse cultures for three reasons: to overcome initial fear and mistrust; to conduct negotiations; and to market our products or services.

A lack of understanding of another's behavior begets mistrust. As a result, some business persons become intimidated and consequently develop what is known as irrational xenophobia, an anxiety or, in the worst case, a hatred of things foreign. National boundaries are "safe", even when sales and profit yields indicate otherwise. From a global business point of view it is not enough to have technical competency—company representatives must also have cultural competency.

Modern aviation dominates global transportation and the world seems much smaller. All economies have become increasingly open to foreign competition. Market barriers have been reduced and competitors have made significant market share gains. The world manufacturing base has changed from smoke stack to high-tech and national survival as well as business survival increasingly depends on reaching out to the people and cultures of the world to sell our goods.

Culture

Let's get the word culture straight in our minds. Most dictionaries give three definitions. In the first instance it is thought of as the act of developing the intellectual and moral faculties; enlightenment and excellence of taste acquired by intellectual and aesthetic training; acquaintance with and taste for fine arts, humanities and broad aspects of science as distinguished from ordinary trade and craft pursuits. That's a good definition, but not what we refer to in this chapter.

A second definition refers to culture as the integrated pattern of human knowledge, belief and behavior that depends on man's knowledge and the capacity to pass on that knowledge to succeeding generations. That's not what we're are referring to either.

The definition that interests us from a business point of view is that which has to do with diverse groups of people—the customary beliefs, social forms and material traits of a racial, religious or social groups. In other words, for us, culture is a set of coded meanings or orientations for a given society, or social setting that affects commerce.

The process of taking the baggage of one's own culture into another is commonly called "cross cultural communications." The ability to be successful in another culture requires an appreciation of theory, time, some practical rules, and an accommodating attitude.

Can one culture be superior to another?

The answer is *no*!

Political systems, armies, navies, and even economic systems may be superior, but cultures are not.

The best way to appreciate the behavior of the people of another country is to "walk in the other fellow's shoes", that is, live there and get a feel for the similarities and differences.

Short of being able to walk in the other's shoes, it is important to study the behavior barriers that create friction and restrict the transferral of wealth across borders and to appreciate the concepts as they relate to global business. To avoid the stumbling blocks to international business, managers need to acquire empathy and tolerance of non-verbal as well as verbal differences and a competency that blends task and behaviorally oriented conduct.

Culture gives us a set of codes to deal with phenomena in a social environment. It sets priorities among the meanings of those codes, and it justifies the need for the culture, usually by means of an associated religion. Whatever a nation's culture is, it works for them. In order to function within it, we, the foreigners, must get on the band wagon.

The Japanese do it very well. They learn how to penetrate foreign markets by sending their managers to live and study in "the other fellow's shoes". Their mission is to develop relationships with contemporaries that will last for years. The Japanese don't try to change the way of life in the other country, they learn about it. When they go home they are specialists in marketing and production in the country which they researched.

Country culture

It's a country's culture that regulates such things as sexuality, child raising, acquisition of food and clothing, and the incentives that motivate people to work and buy products. All of these things are of course major factors in marketing products. Culture is also a complex concept because there are often many cultures within a given nation.

Business culture

Business culture is secondary to a country's general culture, but provides the rules of the business game and explains the differences and the priorities. Thus the environment of international business is composed of:

- relationships;
- language;
- religion;
- values and attitudes;
- laws and the legal environment;
- education;
- technology;
- social organizations.

Relationships

Relationships developed over a long period of time reduce mistrust. To meet this challenge we need to understand the countries, their people, and the cultures where we intend to do business, then spend time connecting with counterparts.

Language

Ask a Japanese businessman what language he speaks, and he will say the language of the customer.

Language is the thing that sets humans apart from other forms of life. It is the way we tell others about our history, and our intentions for the future. Language is the means of communicating within a culture.

For people in a given culture their language defines their socialization. Sometimes, from the substance of some information, it is possible to tell immediately the origin of the speaker. For instance consider this person. What is the country of origin?

"If y'all play ball—we can interface the system architecture, put on a dog and pony show, then split some knock-out profits."

There are more than 3000 languages in the world today and probably as many as 10,000 dialects. Obviously, since there are only about 200 nations on earth, many countries have more than one language and culture. Some of the languages within a country have priority. Some are used for business, others are used for training and education. We need to have an appreciation that there are language hierarchies within nations in order to proceed with such everyday practices as contract definition.

Some languages have become more dominant than others. On a global basis it is generally agreed that English is the world's major language. Therefore, English speakers often have an advantage. Because of its dominant role English is becoming the most useful second language for people of other countries to learn. Although it is not growing in popularity, French is probably the second most useful language in the world. Of course Spanish is essential to do business in Central and Latin America. Languages such as Japanese and Chinese are also growing in importance as these nations grow economically.

The multiplicity of languages and the accompanying cultures in the world economy is having a dynamic affect on global trade. Every time a cultural barrier is crossed there is a potential communications problem and international trade depends on communications. Speaking in the customer's language is the cardinal rule of international trade. Probably nothing deserves your attention as an international manager more than the possibility of language confusion and misunderstanding. It is not uncommon that trade is stifled simply because one or both parties to the relationship misinterpreted the meaning of a simple sentence.

For instance when Coca-Cola was first introduced to the Asian market, the name was translated with Chinese characters that sounded like "Coca-Cola," but read as "Bite the wax tadpole."

The introduction of a Rolls-Royce called "Silver Mist" to the German market failed and its name had to be changed—"Mist" means "dung" in German.

Obviously, on a practical basis persuasive communications requires accurate translation for advertisements, packages and labels. A company whose work is poorly translated runs the risk of being laughed at, offending a customer and, in the end, losing the business deal.

Body language

Example 1
Frank had an appointment to meet Isuko at 11:30 in the morning, but he arrived at 12 o'clock. Their conversation was friendly but Isuko harbored a lingering hostility. Frank unconsciously communicated he didn't think the appointment was very important or that Isuko was a person who needed to be treated with respect.

Example 2
It was important that Jose Arriba and Bill Martin develop a cordial relationship for business reasons. At a party, Jose, in Latin fashion, moved closer and closer to Bill as they spoke. Bill, interpreting this as an invasion of his space or pushiness on the part of Jose, backed away. Jose interpreted this as a coldness. Body language, sometimes called the "silent language," spoke again.

From these examples you can see the subtle power of non-verbal communication. It's the first form of communication you learn, and you use it every day to tell other people how you feel about yourself and them.

This language includes your posture, gestures, facial expressions, dress, the way you walk, and even the treatment of time, material things, and space.

People are very sensitive to any intrusion into their spatial bubble. An American's bubble of psychological distance or space is about eighteen inches. If someone stands too close to an American, he or she backs up. Try it. If they can't back up, they lean away or tense their muscles. In cultures where people have wide psychological distances they try to adjust their space in such a way that he or she feels comfortable. Some protect themselves with a purse, or an umbrella. Others move away to another spot behind a desk or a chair.

The language of the eyes is another age-old way you exchange feelings.

We look away from someone who uses their eyes in a way you are not accustomed. Yet the use of eyes varies worldwide by class, generation, region, ethnic, and national differences. Think about it. Eye contact between men and women is measured in seconds and micro-seconds. In some cultures it's taboo to look at all.

Even the way we listen has a silent language of its own. We know immediately whether or not the person we're talking to is "tuned in". If a person is listening the head will nod, and occasionally the "Hmm" sound will be spoken. The speaker will know the listener wants to terminate the conversation when he or she fidgets and begins to look either at his watch or gaze about the room.

Body language is learned in the same way we learned spoken language—by observing and imitating the people around us when we were growing up. We learned gender signals appropriate to our sex by imitating our mother and father.

These patterns of body language vary widely from one culture to another. American women sit with their legs crossed at the knee, or they may cross their ankles. Young Latin males, in their machismo, sit on the base of their spine, with their legs and feet spread wide apart.

People communicate a great deal by their gestures, facial expressions, posture and even their walks. Can body language affect your business dealings? You can bet on it!

Religion

Nothing destroys the development of relationships more than stereotypes of religious attitudes. Religion plays a major part in the cultural similarities and differences of nations. In itself religion can be a basis of mistrust and a barrier to trade.

A religious group took Bristol Meyers to court where they were punished heavily for selling low-quality formula infant milk in a Third World country. Both Eastman Kodak and General Motors have been targets of organized religious movements in other countries because of management decisions.

Religion is often the dominant influence for the consumer of products. Such things as religious holidays determine buying and consumption patterns. Knowing what is forbidden and what a society expects as a result of their various religions affects market strategy.

Values and attitudes

The roles of values and attitudes in international business are difficult to measure, but vital to success. Work ethic and motivation are the intangibles that affect economic performance. Values, for instance, affect how we view time. The saying is, "the clock runs in English and walks in Spanish and French." One international traveler said: "The only time the Spanish are on time is for the bull fight."

In more modern societies time has become a commodity, i.e. "time is money." As an example, the time horizon of many American firms is measured in quarterly profits, yet for most Asian business cultures, the time horizon is measured in terms of 25, 50 or even 100 years. Building international business and trade across national borders just doesn't happen at big city pace. In countries that have older, more traditional values, time is often measured in the movement of the sun, phases of the moon or relative to planting seasons.

Values of a society determine its attitudes toward wealth, consumption, achievement, technology and change, and we must evaluate in terms of the host culture. Researching attitudes about openness and the receptivity to new technology are the essentials of marketing America's changing products.

> **Japanese Time Horizon:** According to James B. Vaughn, Director of California's Office of Trade and Investment for the Asian region, ". . . Japanese business people have a strong tendency to want to deal with Japanese suppliers. It makes it very difficult for Americans to break into that system." He thinks it may take as much as 10 years to develop the business relationships and understand the market. "It takes a lot of time and a lot of money, and my sense of American business and culture is that it doesn't lead Americans to do business that way."

Laws and legal environment

The laws of a society are another dimension of its culture. They are the rules established by authority and society. On the one hand, laws provide an opportunity to handle the mistrust of doing business across international boundaries and, on the other, they can become barriers and constraints to operations. The laws of nations are often greatly different. About half of the nations of the world are under a form of either Code or Common law, but the other half are under either Muslim, Communist or indigenous laws. In most cases, none of the world's legal systems are pure. Each nation has its own unique laws but, nevertheless, one can find more and more similarities and mixtures within each classification.

Complications among national legal systems could drive the faint hearted from international trade, but international law is growing and there is a set of adjudication practices that has developed over the years. International law is the derived law that, in effect, minimizes the range of differences among national laws. In the interdependent world of today international law is the growth area in the legal environment. There is no international legislative body that makes international laws. What does exist is a set of agreements, treaties, and conventions between two or more nations that represents the dampening of intercultural conflict.

For most dealings we will be most interested in the law as it relates to contracts, but we should always consider litigation as a last resort. Settle disputes in other ways if possible. Litigation is only for the stupid and the rich, because it usually involves long delays, during which inventories are tied up and trade is halted. Law suits are costly, not just because of the money, but also because of the broken relationships that result. Most international commercial disputes can be solved by conciliation, mediation, and arbitration. The International Chamber of Commerce provides an arbitration service that can often be written right into a sales contract for use should the unspeakable happen.

Education

Culture shapes our thoughts and emotions. Our motivation is influenced by our education as well as other things such as values and religion which we have already discussed. The biggest international difference is the educational attainment of the populous. The next biggest difference is the educational mix. In some countries, such as Germany, there is little difference in the mix. Practically all Europeans and Americans are educated from kindergarten through 12th grade. In most industrialized nations education is no longer a function of wealth. A boy or girl from the poorest of families can find a way to get an education. But not so in many countries. It is not unusual to find only the elite of some nations educated to the levels Americans assume for all people. The impact of education is, therefore, profound for marketing products, as well as establishing relationships, because good communications are often based on relative education capacities and standards.

Technology

The most recent change in technology is our growing control over energy and information. The word technology begets concepts such as science, development, invention, and innovation. Some older languages don't even have words to express these concepts. Understanding the technological gap among nations is an essential element to exporting products across borders. Wide gaps still exist between the most advanced nations and those we call "traditional societies." The implications for us are that such things as training needs for technology transfer, and the impact of that transfer on social environments, must be considered. We should always look at technology from the importing country's point of view.

Social organization

International business cannot be conducted without involvement in foreign social relationships. In order to develop market segmentation and target markets the social organizations of a country must be studied. Insensitivity to the customs within the consumer country will not only result in misinformed decisions but also precipitate resentment and, in some cases, recrimination.

Nothing is universal in business organizations. There are no universal theories of motivation, leadership style, or consumer behavior. Such theories are figments of American business schools and do not stand up well in practice, nor do they export well. The truth is humans have invented an amazing diversity of institutions.

Social stratification is the hierarchy of classes within a society—the relative power, social priorities, privilege and income of those classes. Each class within a system has somewhat different and distinct tastes, political views, and consumption patterns. Many countries have a socio-religious ideology that allows rank to be intrinsic and inherited biologically. This implies that different categories of humans are culturally defined as if consisting of different worth and potential for performance. Regardless of how we react to such non-competitive socialization, such ideas are predictable in some countries. Faced with such a system of socio-religious rank it is essential that we learn how to deal with it—not attempt to change it.

Practical applications

As stated earlier, culture affects the behavior of business people in several ways: marketing and negotiating.

Marketing

Adapting your product design, labels, and marketing strategy is driven by the consumer's culture. Here is a short list of examples which convey the importance of culture and how much difference it could make when marketing products across borders:

- Deodorant usage among men ranges from 80 percent in the United States to 55 percent in Sweden, to 28 percent in Italy, and 8 percent in the Philippines.
- Feet are regarded as despicable in Thailand. Athlete's foot remedies with packages featuring a picture of feet are not well received.
- White is the color of mourning in Japan. The color purple is associated with death in many Latin American countries.

- McDonald's failed when they tried to introduce their popular clown into China. The color of the clown's face was white which means death in that country.
- Braun, a German producer of electric shavers tried to penetrate the Japanese market without taking into consideration that Asian hands are much smaller than Europeans. The Braun shavers were much too unwieldy for the Japanese.
- An enterprise selling baking powder in Japan failed when they didn't consider the fact that there are virtually no owners of ovens in Japan because their apartments are too small for this kind of furniture.

Negotiating

Some nations operate on a fixed-price system where most consumers grow up with the notion of buying off the shelf at the price offered or don't buy at all. On the other hand, people of many nations are born cultural negotiators.

What makes global negotiation different? Such cultural factors as the use of time; the individual versus the group; orderliness and conformity of the society; patterns of communications, pace of negotiations; strategies; emphasis on personal relationships, decision making; and gender issues. Negotiations can even differ from region to region.

Unfortunately, too many firms wander into international bargaining situations with no plan and no idea how to proceed. For them, it's an ad lib and ad hoc operation all the way. For some, lack of preparation is the result of a sense of corporate superiority, but for most it's pure ignorance of the number and competence of the ferocious competitors out there scouring the world for scraps of business.

The first step in preparing for international negotiations is to develop a complete assessment of our firm's capabilities. Analyze our strengths and weaknesses, particularly in terms of managerial skills, product delivery, technical abilities, and global resources.

Next, analyze our target—the company or country we intend to sell our product to. Keep in mind that the human and behavioral aspects of our negotiations will be vital.

- Understand the place in the world we will be traveling to.
- Know their culture, history, and political processes.
- Pay particular attention to the importance of face saving to the people of the country where we will be negotiating.
- What is the host government's role in country negotiations?
- How important are personal relations?
- How much time should you allow for negotiations?

In Ethiopia the time required to make a decision is directly proportional to its importance. This is so much the case that low-level bureaucrats attempt to raise the prestige of their work by taking a long time to make decisions. If we foreigners attempted to speed up the process, we could innocently downgrade the importance of their work.

The third step is to know our competitors. What is their financial position, their strengths and weaknesses, and what are their capabilities in terms of negotiating gambits?

The last step is to prepare and train the negotiating team. In today's increasingly competitive business world, there is no substitute for extensive advanced preparation and thought. Many companies have taken to role playing their negotiations long before the initial quote is submitted or the actual marketing of a product begins. Teams are formed and each team is given a set of negotiating alternatives. Each team pretends to represent a product, company, or country which might be in the line up of competitors. With a chalkboard nearby on which a team presents its position, the negotiators go through sufficient rounds to get a sense of the process. Sometimes price is reduced by 10 percent, or service warranties are offered. Even specific advertising concepts are discussed. Little is left to chance.

Competence in formulating strategy and negotiating skill is seldom learned from books–both subjects are ruled by so many variables that there is no substitute for experience and knowledge. Nevertheless, preparation and role playing acts as an excellent training device and serves to sharpen the skills of even the most experienced.

Key elements of cross-cultural negotiations

- Use the team approach. Take along financial and technical experts. Have someone take notes while the negotiators focus on the action.
- Dress for business. Show by your appearance that the event is of major importance.
- English is often the negotiating language, nevertheless take along someone on your team who speaks the opponent's tongue. Rudimentary knowledge of key foreign terms and numbers might ease the process.

Bribery

People prefer not to talk about it, but it happens and we must be aware that bribery is part of doing business worldwide. Not every person in a country views it in the same way. There are ethical people in every country, but bribery is more prevalent in some countries than others.

The names for bribery vary from country to country but the act is the same. In the middle East it is called *backshesh*; in Italy, *la busterella*; West Africa, *dash*; *Grease* in the U.S.A.; *la mordid* (bite) in Latin America; *kumshaw* in Asia; and *pot du vin* (jug of wine) in France.

Americans are prohibited by law from participating. The Foreign Corrupt Practices Act (FCPA) forbids below-the-table exchanges except in the case of small facilitating payments. After standing alone since 1979 when the FCPA was enacted, the United States was joined in January 1998 by 29 members of the Organization for Economic Cooperation and Development. This body, which represents the globe's largest economies, signed a treaty outlawing the bribing of foreign governmental officials. Five other non-OECD nations, including Argentina, Brazil and Chile, also signed the agreement.

Summary

We may think culture will take care of itself after the technical business studies and analysis are complete, but maintaining global competitiveness means changing viewpoints and adjusting to the demands imposed by the new global environment of interdependence. To cope and compete in international markets, one must factor foreign cultures into global business strategies.

If we let it, culture can be a deterrent to international business. It can get in our way with regard to even thinking about challenging another country's markets, in negotiations, and in the selling of our goods. But when we discover that people in other lands are more like us than different, and if we understand the underlying issues that make up the differences, we can overcome frictions and easily do global business.

The next chapter explains the early international trade theories issues a global business faces when trading across borders.

CHAPTER SIX

Conflicting trade theories

I simply imagine it so, then go about to prove it.

Albert Einstein

Why do international business managers care about theories? Because professors teach them, students and laymen believe them, and politicians attempt to practice them.

Rulers ask, "Why not remain independent and trade only within our national borders? Why should we join the global economic system?"

Over the ages those who advise governments: thinkers, theorists, and writers, have attempted to explain why trade takes place across borders. One answer is, not all nation-states are equally endowed. In fact, no nation is an autarky, that is, no nation has 100 percent of the things it needs within its borders. Even if a nation was self sufficient, in today's world it is unlikely it would manufacture all the goods its people might like to have. Another answer is that left unregulated, trade is a very random process which follows profit. Trade could be within borders but . . . if profit is better beyond, why not?

The question of "why" people and firms trade across national borders has been studied by economists and writers over an expanse of about 450 years. Figure 6.1 shows the spectrum of that thought on a time scale that indicates the time span when each theory was in vogue.

Early theories of international trade

Economists and other advisers have always influenced governments. The earliest of their arguments and probably the most influential was the theory of Mercantilism (1500–1800). Later came the Classical Era theories (circa 1700–1850), which included absolute advantage and the theory of comparative advantage. Alternative theories have emerged sporadically over the years each bringing clarification to the question: "why trade beyond our borders?"

Each will be discussed in the following paragraphs, but not in the depth one might find in standard economics texts. Rather, the intent of our discussion is to provide for the working manager an overview of

Figure 6.1 The time spans of international trade theories

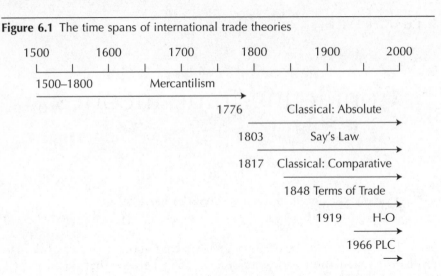

the many explanations of international trade so they might better understand the thoughts that influence governments.

Mercantilism

No one knows when the label "mercantilism" was put on what is generally acknowledged as the first international trade theory. This notion had it that overseas trade was really about grasping leaders of foreign nations. In those days, they wanted to accumulate gold and silver in order to increase their power in the world. Gold and silver was the currency acceptable to pay armies which were, and to a certain extent remain, the expression of power. Expounded in Thomas Mum's *England's Treasure by Forraign Trade* (1949), the public policy implications of mercantilism were to influence a favorable balance of trade. This was accomplished by keeping the costs of production low, taxing imports, and waging an offensive in export markets. In other words, international trade was a zero-sum game and the seed of war because it inherently brought about conflict between nations.

Government policies of the time were outward, controlled, and competitive. This theory explains the great expansion of England, France, Spain and Portugal during these times. Without gold as a medium of exchange, obviously the original theory is voided. The private business policy implications of that time were the utilization of cheap labor, often exploiting children, women, and slaves.

This theory remains in practice today, but modern versions differ from the original in that today the accumulation of convertible currency instead of gold is often the goal of governments. The utilization of inexpensive labor remains in practice.

Classical: absolute advantage

The theory of free trade took hold toward the end of the eighteenth century when Adam Smith suggested that trade was more correctly explained as an unregulated, laissez-faire activity which had significance in the division of labor. In his book *An Inquiry into the Nature and Causes of the Wealth of Nations*, 1776 (1937), Smith offered the concept that nations traded those goods for which they had an *absolute* advantage, that is a low-cost advantage based on its natural endowments. Smith argued that it was the invisible hand of an unfettered market that brought about social harmony and public benefit.

Classical: comparative advantage

Later, in 1817, David Ricardo's *On the Principals of Political Economy and Taxation* was published (1948). In his work, Ricardo expanded on the thoughts of Smith and suggested free trade was based on *comparative* as well as absolute advantage. The "labor theory of value" suggests that the value of commodities ultimately depends on the human labor time expended in their production. In reality the theory of comparative costs is the same as the notion of opportunity costs which is the idea that a country can use its productive resources only once, so a choice must be made.

These two theories are often packaged by economists under the heading called "classical economic science" which suggests that trade between free countries furthers the welfare of both. That is, that harmony, not conflict, governs commercial relations between nations. Exports are profitable for exporters, but the country as a whole benefits from imports. In other words, imports are consumed and consumption is the most conspicuous end of economic activity. The public sector implications of this policy were the movement away from regulation. The private sector implications were the validation of free markets.

Alternative explanations

The principal changes in the theory of why enterprises trade across national borders since David Ricardo's time have been the adapting of the earlier work to a more complex world and a significant increase in world trade. Neoclassical theories, as they are called, are those that explain why economic transfer takes place across borders in terms of supply and demand such as Heckscher-Olin (H-O), Terms of Trade, Say's Law, Leontief Paradox, and Product Life Cycle.

Heckscher-Ohlin (H-O) theory

In a brief article published in 1919, Eli Heckscher, a noted Swedish economic historian, introduced the concept that businesses export those goods that use the most abundant factors of endowments available to that country.

Drawing from this earlier work, Bertil Ohlin, one of Heckscher's students, more fully explained, in papers also published about 1919 and later in *Interregional and International Trade* (1952), that this concept replaced Ricardo's theory of value (comparative advantage) with the notion that factors of endowment are the determinants of trade. Those factors of production were: natural resources, capital, management, labor, and technology (know-how). Today we add *intelligence* to the list—intelligence being the ability to search information that enhances the competitive position of firms in the global arena, such as technology, competitors, opportunities, etc.

Sometimes called the "modern theory of international trade," the Heckscher-Ohlin (H-O) model believed the factors of production did not easily move across frontiers. Land didn't move at all, and labor preferred to stay. This theory assumed fixed supplies of homogeneous factors of production, absence of technology innovation, and sameness of production functions in different countries. The public sector policy implications are less control. Private sector business policy implications were competition, market theory, and self interest.

Terms of trade

John Stuart Mill (1806–1873) in his *Principles of Political Economy*, 1848, (1920) suggested that there is a theorem related to reciprocal demand that explained the price paid to foreigners for a good *vis-à-vis* the price charged to foreigners for exported goods. Mill defined this as the "terms of trade" which a country is willing to buy and sell on world markets. Further explained as a "country offer curve" which shows simply that price is low if demand is low, price is high if demand is high.

Say's law

Jean Baptiste Say published in 1803 in *Traite d'economie politiques*, an expression of the naive thought that supply creates its own demand. Thus his theory suggested that creation of full employment ensured the full capacity loading of existing plants and therefore that imports, however cheap, can do no harm to the internal domestic situation. The theory has been generally discredited, but it may hold in some areas of high technology.

Leontief paradox

Nobel laureate economist Wassily Leontief used input-output analysis to test the Heckscher-Ohlin (H-O) theory in the case of America. Since the United States is a capital-intensive economy it was assumed that it exported capital goods in exchange for labor-intensive products. Leontief's results contradicted the thesis by concluding just the opposite. His data showed that the U.S.A. exported products the contents of which contained less capital and more labor than the goods it was importing.

Product life cycle

The theory of product life cycle may partially explain the Leontief Paradox. This theory, credited to the American economist Raymond G. Vernon in an article published in 1966 titled *International Investment and International Trade in the Product Cycle*, has it that international trade proceeds in four stages: (1) a developed country introduces and has a monopoly on a new product for export; (2) foreign production begins; (3) foreign production becomes competitive in export; (4) the originating developed country imports the product.

The paradigm suggests that products live through four stages of life: (1) introduction or innovative, (2) growth or process development, (3) maturity or standardization, and (4) declining. As the product reaches maturity then passes into its declining phases, international markets change, thus providing various trade opportunities. Public and private sector implications are the same as classical.

Government control

To the extent they are influenced by, believe and practice these theories, governments apply more or less interstate controls. Figure 6.2 shows the implications of the various international theories on government controls.

Figure 6.2 Government control of trade

Less Control	Terms of Trade
	H-O Theory
	Product Life Cycle
	Classical
Most Control	Mercantilism

Summary

The question of "why" people and firms trade across national borders as studied by economists and writers is fairly new, covering only an expanse of about 450 years. Figure 6.1 showed the spectrum of that thought on a time scale. The mercantilist's original premise was that a nation must export for the purpose of accumulating gold in order to increase that nation's power in the world. Today mercantilism has been modified to accommodate convertible currency at the expense of inexpensive labor.

Adam Smith brought us absolute advantage and market theory as the reason for international trade, while David Ricardo introduced the concept of comparative advantage. Heckscher, as modified by Ohlin, introduced the concept that nations traded because they had a comparative advantage in the factors of endowment.

As a result of the influences of these theories and differing approaches, governments apply more or less interstate control, shown in Figure 6.2.

The next chapter deals with opposing development theories, which are often the basis of public policy debates and have implications for cross-border business.

CHAPTER SEVEN

Competing development theories

We need to learn how to spend our time and effort working on the future, instead of continually rearranging the past.

Philip Crosby

The global business system includes nations that are not equally developed economically. Of course, not all cities are equal nor are all communities and certainly not all markets. There are "have" and "have-not" nations. Some countries are wealthy and on average their people live reasonably satisfying lives. But in other parts of the world the people of other nations live in abject grinding poverty, destitution, and squalor.

Of course, like nations, not all humans are equal in terms of personal capacity or wealth. In some countries there are three classes of people: the rich, the middle class and the poor, and in those countries even the size of the classes vary. In other nations there are only two classes of people: the "haves" and the "have-nots."

This chapter examines the "have" and "have-not" nations in terms of historical theories, i.e. what has been said by thinkers to explain the uneven growth evident in the world today and what nations do to change.

Economic (growth) development

Economic development has different meanings for different people. For the international economist it typically means improving growth for the least developed countries (LDCs). For local governments it may simply mean creating jobs for their constituents—provincial politicians may not even know that the process has a name. For others, economic development means land reform and the redistribution of agri-business.

Development is measured in terms of growth because the intent of most governments is a continuing rise of gross national product (GNP) percapita income, and better lives (the elimination of poverty, inequality, and unemployment) for their people through improved techniques of production and marketing.

We know that country markets can be artificially stimulated by governments through the process alternately known as "growth" or "economic" development. It is a comprehensive term that includes the many improvements to a nation, such as infrastructure, education, and capital formation, but the major element of growth development is private sector business development.

Nations can change. As a result of government stimulation and private sector business growth they can graduate to higher classifications, or by competition, natural disasters, or war a country can be demoted.

Graduation

Graduation is the assumption that individual developing countries are capable, as a result of economic growth, of assuming greater responsibilities and obligations in the global business system.

Within the World Trade Organization (formerly GATT), International Monetary Fund (IMF), United Nations Conference on Trade and Development (UNCTAD), and the World Bank there are rules for graduation that relate to import restrictions, the generalized system of preferences, and low-interest loans. As developing nations advance their standard of living, donor countries may remove the more advanced from these special eligibility programs. The generalized system of preferences (GSP) is a non-reciprocal preferential treatment of tariffs in favor of developing nations and is a major success of the UNCTAD Conference. The World Bank may also move a graduated country from dependence on concessional grants to non-concessional loans.

Demotion

Of course the reverse can also happen. A country can be demoted in terms of need due to a reversal of economic conditions caused by drought, floods or war. In such a case the nation may become the recipient of economic assistance or preferences from various supranational organizations and developed nations.

Country development classifications

For purposes of providing assistance, the United Nations (UN) labels countries in terms of their relative wealth. However, no matter how nations are labeled, *no inference of superiority or inferiority is intended*.

The UN groups are: developed, developing, and less developed. In reality, as countries grow, labels blend and the positions of nations relative to others can change.

In addition to the labels given by the UN, pundits (print and audio/ video journalists) have also characterized the relative wealth of nations. Prior to the disintegration of eastern and central European command economies, they invented the term "four worlds." The *first world* meaning the industrial (developed) nations. The *second world* the communist nations, the *third world* the developing nations, and the *fourth world* the least developed, or the bottom 30 nations. Figure 7.1 shows these groupings.

Figure 7.1 Four worlds

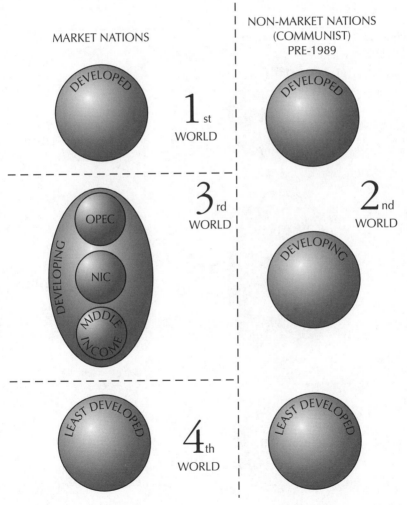

Three worlds from four

Later, as a result of the peaceful revolutions of 1989 and 1991, wherein the nations of Europe rebelled against political and economic tethers and the Soviet Union splintered into 15 separate states, pundits began to speak of three worlds: developed (rich industrialized); developing (middle income); and the less developed. Others see only two: the "haves" and the "have nots".

Although there are a few remaining Communist (non-market) nations, Cuba, North Korea, the People's Republic of China (PRC), and Vietnam, most countries today have mixed market economies. Figure 7.2 is a pictorial of the free market countries organized into three worlds by percapita income, but also showing the "have" and "have-not" worlds.

Figure 7.2 Three worlds from four

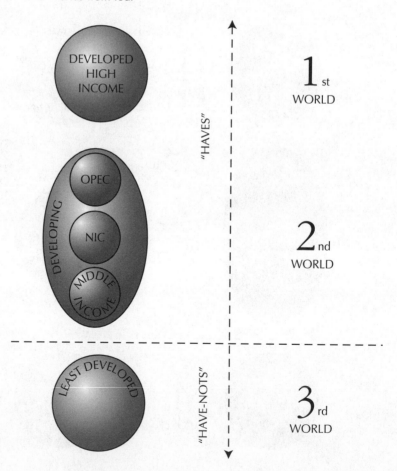

Other ways to categorize nations

Classifying nations in terms of developed, developing, less developed or two, three, or four worlds is too simplistic. Countries can be classified by many variables and there are no finite divisions. Here is a sampling of the other ways we categorize nations:

Percapita income

Nations can be classified by percapita income as high-, middle-, or low-income. Today, the average percapita annual income of people in countries can be less than $400 per year and as high as more than $25,000 per year. However in recent times, UN macro data indicates that percapita incomes of high- and middle-income nations are moving toward parity.

Developed nations (high income)

In this category we include nations whose citizens have at least $10,000 percapita income. This includes Canada and the United States, all of Western Europe (except the former Yugoslavia), together with Australia, Israel, Japan, New Zealand and South Africa. In many countries percapita income exceeds $25,000 a year.

Developing nations (middle income)

This grouping includes those countries where the people have a percapita income greater than $2000 but less than about $10,000 and, as shown in Figure 7.2, includes the Organization of Petroleum Exporting Countries (OPEC) and the newly industrialized countries (NICs), such as Singapore, South Korea, Thailand, Taiwan, and Hong Kong. Although percapita income of some OPEC nations exceeds $25,000 they are still considered developing because the national education system and other infrastructures are still considered to be weaker than most industrialized nations.

Least developed

This grouping contains about 36 countries—the poorest nations whose people have percapita incomes of less than $400. Most are in Africa, but a few like Afghanistan, Bangladesh ($130), Bhuta ($80), India ($240), Laos, and Nepal are in Asia. Haiti is the only country in the Western Hemisphere so classified by the United Nations.

Gross domestic product (GDP)

Nations can be classified by gross domestic product (GDP) as developed, developing, or underdeveloped.

Geographically

Because most of the developed countries are in the Northern hemisphere and most of the developing nations are in the Southern hemisphere, the terms "north" and "south" also often are used as identifiers.

Free markets

Typically, the people of developed nations have money so you should logically expect those nations to have the greatest market potential, while developing countries might have average or low market potential. The major consumer markets of the world coincide with the most developed nations, which coincides with a leverage toward free markets. Europe, North America and Japan dominate because they are highly industrialized and the people there have funds to spend.

Trade theories

Another measure of economic growth may be attributed to the adoption of one international trade theory over another. Those nations that adopted Adam Smith's free market theory and outward orientation have generally developed at faster rates than those that adopted Marxism (controlled markets) and inward trade orientations.

Entrepreneurial rewards

Overall, nations that place greater emphasis and reward on entrepreneurship have achieved higher growth rates.

Type of industry

Nothing is discussed more among social scientists and economists than the changing environment of growing nations. Some suggest that nations begin their growth as agriculturally based, move through an industrial stage, then arrive at a post-industrial stage where the industry is more service oriented than manufacturing oriented.

Political stability

A high degree of political stability is generally recognized as a prerequisite of growth. Countries that have frequent coups and revolutions tend to be less developed than those which change governments peacefully.

Population

Much of the literature about population points to an inverse relationship between population growth and economic development. Nations experiencing low or no population growth have less unemployment and tend to be better off than those with high population growth rates.

Classes

Economies tend to do better where a nation has a strong middle class. Yet there are still some countries that have been unable to cast off religious or colonial roots that brought only two classes: the rich and the poor—the "haves" and "have nots".

Management

Typically found in the higher classifications of economic growth are the managerial skills to handle day-to-day problems and the know-how of finance, R&D, production, and strategic planning.

Education

For development purposes, defining education is often difficult. Do we mean trainable workers, quantity of education, quality, or methods? For purposes of this book we mean education throughout the population spectrum, not just the elite class. A mass of people capable of responding to an increasingly complex, scientific, social, and technical life.

Technology

Those nations that place high value on human capital leading to education, inventiveness and technology tend to have higher economic growth.

Business maturity

With the advent of the expansion of global businesses, there is a new classification with only two descriptions for nations. Those that have matured or maturing global businesses. Closely related to entrepreneurship, this classification focuses on the success a nation has had in developing outward oriented businesses capable of competing in global markets.

Table 7.1 shows these groupings as they relate to the various ways to measure a nation's economic growth.

Economic development theories

All nations, regions, and cities have development strategies. Understanding the historical theories upon which governments have built their strategies provides a foundation for building a global business.

The fundamentals of growth development are the same for the inner city of Los Angeles, the *barrios* of Mexico City, or the nation of Nigeria.

Governments design schemes to stimulate job creation. They experiment, within the cultural norms of their nation, with various models. Whether it be a community or a nation, there have historically been three general economic theories (ideologies) and several theoretical intervention growth models which, over the years, have been used to actively stimulate growth:

General theories or ideologies

- Capitalism
- Socialism
- Communism

Intervention growth models

- Fiscal manipulation
- Monetary manipulation
- Traditional (Harrod-Domar)
- Structural-change
- International-dependency
- Neo-classical counter-revolution
- Balance of payments (BOP).

Figure 7.3 shows the various economic growth strategies in relation to a time line of history.

General theories or ideologies

Most people don't think of them as economic theories, but the three major bodies of development thought which have been the primary influences of national growth are: capitalism, socialism, and communism.

Table 7.1 Economic development classifications

Percapita income $$	GDP	Geography	Free markets	Trade theory	Entrepreneurship	Type of industry	Pol. stab.	Pop./unempl.	Classes	Mangement	Educat.	Technology	Global bus.
High	Developed	North	High	Outward	High	Service/Manufact.	High	Low/Low	3	High	High	High	Mature
Middle	Developing		Med.	Mixed	Med.	Manufacturing	Med.	Ave./Low	2½	Med.	Med.	Med.	Mat'ing
Low	Underdevelop	South	Low	Inward	Low	Agriculture	Low	High/High	2	Low	Low	Low	Mat'ing

Figure 7.3 Time line of economic development theories

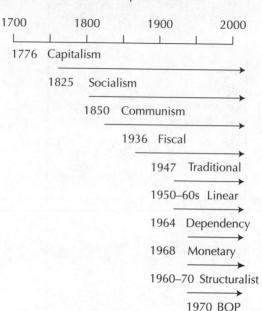

Capitalism (market theory or free enterprise)

This is the oldest general theory and is the notion of private ownership of the means of production. The foundation theory associated with capitalism is Adam Smith's "invisible hand" or market theory. Democracy is the social/political system usually associated with capitalism, although its economic aspects could operate under a ruling dictator.

Under capitalism, all factors of production are privately owned. The market determines success and survival. Profit is the motivation and risk of losses is accepted by those who provide the infusion of capital which provides the engine for growth; therefore, the capitalists are those who principally gain if there is a profit. The private sector motivations of capitalism are that investment may pay off with great rewards.

The assumptions of capitalism are:

1 private property;
2 free enterprise;
3 free choices;
4 competition and unrestricted markets;
5 self-interest;
6 market or pricing systems;
7 low regulation or control by government.

In theory, the public sector policy implications of capitalism are "hands off," but in reality no nation practices pure capitalism. Most often they blend other economic theories with capitalism. Often, as in the case of the United States, this is not openly acknowledged.

Socialism

Socialism is a term first used in Great Britain in 1827 and later attributed to the ideals of several writers including, among others, Frenchmen François Marie Fourier and Louis Blank. In its purist sense a socialist government owns the productive resources. Individuals may own items of wealth and major consumer durables, but they may not own factories, or machines that produce what society wants. Socialism is usually democratic but it could function under the rule of a dictator.

The assumptions of socialism are:

1 people are induced by wage differentials;
2 there are heavy taxes on large incomes to redistribute incomes;
3 rewards people receive from producing are set by the state not by the market;
4 people cannot become entrepreneurs, their endeavors are determined by the state.

Government policy implications of pure socialism are similar to that of communism, that is there is a great deal of central planning. In the real world there are varieties of socialism most of which permit individual ownership of smaller businesses, while government controls large industries.

Communism (Marxism/Leninism)

This theory, much older than mercantilism, argues that world capitalism is the victim of deep-rooted conflict between labor and capital which also governs capitalistic trade. Accordingly, poor countries have a shortage of markets because workers are too poor to buy domestic goods. Consequently, manufacturers sell overseas and they encounter competitors. Mortal struggle for the market begins and trade leads to war between capitalistic states. Attributed to Karl Marx (1818–1883) the theory of communism is a social organization based on government ownership of the means of production and distribution, and a worldwide classless society.

The assumptions of communism are:

1 all resources are owned by the people;
2 the populous is motivated by altruism;
3 workers contribute according to their productivity;

4 people receive according to their needs;
5 goods are produced for use, not for profit.

The public policy implication of this theory is the development of economic monopoly. With minor exceptions, the government owns all major factors of production, factories and farms. In the pure theory, government is to ultimately disappear and be replaced by the new populous motivated by altruism. From a free market point of view, the private sector implications of communism are deadly—the notion of private enterprise is nonexistent.

Figure 7.4 shows the primary spectrum of general economic theories as they relate to control by governments.

Intervention growth models

Governments continuously search for and adopt whatever theories seem to improve the welfare of their nation. In addition to adhering to one of the general ideologies, seven theoretical models have historically been used to artificially stimulate growth:

1 Fiscal Manipulation;
2 Monetary Manipulation;
3 Traditional Model (Harrod-Domar);
4 Structural-change Model;
5 International-Dependency Model;
6 Neo classical counter-revolution,
7 Balance of Payments (BOP).

Fiscal manipulation model

In modern times, industrialized nations such as the United States have adopted economic growth strategies that include various methods to stimulate private sector business. Most significant of these is the manipulation of fiscal policy. This is the theory, introduced by the British economist John Maynard Keynes (late 1930s), suggests that national and therefore business growth can be changed by the intervention of government spending. The theory is most simply explained by the formula $GNP = C + I + G = (X - M)$ where C is consumption, I is

Figure 7.4 Government economic control

Least Control	Capitalism
	Socialism
Most Control	Communism

business investment, and G is government spending. This intervention model, does account for international trade by showing X as exports and M as imports. If a picture is worth many words, the traditional bath tub illustration best explains Keynes' framework and is shown in Figure 7.5.

Monetary manipulation model

Monetary manipulation policy is not new. The model suggests that business is stimulated by regulating interest rates and the flow of money. As a means of financing their revolutionary war, the United States has had a monetary policy since the Continental Congress first printed money. The concept is often attributed to the American economist Milton Friedman (about 1968) due to his advocacy of monetary policy over other means of stimulating economic growth. Industrialized nations usually rely on monetary policy as a primary means of buoying growth and controlling inflation.

Traditional model (Harrod-Domar)

Dutch economists, Harrod and Domar (about 1947) developed an equation known as the traditional model. In its simplest form it assumes that

Figure 7.5 Fiscal manipulation – bath tub model

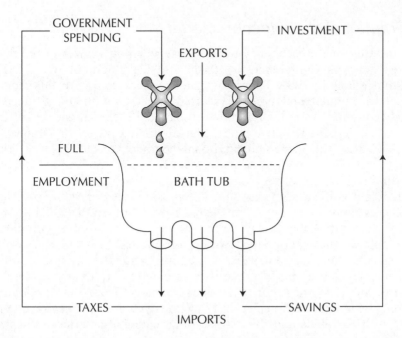

every economy (large or small) must save a portion of its national income, if only to replace worn out or impaired capital goods (buildings, roads, equipment, etc.). To grow, a community or nation must also invest net additions to the capital stock. It also assumes that a relationship, called the capital/output ratio exists between the size of total capital stock K and GNP, G.

If we define the capital/output ratio as k and assume further that the savings rate, s, is a fixed proportion of national output and the total new investment is determined by the level of total savings we can construct a simple model of economic growth which states that the change in G divided by G is equal to the savings rate (s) divided by the capital-output ratio (k), or

$$\Delta G/G = s/k$$

It says that the growth rate of national income will be positively related to savings ratio and negatively related to the economy's capital/output ratio.

Used by governments as a tool to estimate levels of investment needed to stimulate growth, the Harrod-Domar growth model demonstrates the importance of a high level of domestic savings in order to give a high capital-output ratio. It also suggests there is strong linkage between savings and investment. Given the absence of each, foreign capital becomes the most important factor in the development process.

International-dependency model

The international-dependency model arose as an outgrowth of the first United Nations Conference on Trade and Development (UNCTAD) conference held in 1964. Those governments that hold with this model believe that underdevelopment is caused by the contemporary international economic system. Underlying this model is the classical Marxist view of capitalism which includes the Leninist concept of "imperialism," that is, the giant multinationals corporations (MNC) are the enemy and the economies of some countries are conditioned by the growth development of the dominant (imperialist) countries.

Graphically this is seen in Figure 7.6 where the center or "metropole" represents the power struggle of the capitalists (imperialists) led by the United States of America. Under this model, the metropole dominates and exploits the "periphery" which represents the less developed nations. The outer circle represents the international economic system.

Advocates of this model argue that economic surplus (which in the Marxist model is the labor of workers) transfers from the developing nation to the advanced nation only by the systematic behavior of the giant multinationals and the institutional, coercive practices of supra-

Figure 7.6 Dependency model

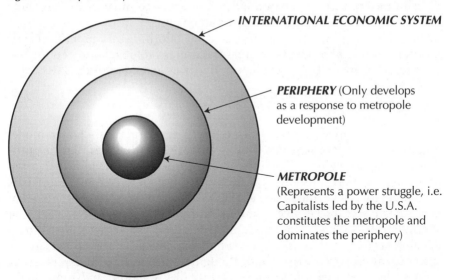

INTERNATIONAL ECONOMIC SYSTEM

PERIPHERY (Only develops as a response to metropole development)

METROPOLE
(Represents a power struggle, i.e. Capitalists led by the U.S.A. constitutes the metropole and dominates the periphery)

national organizations, such as the IMF, World Bank, etc., which exploit cheap labor and extract raw materials. In other words, only the metropole countries can develop on a self-sustaining basis; the periphery countries can only develop, if at all, as a response to metropole development.

From the belief in the international-dependency model has come the development of a United Nation's declaration and action program to establish a new international economic order (NIEO) for (at the time) the group of 77 developing nations. In May 1974 the United Nations General Assembly adopted the "Charter of Economic Rights and Duties of States," which called for the "full and complete economic emancipation" of the developing world. This charter was accompanied by a six-point program of action:

1 cartels (develop producers associations);
2 institute international commodity agreements;
3 improve access to developed markets by removing tariff and non-tariff barriers and providing preferences;
4 collective self-reliance, regional cooperation;
5 increase financial resources to mitigate external debt;
6 develop a code of conduct for transnational corporations.

A major success of the NIEO was the preferential treatment of manufacturers goods called the generalized system of preferences (GSP). "Generalized" meaning that all developed countries were intended to participate. "Preferences" meaning that all developing countries were to receive the same preferential treatment. GSP is a non-reciprocal, non-discriminatory tariff reduction (duty-free entry to most of the products granted preferences) based on the suspension of most favored nation (MFN) treatment and reciprocity. Textiles, clothing and processed agricultural products (products of greatest interest to developing countries) are excluded. In 1970, 18 developed countries agreed to offer GSP.

Structural-change model

Alternatively called "growth with equity," the structural-change model argues that development is rooted in historical influences. For instance Appalachia, a region of historical underdevelopment in the United States, is arguably a product of the company store syndrome. Similarly, underdeveloped nations are explained in the historical context of colonialism, which allowed a small minority to own the majority of the most fertile land. Governments that adopt the structuralist model develop strategies that attempt to change a nation's cultural pattern by introducing import substitution, thoughtful use of foreign capital, land reform, less reliance on primary commodity exports, and more high-technology differentiated products. Although developed and expounded primarily during the late nineteenth and early twentieth century the model is still applicable in those nations wishing to strengthen their middle class.

Neoclassical counter-revolution

The neoclassical counter-revolution model is simply a call for dismantling of private ownership and privatization of public corporations. It argues that the intervention of the state in economic activity slows the pace of economic growth. By permitting free markets to flourish, privatizing state-owned enterprises, promoting free trade and export expansion, welcoming foreign investment and eliminating distortions caused by governments, economic efficiency and growth will occur.

Managing by balance of payments (BOP)

This concept thinks of a nation as if it were a corporation with a set of financial statements, which over time give the country's managers sufficient information to make business decisions. By analyzing the data, as a corporate executive might, government officials can isolate problems and generate solutions. For example, if wage rates are significantly above the world labor market the country will suffer high trade deficits because imports will be a bargain. On the other hand, if wages are significantly low the country may experience high inflation due to lack of competition.

Bankers sometimes push money onto borrowers. The problem with recipient countries is that some are all too often "inward" oriented in their international trade policies. When they don't exchange enough products in global markets to generate convertible currency cash flow they can't even pay the interest on their debt. To service even a partial amount, nations begin capturing foreign currency at the borders from exporters and rationing it to those who import national priority goods. This tends to acerbate any economic growth problems by causing black markets and inflation.

Whatever the causes, when a nation's balance of payments goes into a deficit position it sends a signal to global businesses that government policy makers of that country must begin to consider means to return the balances to a more neutral position. This can be accomplished by several methods:

- Curtailing imports and emphasizing exports in the hope that a surplus of foreign currency will be introduced to bolster the balance.
- Deflating the domestic economy by adjusting monetary and/or fiscal instruments.
- Devaluing the exchange rate.
- Imposing exchange controls over international transactions, all of which become barriers to international trade.

The ledger

How do managers of a given nation know they have an international debt problem? Every nation keeps a set of books called the balance of payments (BOP). Using a double-entry system, BOP accounts classify and aggregate all the international trade and payments of the economy. How do modern nations collect the data? By requiring each transaction which crosses the border to be recorded on special collection forms and then entered into a central computer.

This summary of all transactions between residents of one country and the residents of another country, which usually covers a period of one year is kept in three accounts: (1) current account, (2) capital account, and (3) official reserves account. (Residence of businesses is generally determined by the country in which they are incorporated). Table 7.2 shows a conventional presentation of a nation's balance of payments.

The balance of payments of a country then, is really the summary of three balances: the balance of the current account (BOCuA), the balance of the capital account (BOCaA), and the balance of the official reserves account (BOORA). These accounts are the record of the imports and exports of merchandise and services, cash payments, gold flows, gifts, loans and investments, and other transactions. The result is an overall

Table 7.2 Balance of payments

	Debits	Credits	Net debit (−) or credit (+)
A. Current Account			
1. Goods	600	500	
		25	
Net Balance on Merchandise Trade (BOMT)			−75
2. Services			
a. Travel	100	50	
b. Transportation	75	60	
c. Investment	50	100	
d. Other	25	50	
Net Balance on Goods and Services (BOGS)			−65
3. Unilateral Transfers	75	25	
Net Balance on Current Account (BOCuA)			−115
B. Capital Account			
1. Long-term Capital			
a. Direct Investment	100	50	
b. Portfolio Investment	25	50	
2. Short-term Capital	500	600	
	260	250	
	25	50	
	50	100	
	50	25	
		100	
Net Balance on Capital Account (BOCaA)			+215
C. Official Reserves Account			
1. Monetary Gold (net)	5		
2. Reserve Assets (net)	100		
3. Liabilities to Central banks (net)		15	
Net Balance on Official Reserves Account (BOORA)			−90
Net Errors and Omissions	10		−10
Total Debits and Credits	2050	2050	

view of a nation's international economic position and is particularly valuable in the formulation of governmental, as well as business, policy.

The balance of current account is composed of two sub-accounts: (1) balance of merchandise trade (BOMT), and (2) balance of goods and services (BOGS). The balance of capital account records the net changes in capital imports and capital exports. The official reserves account shows the net foreign transactions of the nation's central bank.

Balance of merchandise trade (BOMT)

Balance of merchandise trade is a component of the balance of payments, and is the surplus or deficit that results from comparing a country's expenditures on merchandise imports and receipts derived from its merchandise exports. Simply put, the BMOT = Exports − Imports.

Balance of goods and services (BOGS)

The balance of goods and services is the BOMT plus or minus net services. Services includes sales and purchases of such things as transportation, insurance, travel, return on investment (interest, dividends, profits, royalties, speculation on currency, etc). Simply put, the BOGS = BMOT + or − Net Services.

To summarize then, the balance of payments consists of the summary of three equations:

1 BOMT = Merchandise imports − Merchandise exports
2 BOGS = BOMT + or − Net services*
3 BOCA = BOGS − Unilateral transfers

*Services includes ROI (interest, dividends, royalties, speculation)

4 BOCaA
5 BOORA

Summary

The people who manage all governments struggle to discover the right management mechanisms that will contribute to the growth of their nation. They experiment with economic theories, ideologies and growth models. Most models advocate free markets as best choice for national growth but, today, all nations have development strategies which are intended to stimulate market development. Understanding the historical theories upon which governments have been built provides a foundation for understanding the implications of trade upon global economic development.

The next chapter offers insight into the debates about trade and development as they affect public policy.

CHAPTER EIGHT

Opposing public policies

Why do some companies based in some nations innovate more than others? Why do some nations provide an environment that enables companies to improve and innovate faster than foreign rivals?

Michael Porter (Professor Harvard Business School).

Globalism is not a universally accepted fate and the global business system is not without debate. International trade and investment are constantly battered by argument. Within every country disagreements rage about the correct mixture of interstate controls, erosion of sovereignty, or the impact of another nation's changing policies. Heard in the chambers of Congress and Ministries every day are, "Those foreigners are causing . . ."

The major arguments for and against globalization are discussed in the following paragraphs, all of which must be considered by the international business person when formulating a strategy.

Concerns about globalism

As the nations of the world become more and interdependent, debates rage about home production and markets. Highest among them are the arguments about the impact on jobs.

Nationalism versus globalism

In this sense the term "nationalism" mainly means economic nationalism but includes concerns about uncontrolled immigration and threats to national sovereignty which advocates argue diminishes national independence. Those in favor of globalism counter by arguing that to be a player in the global community, just like a family in a local community, there must be give and take. Every one is a winner in a world where cooperation and collaboration is accepted.

Consumers versus jobs

One of the major issues faced by every country is how to keep its population at work. Jobs are of major concern when they are connected to industries impacted by imported competitors. Yet it is often these very imports that provide the consumer with a greater selection of products and stretches personal income to provide a decent lifestyle for the family of the very workers who are impacted by the potential loss of work caused by the imports. In fact imports are generally good for production and the creation of jobs because imports tend to stimulate competition and keep inflation in check.

Free trade versus managed trade

Managed traders, also known as protectionists, urge restrictions on imports to enable domestic producers to compete successfully against global producers. Free trade advocates argue that if domestic businesses are so inefficient and they cannot compete with imports they should either get out of business or formulate a new strategy.

Imports versus exports

This argument is heard less and less in today's interdependent world, yet there remain those who classify imports as bad and exports as good. These people are considered to be protectionist oriented. Those for imports argue exports help only the producers side and that imports help everyone.

Private versus public

This is an argument expressed by politicians who must consider the mix of private enterprise versus governmental operated organizations. The question relates to equity and efficiency. Those who argue for more private management suggest that the profit motive is more efficient. Those who take the opposite position say that free enterprise is not equitable nor controllable—that only public management with its easy regulation can bring equity to work forces.

Plan driven versus market driven

Some governments believe that market forces alone do not create the desired effect; therefore, these governments establish yearly plans, sometimes five, sometimes ten, and announce industrial policies that identify strategic industries, protect domestic industries, provide incentives to achieve their goals, place emphasis on exports, and promote business cooperation instead of competition. Whether by directed or indicative (more fully explained in Chapter Nine) planning methods these governments then give administrative guidance which amounts to managing international trade and investment. The issue then, is whether or not these plan-driven policies are a barrier to free trade? To the extent that planning is transparent and all business is permitted to participate, the effects are minimal. However, when the interstate controls used to achieve the planning goals are in conflict with and curtail business, the plan-driven policy can have a distorting effect on free trade.

Workers (unions) versus business

This argument makes a case that workers may become the losers in the expansion of globalism. That unless there are strong international unions to organize them, global businesses will take advantage of workers, exploiting them for profit.

Environment versus globalism

If more businesses get into the global market doesn't it follow that the earth's resources will be consumed at greater rates, thereby threatening mankind's survival? Wouldn't the increase in industrialization multiply the threat of global warming and other environmental issues? These are the arguments from those who see a significant danger if environmental issues are not addressed as the globalism movement grows.

Factors affecting the degree of globalism

Globalism does not have equal impact among nations or even regions. It is does not have instantaneous results. Governments continue to debate how to control the degree of its effects.

Balance of payments

This is the argument that a nation is out of market equilibrium with the world market when its balances are out of adjustment. It is a macro concept which can be visualized as if a nation were like a corporation. When the balance of payments is in deficit it could be argued that the endowments, such as labor, or the products which flow from those national endowments are not competitive in the world's free market, or that the economy as a whole is not competitive in the market. Advocates of this argument often want to artificially restrict imports, promote exports, or tinker with exchange rates.

The counter argument has it that over the long term, nations will adjust naturally when wage rates, prices and interest rates move with the world market.

Others suggest that international capital flows determine trade flows, and a nation's overall economy is strong when it shows a surplus in its capital account. They say that capital is attracted to higher interest rates and strong economies and a growing stock of productive capital ensures a bright future regardless of payments deficits.

Infant industry argument

Infant industry argument is the view that "temporary protection" for a new industry or firm in a particular country through tariff and non-tariff barriers can help it become established and eventually competitive in world markets. The counter argument is industries that have been established and operated with heavy dependence on direct or indirect government subsidies or protection have found it difficult to relinquish that support. It is better that uncompetitive businesses decline naturally and government support be thrown to new competitive industries.

Peril point

Peril point is a hypothetical limit beyond which a reduction in tariff protection would cause injury to a domestic industry.

Control versus globalism

This is the argument that national governments are losing control of their economy to private and public forces that overlay boundaries. Those that support this view want participation in supranational organizations to be curtailed to the extent that sovereignty could be eroded.

The other side of this argument supports stronger world governments, even a "one world" approach.

Regionalism versus global rules

Globalism infers a multi-lateral approach to harmonizing international trade processes. Regionalism, on the other hand, gives preferences to those players who are members of a given regional treaty. To the extent that regional preferences are more or less liberal than global multi-lateral rules free trade is distorted.

Economic development and the global economy

As the affects of globalism are realized to economic development more and more arguments are raised concerning its usefulness.

Preferences versus sameness

Nations that are behind in their development argue that they need advantages given to them by the more developed nations in order to compete. Preferences might be in the form of tariff reductions or they might be in terms of richer nations opening their markets while the less developed keep theirs closed.

Growth development

Development varies among countries, populations and regions. Arguments about the causes of economic conditions vary. Growth development experts are equally diverse in their debate about what makes lasting changes in economies. Most agree that the "haves" of the industrialized world have a responsibility to contribute to the stimulation of development of the "have nots" of the less developed nations. *Growth development*, sometimes termed "economic development," is recognized as a problem area for the world at large. There is growing recognition that industrialization is the answer and that international trade and investment makes a significant contribution to growth and improved welfare. For others the answer is simple: focus money on the problem and underdevelopment will go away. Others argue that the solutions are too complex, that is, to change the aspirations and wants of people requires cultural changes and that takes time. They ask, "Where there is no middle class, how is one developed?"

Even within a nation the argument of development is debated as to how much foreign trade and investment should be induced and how much growth should be "home grown".

"Have nots"

Some people from those nations categorized in one of the less than fully developed groupings, the "have nots," argue that their conditions are the result not just of inadequate financial capital, but also social overhead capital which includes:

■ infrastructure;
■ education, literacy;
■ inadequate managers, private and public;
■ insufficient entrepreneurs.

Others argue that their culture gets in the way—their people are happy as they are. They just don't want to be better off through industrial development. Still others argue that the causes are population growth or the adoption of the wrong ideology or economic strategies.

Many argue that it is the economic war between Marxism and the imperialist capitalists that have caused the conditions.

"Haves"

The "haves" of the developed nations argue, "Come and get it." They say, "We opened our markets, you should do the same. Change your economic system. Your policies are too protectionist, there is too much government intervention." . . . "Shift to a market economy," they say. "We know that free trade benefits all. Join the global economic system and compete."

The United States' Foreign Aid policy during the 1980s, for example centered on privatization. The Brady Plan, designed to mitigate Third World debt problems of the time, stipulated the institution of market-oriented reforms. Other developed nations offered mixed credits with "tied aid" conditions that benefited the giver.

Country risk argument

The "haves" say the economic conditions of the "have nots" are brought about by not having political stability, resulting in fragile economic or financial policies, diverse labor conditions, changing laws, and terrorism. They argue that economic exchange cannot occur when country risk is high and those nations that do not achieve stability invite economic suicide.

Host country argument

The host country debate argues that the giant multinationals siphon off the profits, leaving the host country's condition unchanged.

Inward (provincial) orientation

Some argue that provincialism is the cause of underdevelopment. *Inward orientation* is a strategy which biases government incentives in favor of domestic strategy and against global business. Those who oppose this strategy believe inwardness tends to cause people, businesses, and governments to become absorbed in getting through the day, paying the bills, and meeting immediate obligations. Inward orientation involves overt, high protectionism and is often associated with high inflation and extensive bureaucracies. Those who argue against this say that inward government strategies gradually cause businesses and nations to become isolated and self-absorbed. Their intellectual and emotional horizons shrink and they lose contact with the world outside, thus becoming myopic to larger meanings and roles.

Import substitution

Import substitution is the name of an inward strategy whereby a nation attempts to reduce imports (and hence foreign exchange expenditures) by encouraging the development of domestic industries.

Those who are against this strategy argue it is extremely protectionist by restricting imports of consumer goods. They argue that the encouragement of local enterprise to manufacture to replace the imports is good, but without competitive imports this strategy tends to build high-cost industries that eventually become a drag on the economy and bring high prices to the consumer. An additional pitfall is that without competition the products, over time, become non-exportable because they lose world-class quality.

Outward (cosmopolitan) orientation

An *outward oriented* strategy can be characterized as being neutral between productivity in the domestic or export market. The "haves" argue that the outward process of joining the global economic system brings growth. Because international trade is not discouraged, outward orientation is often, though sometimes misleadingly, referred to as an export promotion strategy.

Grappling with a global economy and an emerging democracy, Mexico, in the mid-1990s (then under President Salinas) attempted to move rapidly from nearly eight years of crisis marked by stagnation and inflation toward an outward orientation. By dropping barriers and eliminating protection for the country's domestic producers, the nation's policies now encourage an export strategy and an open invitation for foreign investment which could, in the long run make Mexico a world-class trading partner, create jobs and raise the standard of living for its citizens.

Miscellaneous arguments affecting globalism

Public policy makers grapple with many of the newer issues associated with the globalism phenomena.

Two worlds or three?

November 9th, 1989 was one of the most significant days of the twentieth century. It was the day that the Berlin Wall crumbled, signifying the peaceful revolution of central European nations retreating from non-market economics. Even more significant was 1991. It was the year the Soviet Union splintered into its individual parts. Some argue it was the year the world sifted into two worlds: the "haves" and "have nots". If so, the debate between the two takes on new meaning because the conversion from command economics to market economics can be chaotic and must be carefully controlled.

North/south argument

The "haves" argue that growth development is simply a north/south issue. They believe that those north of the equator are naturally better fit to be wealthy. These are the arguments that climatic conditions explain the differences in the economic development of humankind. Those who espouse this argument point to the economic and intellectual growth at the extremes of the globe, i.e. northern Europe, Japan, and the United States in the north and Australia, South Africa and Argentina in the south. They argue that less temperate climates limit human energy and mental powers and suggest that those within twenty degrees above and below the equator are destined to suffer forever because temperature and climate have arrested their desire to improve. Those who dispute this argument point to Singapore, Malaysia and Indonesia as examples of progress despite climatic conditions.

Equidistant denationalization

Equidistant denationalization is the approach by some corporations wherein their home office is one of convenience without allegiance to any particular nation. They view the world as one big market with an untold number of sub-markets, and their employees and managers are of every conceivable national origin. This argument has it that markets should be mapped in a common-sense way. Such as, where are the best country markets for products? Where will they be in the future? The home market may be a comfortable decision—no cultural problems—no currency problems, but it may not ensure business survival during the era of global interdependency. The real issues, they argue, are who has the purchasing power to buy products and what products satisfy their want? Even if there is a need and a market in the home country there may be a better (larger) market in another country. They argue: no jobs, no money, no market, no interest.

The counter argument has it that businesses should reflect a greater degree of patriotism and nationalism, that the founders owe much to country in which they are born.

Foreign direct investment

This is the argument, steeped in nationalism, that businesses and people of one nation should not own property in another. Those who argue against foreign investment believe at its greater limits that people and or governments of one nation could own another and, therefore, be able to control the other.

The counter discussion is that there is insufficient money for any one group or person to own another country. They argue that the sovereign nation always has the political might to expropriate, and thereby nationalize, that which it does not like and foreign investment brings new ideas, competition, and jobs.

Summary

A nation-state is defined as a form of political organization under which a relatively homogeneous people inhabits a sovereign state. Very often equity versus efficiency is the root of the public/private debate.

There are many arguments that drive public policy. Some are based on mores, some on historical results. Because sovereignty is freedom from external control, the debates of nationals versus foreigners is a continuous debate in every country. Free traders argue that competition not protection should decide survival.

Some believe that because economic development is trade related the equilibrium of the balance of payments is, over time, self righting and need not be artificially controlled.

The next chapter discusses today's reality with regard to international business and its relationship to governments and offers a new paradigm for consideration.

Competition at the borders

CHAPTER NINE

Today's reality: the trade-development link

Plan for the future because that's where you are going to spend the rest of your life.

Mark Twain

The theme of this, the third part of the book, is that too many business and political leaders throughout the world, blind to modern realities, are unaware of the new paradigm called artificial comparative advantage (ACA), which links international trade to economic development. Too often they forget they are in global competition where resources are fully mobile and fickle businesses change locations in a blink, no longer tied to "natural capital."

Part Three consists of three chapters which, when considered as a whole, show how the trade-development linkage has benefited nations but also offers strategic opportunities for global businesses. In this part we discuss the real-world methods used by governments to develop their economies.

- Chapter 9: Today's Reality: The Trade-Development Link
- Chapter 10: Trade Creation
- Chapter 11: Trade Barriers

In earlier chapters (about trade and development theories) it was noted that over the ages rulers have asked thinkers, theorists, and writers to answer the same questions: "Why trade across national or regional borders? Why not remain independent? Why should we join the global economic system?"

Would icons of economic and trade thought, such as Ricardo, change their fields in today's booming world economy? Maybe they would not alter their direction completely but they would modify their thinking for three reasons:

1 In their time they believed the factors of endowment were immobile and did not easily move across frontiers. They assumed fixed supplies

of endowments, absent technology innovation, and sameness of production functions in every country. Of course today rapid technological developments, and a decline in transportation costs has permitted producers to separate production functions that were once integrated. For each part of the process companies now seek the most cost-effective method throughout a world that has an increasing number of potential locations.

2 They were not yet aware that information (intelligence) would become the sixth factor endowment.

3 The "classical" theorists were also not yet aware of the influence of cross-border trade on economic development.

Have governments changed their policies based on these modern realities? Yes, because in the age of globalism international business does link nation-state economies; therefore, international trade and investment does make a significant contribution to economic development.

Major economic events strengthening globalism

Any attempt to understand the changes that strengthened globalism, interdependence, and the trade linkage requires a review of the most significant economic events since World War II:

1 The Marshall Plan and the recovery of Germany, Japan and Italy.
2 The incredible success of the Four Tigers of Asia.
3 The use of government planning and industrial policy.
4 The failure of directed economies to satisfy the expectations of people, leading to the restructuring of Central and Eastern Europe, and the evolvement of two worlds from three.
5 The trend toward parity of living standards among nations.

Marshall plan

The major factor that contributed to the post-war recovery of Western Europe and Japan was the program called Government Aid and Rehabilitation in Occupied Areas (GARIOA), better known as the Marshall Plan. This plan essentially provided the financial resources for those war-torn and disrupted countries to import capital equipment, start peace-time production, and begin exporting. It also offered preferences and opened markets in other industrialized states for those goods. The primary reason for its success was the lowering of trade barriers and the formation of the Organization for European Economic Cooperation (OEEC) through which the Europeans made their own plans as to how to maximize the use of the $12.5 billions of long-term loans and liquid short-term funds channeled from the United States through the Marshall Plan.

Tigers and Japan

Over the last half of the twentieth century there are important examples of nations graduating to higher economic levels of development. Most notable of those nations that gained economic promotion from "less developed" status to "developing industrialized" status were Japan and the Four Tigers of Asia. After World War II those nations discovered a new model by which nations could grow economically. As small island or insular properties, with low percapita incomes and commensurably small domestic markets, and without significant natural resources, the "Tigers Model" showed a way to make incredible growth changes (Rabushka (1985) or Perkins (1983)).

Government planning

Didn't planning die with the fall of the Soviet Union? Look around the world and decide for yourself. Not all nations adhere to pure market economics. China (PRC), Taiwan, Japan, South Korea, and many others continue to develop extensive economic development plans even though they permit a modified market economy.

Comprehensive planning is a twentieth-century innovation. It was virtually unknown before 1900, but by 1975 planning had become pervasive in the world economy.

Early thought, such as Adam Smith's "invisible hand" theory, had it that business would respond quickly to consumer demand with minimum government intervention. However, over time most nations have adopted either "directed" or "indicative" economic growth policies. Perkins (1983) said, "Development planning or investment planning is thus a modern institutional innovation which, over the last fifty years, has been increasingly applied successfully to giant multinational business firms pursuing a strategy of diversified growth and almost equally to nation states to maximize returns on allocation of limited capital resources."

Directed: "To plan the action and to supervise and instruct in the carrying out of such plan."
Indicative: "Giving an indication, suggestion, or intimation; showing; signifying."

Webster's New World Dictionary

Directed planning

Frederick W. Taylor had no idea the impact his work would have on the world when he began his labor at the Midvale Steel Company in Western Pennsylvania in the 1880s. Now known as the father of "scientific management," he was simply applying an engineering approach to factory management. The time and motion studies he pioneered not only resulted in improved efficiency and productivity, but better planning processes that altered capital investment techniques.

His science soon invaded the boardrooms of corporate America, principally in such private sector giants as General Motors and DuPont. But before long it was also adopted by governments.

According to Perkins, Karl Marx never advocated central planning, but Taylor's Midvale work so influenced V. I. Lenin that he introduced it to Stalin, who installed planning techniques in the public sector as a strategy for national industrial development. In 1928, the Soviet Union's GOSPLAN (State Planning Commission) developed three plans:

1 General Plan (10–15-year goals);
2 Perspective Plan (five-year goals);
3 The Control Plan (12-month goals).

The GOSPLAN staff expanded over time from only 40 personnel in 1921, to 300 in 1923. In 1926, the staff grew to almost 1000 people and were organized into 12 regions with 43 local planning committees reporting to it. By 1928, it implemented its first five-year plan.

Poland, Romania and Albania also adopted central planning. Hungary and Czechoslovakia chose a quasi-market road. The former East Germany and Bulgaria attempted the middle of the road. Yugoslavia used what they called guide-line planning coupled with market theory. Other members of the Communist bloc established centrally planned economies.

During World War I, even the United States government developed a comprehensive plan. It enlisted the aid of a core group of civilian experts to gain the cooperation of private enterprise and focus the economy on the war effort. Again, during World War II, with James F. Byrnes, one of America's most able managers at its helm, President Roosevelt established the Office of War Mobilization to centrally plan the resources to defeat foreign enemies. Later, in the 1950s, Robert McNamara implanted the Joint Strategic Planning System (JSPS) with direct ties to the Planning, Programming and Budgeting System (PPBS) in the Department of Defense (DOD). It has become the most sophisticated strategic planning process in the world. However, except for defense, the United States remains a peace-time paradox. Big American businesses adopted Taylor's planning philosophy long ago but the United States government has not, ostensibly because economic planning, although never intended, became linked to Marxism.

Indicative planning

Planning helped build Western Europe after World War II. As stated earlier, the OEEC was formed to improve planning for distribution of Marshall Plan aid.

To attain their own growth strategies, France implemented an "indicative" planning process. They solicited voluntary cooperation by using the persuasive powers of government (incentives such as preferred taxes and low-interest loans). The aim of France's indicative planning process was to improve per capita growth, develop investment priorities, and direct the flow of capital to advantageous sectors.

Rabushka (1985) explained that after World War II, Japan made the greatest gains using an indicative planning strategy. The government's Ministry of International Trade and Industry (MITI) set rough, general targets every 2–3 years. No exact details were ever given for most of the plan, but for a small number of high priority industries it issued a comprehensive plan.

The Four Tigers of Asia followed suit when they discovered that the factors of endowment: land (natural resources), labor, technology, management and capital moved easily across borders, and those factors could be controlled through a mixture of directed and indicative planning and industrial policy schemes.

De facto, even the U.S. government offers various tax and low-cost loan schemes to achieve its industrial aims.

Industrial policy

Industrial policy, also known as "country-international strategic market planning," is a strategy used by a nation to strengthen its industrial base and develop competitive export industries to improve its balance of payments position.

Historically, the term "industrial strategy (policy)" has been associated with at least some degree of centralized economic planning—directed or indicative. The underlying assumption is that market forces alone do not create the effect desired by a given nation. The need for strategic economic development direction thus becomes the basis of government policy and interstate controls.

Mr. Masaaki Kotobe (1985), a Japanese expert explained industrial policy as, "The sum of a nation's efforts to shape business activities and influence economic growth."

An American specialist, Chalmers Johnson (1982, 1985) suggested that it is, "The initiation and coordination of government activities to leverage upward the productivity and competitiveness of a whole economy and of particular industries in it".

All nations, including the United States (de facto), have some form of industrial and international trade policy, some written, some unwritten, some articulated to the public, some not. Japan and France are the best-known examples of free world indicative planning. Executives of the Japanese Ministry of International Trade and Industry (MITI) believe that although business and labor are conscious of world competitive challenges, they lack the credibility to speak from a broad, national point of view. Therefore, government must concern itself with the strategic management of the economy by attempting to understand which sectors are likely to find better opportunities, and assist key sectors to achieve better positions in world markets.

Typically, the industrial planning objectives of nations which have adopted industrial policies are:

- Improve the country's competitive position in key "sunrise" and high value-added industries as well as rationalize its position in "sunset," low value-added, and key linkage industries.
- Promote the shift of resources out of declining industries and into more promising sectors, which create new and higher value-added jobs.
- Intervene in a few key markets with the intention of helping domestic businesses establish or improve positions in new international markets.

Development of strategic industries

Sunrise and high value-added industries are industries growing fast relative to more matured or declining industries. Governments make wisest use of factors of endowment by placing emphasis on higher value-added industries. This technique, called "industry rationalization," calls for adoption of techniques such as:

- using the carrot and stick approach;
- giving administrative guidance;
- stressing a free enterprise environment;
- ensuring a sound infrastructure;
- developing standards;
- encouraging economies of scale;
- protecting domestic industries;
- stressing market driven business;
- encouragement of cooperation, i.e., economies of scale through the formation of cartels and 'bigness' of corporations.

Failure of directed economies

In recent times the Soviet directed economic system came up short in its goals, while mixtures of indicative planning and *laissez-faire* market mechanisms continue to flourish in other parts of the world. The failure of the Soviet system was instrumental in bringing Eastern Europe into the global economic community. There is a difference between directed economies and indicative market economies. The former is the attempt by governments to publicly control the manufacturing and trading processes of a nation in lieu of letting Adam Smith's invisible hand work its magic. The latter are macro development visions that are distinctly tailored for a given nation to improve its economic lot.

In the case of the former Soviet Union, directed economic planning failed for many reasons, including the impossible task of satisfying consumer wants/choices through directed planning and because profit as a human motivation was the missing element.

Parity

Over the fifty years of freeing trade, since World War II, the percapita GDP of the industrialized nation-states as well as some newly industrialized nations (including Japan, the Four Tigers, and Western Europe), as shown in Figure 9.1, has tended toward parity ranging, in 1987 U.S. dollars, between $15,000 to $23,000 per person based on both market exchange rates and purchasing power parity. Similarly, as shown in Figure 9.2, regions with medium percapita GDP have achieved parity at about $5,000. Unfortunately, as shown in Figure 9.3, countries in regions with low percapita GDP have not gained similar parity (United Nations, 1993).

Search for a new paradigm

The questions facing governments and businesses today are:

1 What is the significance of the major economic events?
2 Is there a new paradigm that permits governments and businesses to take advantage of the trade-development linkage?

Can we use a scientific method, like an econometric model, to test every variable and isolate the elements of these very complex questions? Possibly, but more realistically we must search empirical evidence for what practically explains what happened and the "Tigers Model" provides that data. The linkage of growth to trade is a major factor in what has and can happen as the world moves toward more globalism and interdependence. Thousands of years of adaptation has led Asians to put into practice those models that work. Their paradigm includes economic freedom but also a great deal of government intervention.

Figure 9.1 High percapita income trends

(a) Percapita gross regional product, based on market exchange rate

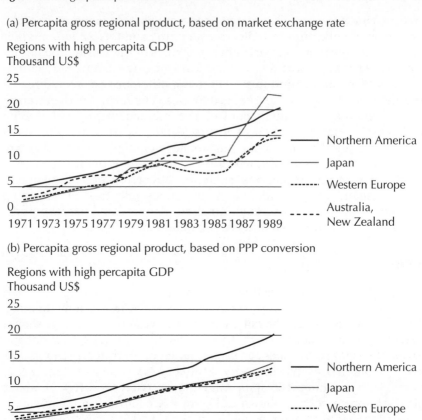

Regions with high percapita GDP
Thousand US$

(b) Percapita gross regional product, based on PPP conversion

Regions with high percapita GDP
Thousand US$

Source: Trends in international distribution of gross world product, Special Issue National Accounts Statistics, Series X No. 18, Department for Economic and Social Information and Policy Analysis, Statistical Division, United Nations, New York, 1993. Reproduced with permission.

Paradigm

The buzzword "paradigm" (spare-a-dime) has spread, some believe like a bad virus, such that it now has common usage in the business world as well as in scientific jargon. The origin has been traced to a book published over 30 years ago by Thomas Kuhn, now professor emeritus at MIT, titled *The Structure of Scientific Revolutions* (*Fortune* 1991). He used the word to describe archetypal scientific constructs, but over time it came to mean basically any dominant idea.

Paradigm is used in this book as a synonym for model or concept.

Figure 9.2 Medium percapita income trends

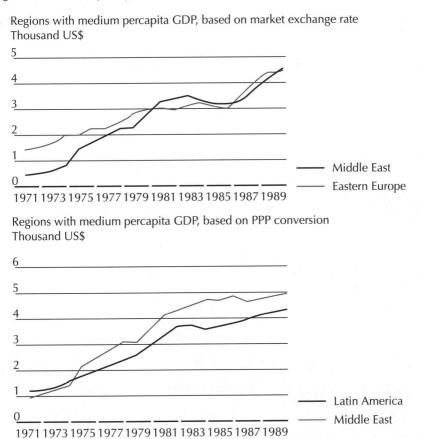

Regions with medium percapita GDP, based on market exchange rate
Thousand US$

Regions with medium percapita GDP, based on PPP conversion
Thousand US$

Source: Trends in international distribution of gross world product, Special Issue National Accounts Statistics, Series X No. 18, Department for Economic and Social Information and Policy Analysis, Statistical Division, United Nations, New York, 1993. Reproduced with permission.

During the 45–50 year period following World War II, these newly industrialized countries (NICs) significantly changed their economic lot by using "intelligence," the sixth endowment factor, to induce the other factors at the same time that they artificially controlled their economy. Their growth is clearly shown in Tables 9.1, 9.2 and 9.3.

Table 9.1 shows the ratios of exports to GDP (%) and growth rates of Asia Pacific Economies. Table 9.2 shows South Korea's growth change as it relates to changes of international trade strategy. Table 9.3 shows manufactured exports as a percentage of total exports.

Figure 9.3 Low percapita income trends

Regions with low percapita GDP, based on market exchange rate
Thousand US$

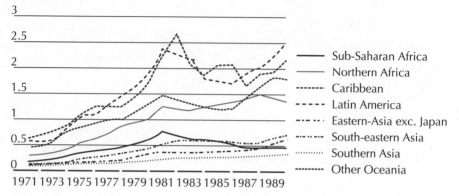

Regions with low percapita GDP, based on PPP conversion
Thousand US$

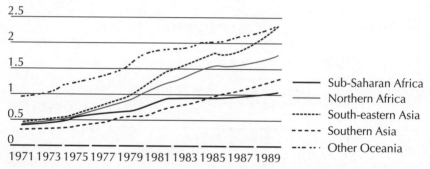

Source: Trends in international distribution of gross world product, Special Issue National Accounts Statistics, Series X No. 18, Department for Economic and Social Information and Policy Analysis, Statistical Division, United Nations, New York, 1993. Reproduced with permission.

Table 9.1 Openness and income growth of key Asian Pacific economies, 1965–1988 *Source*: CEPD 1990

Country	Ratio of Exports to GDP (%)		Annual growth rate (1965–88)
	1965	1988	
Japan	11	13	4.3
Hong Kong	71	136	6.3
Korea	9	41	6.8
Taiwan	19	61	7.1
Singapore	123	138	7.2

Table 9.2 Trade strategy, export growth, and gross domestic product (GDP) South Korea 1953–1976. *Source*: Krueger 1983.

Country	Period	Trade strategy	Export earnings	Real GDP
South Korea	1953–1960	IS	−6.1	5.2
	1960–1970	EP	40.2	8.5
	1970–1976	EP	43.9	10.3

Note: IS (Import Substitution); EP (Export Promotion)

Table 9.3 Manufactured exports as a percentage of total exports. *Source*: UN 1984

Country	1965	1970	1975	1980	1983
Taiwan	46.0	78.6	83.6	90.0	93.1
S. Korea	52.0	74.9	76.8	80.1	83.4
Hong Kong	92.4	95.3	96.7	95.6	95.3
Singapore	28.9	26.7	39.9	45.6	48.2

Artificial comparative advantage

The "Tiger Model" is the basis for a new paradigm labeled "artificial comparative advantage (ACA)" which is somewhat like the old mercantilism (1949) theory but convertible foreign exchange is the prize instead of gold.

ACA explains the linkage of international trade and investment to economic development and encapsulates into one framework the elements which brought success to the Tigers and Japan. The bases of the new paradigm are:

- there are no dissimilar factor endowments because those that are not provincial (natural) to a country can be artificially induced;
- there is a great deal of technology transfer;
- factors of endowment differ among countries but are transferable.

Just as national poverty is man-made, so is wealth. The lesson is that modern governments no longer take a hands-off, management by "gaggle," *laissez-faire* approach. Increasingly, as Thurow (1992) tells us, they look and act like businesses. They organize to gather intelligence, assess their domestic position against long-range objectives, and develop plans that drive industrial policy and strategic industries. Underlying this framework is the notion that international policy drives domestic policy and, therefore, economic growth. Export industries create new labor skills, employment, and stimulate the general economy. International trade is not only sufficient for economic development, it is inseparably linked to it. Global trade has become a major stimulus for nations without sufficient domestic markets to create production demand. Non-traditional products and entrepreneurship are the keys to success and every sector seeks exports, not just traditional commodities markets.

The newly industrialized countries significantly changed their economic lot by artificially inducing the factors of endowment that offer one nation an advantage over others at the same time they artificially control their economy. Therefore, the paradigm cannot be simplistic because it must incorporate planning, industrial policy, and torquing into an outward-oriented world focus.

Artificial comparative advantage isolates ten elements which characterize the Tigers model:

1 political stability;
2 market theory;
3 hybrid capitalism;
4 entrepreneurship;
5 outward orientation;
6 fully mobile factors of endowment;
7 planning;
8 industrial policy;
9 strategic industries;
10 "torquing," to meet development goals.

Political stability

Notwithstanding near eruptions between Taiwan and Communist China, the Korean War, and continual irritations along the border between North and South Korea, each of the "Tigers" maintained political stability in terms of economic focus.

Market theory

Each of these nations elected to adopt market theory in lieu of the communism-directed approach.

Socio-capitalistic hybrids

Most nations of the world have experimented with pure notions of one of the classical general theories or another. The truth is politicians adjust to whatever works for the good of the general welfare. Nations develop strategies to artificially stimulate the growth of their economies. Governments are continually searching for means to put people to work. Job growth equates to market development. Even smaller sectors such as provinces and communities have schemes to advance local output.

In practice, the Four Tigers and Japan adopted policies that encouraged free enterprise and capitalism, while at the same time establishing socialistic laws which ensured a reasonable distribution of welfare in those areas of public life where capitalism was not efficient.

Entrepreneurship

One visit to any of these nations enlightens the disbeliever. Free enterprise is in the hands of thousands of self-employed entrepreneurs who dot the landscape of these countries. They are the seeds of the new economic growth.

Outward orientation

Outward theories can be characterized as being neutral between productivity for the domestic or export market. Born with small home markets, Japan and the Tigers encouraged export promotion.

Factors of endowment

Not being self sufficient, each of these "newly industrialized" countries learned that the factors of endowment moved easily across borders, and they could be controlled.

Planning

These nations developed central planning that included five-year plans which had observable and measurable development goals linked to indicative techniques.

Industrial policy

The underlying assumption of industrial policy is that market forces alone do not create the effect desired by a given nation. The need for strategic direction thus becomes the basis of government policy and interstate controls.

The Tigers and Japan early on adopted industrial and international trade policy. Executives believed that business and labor lacked the credibility to speak from a broad, national point of view; therefore, those governments concerned themselves with the strategic management of the economy. By attempting to understand which sectors were most likely to find better opportunities, they assisted key sectors to achieve stronger positions in world markets.

Strategic industries

The Tigers also recognized that exporting "labor" tended to relegate some nations to perpetual second-class citizenship. They learned that sunrise and high value-added industries grew fast relative to more mature or declining industries. By making wisest use of the factors of endowment these governments placed emphasis on human resources and high value-added industries. The technique, called "industry rationalization," called for adoption of these new techniques.

Torquing/discounting

To put their plans, industrial policy and strategic industries into operation, the Tigers adopted the technique of "torquing", and one way to visualize ACA is to compare it to torque.

Torque is a term learned in high-school physics. It is most often used in engineering projects wherein a rotational force is measured about a point. The twist or rotational effect of the torque moves an object in a desired direction. Greater torque is required when output is low. The concept has usefulness outside of physics because of its general instructive nature. For instance, visualize the wheels of a locomotive at rest in the train station. To get the train moving, the engine must turn the wheels, and the greatest torque is required at the beginning in order to overcome the friction between the wheels and the track. Once the train is underway, less torque is required.

Now visualize the application of interstate controls: *barriers* and *incentives* in such a torque-like fashion as to move a nation's economy forward. Like a locomotive, more torque (interstate controls) are required to get it started, once moving less torque is required.

One would expect the "have not" nations of the world to require the greatest long-term torque. Their goals would be to apply it until their entrepreneurial, capital, and technological levels were at competitive levels. The "have nots" offer greatest opportunity, but the highest risk.

Industrial nations need less but change their applied torque more rapidly, that is, today a region may be booming and the next it must be discounted to prevent short-term fall-off of employment.

Another way to visualize the torquing concept is to consider it synonymous with the notion of discounting. Think of a nation as if it were a business. Some products, those with the best attributes and high demand (like Mercedes Benz) seldom need discounting, but others experience low demand and must offer enormous discounts. Nations and even sectors of nations vary in their need to offer discounts to spur their economic growth.

Interstate controls

Interstate controls are the incentives and barriers nations use to create economic development through the use of torque or discounting. ACA accounts for the torque-like interstate controls or discounts which are applied by governments as strategies to propel an economy to higher levels of development and welfare. Using planning and industrial policy, governments enact laws and activities which serve to act as barriers to free trade, protect certain industries, while at the same time, other laws act as trade creation incentives. Examples of barriers (to name but a few) are:

- tariffs and other import charges;
- quotas (quantities at borders);

Figure 9.4 Artificial comparative advantage–I

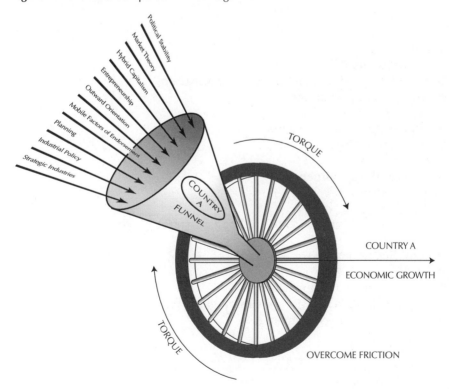

Figure 9.5 Artificial comparative advantage–II

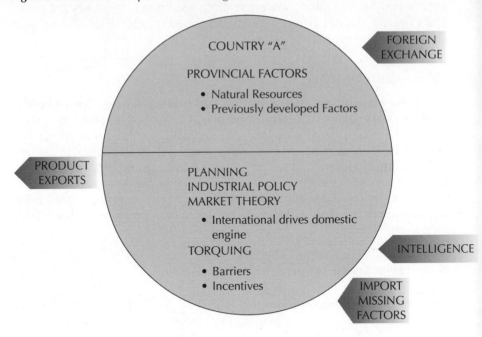

- import licenses;
- customs valuation;
- standards, testing, labeling, and certification;
- government procurement;
- export subsidies;
- intellectual property rights;
- investment barriers;
- excise taxes;
- structural impediments;
- discriminatory exchange rates.

Examples of incentives (to name but a few) are:

- subsidies to encourage targeted production;
- low-interest loans to target industries;
- special depreciation measures;
- forgiveness or relaxation of capital gains taxes;
- foreign technology licensing;
- R&D funding;
- tax holidays;
- free training;
- repatriation of profits.

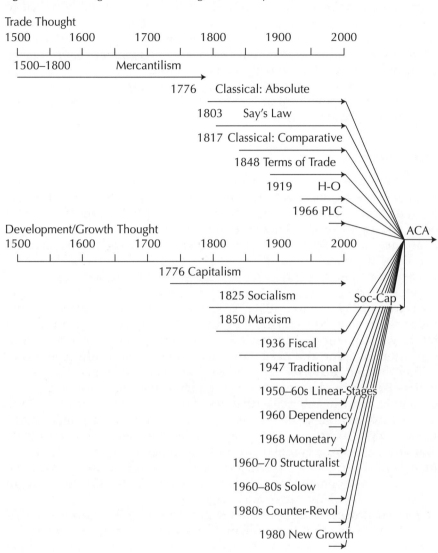

Figure 9.6 Convergence of trade and growth theory

Visualizing ACA

In the real world, theory follows reality and modern theory is not simplistic. During the period since World War II, a new framework has evolved which explains the world business explosion. The paradigm of "artificial comparative advantage" has evolved over the past 25 years as the fastest growing nations have taken advantage of the fact that the factors of production are fully mobile. The framework is complex and includes the growing use of planning and industrial policy and establishes that international trade is inseparably linked to economic development through interstate controls. Figure 9.4 and 9.5 show pictorially the elements of this framework.

The ACA paradigm is different because it is a pragmatic convergence of the older theories into one that links planning and international trade to economic growth. Figure 9.6 depicts the convergence of former trade and economic growth models into ACA, the new framework that explains worldwide growth.

Summary

The government's place is to steer and guide a nation, thus insuring that whatever welfare accrues is distributed according to the needs and preferences of the people of the sovereign lands. In practice, the preferences of people vary greatly. Therefore, modern government policy makers constantly search for what works and their methods affect the strategic decisions of global businesses.

The six major economic events since World War II discussed in this chapter show how Western Europe, Japan, and the Four Tigers of Asia recovered using a mixture of government indicative planning and industrial policy. Notwithstanding the failure of the directed methods by the government of the former Soviet Union, planning is a twentieth-century innovation and has become pervasive in the world economy.

Today nations do formalize their strategic vision in terms of industrial policy. Reality is that international policy drives domestic policy and economic growth and trade theories have converged. Japan and the Tigers took advantage of the fact that international trade and investment made a contribution to economic development. They invented a new strategy using a complex mix of socio-economic factors. The Tigers Model provides empirical evidence of the linkage between trade and economic development into the ten elements which define a paradigm called artificial comparative advantage (ACA).

In the real world, theory follows reality and since World War II, artificial comparative advantage explains the world economic explosion. The success of Japan and the Four Tigers of Asia has proven to be so effective that most lower income nations, as well as the newly democratized of Central and Eastern Europe, are adopting these techniques.

The next chapter discusses the various ways in which nations use trade creation as a torquing measure to grow their economies.

■ CHAPTER TEN ■

Trade creation

In a price sensitive marketplace, the lower costs achieved by offshore production often enhance volume. We must integrate the labor resources of the Third World, where a tremendous number of workers are desperately in need of jobs, with the purchasing power of the developed countries.

Peter Drucker

This chapter discusses one half of the torquing process visualized by the artificial comparative advantage (ACA) paradigm discussed in Chapter Nine. Think of this chapter as a menu of "incentive" and "discount" schemes offered by governments to global businesses to stimulate economic development in their respective countries. Financial capital, human capital and technological opportunities are the key topics of this chapter because they are the elements nation-states use to stimulate economic growth. The astute global manager who understands the schemes and makes use of international intelligence can gain a competitive edge.

The schemes

Most business managers believe that free enterprise is the most efficient means to allocate the seeds of trade and economic growth creation. Private business provides jobs, know-how, and new products and has the search capability to find new markets, and to transfer capital and technology. The interesting thing about this notion is that most governments agree it is the most efficient way. Because the factors of endowment are mobile, many nations take an active role, through the use of interstate controls, to promote international trade and investment as an adjunct to the local engines of growth development. Supranational organizations such as the World Bank also offer economic development incentives that promote global business.

Used by nations and supranationals alike, various schemes are offered to induce capital, technology, and know-how to achieve growth development ends. Nations offer a seemingly inexhaustible list of schemes to entice the elements of trade creation. Many nations preclude foreigners from owning property; however, to promote export-only enterprises, exceptions are often made for 100 percent ownership of land and enterprises. Beyond subsidies and tax schemes, some nations offer special program incentives such as product development assistance, trade consultancy services, venture capital schemes, and skills training grants. As shown in the following paragraphs, these amount to "good deals" or "opportunities" offered to growing global enterprises. As an example, see Appendix A for a summary of the inducement package offered by the government of Singapore.

Of course, capital is the major engine of growth for free enterprise. It is also a major influence (stimulant) of international trade and investment. All forms of capital (financial and human) contribute to increasing business productivity and, therefore, the competitiveness of a nation's products. With capital, nations are able to move toward outward orientation and world competition.

Global enterprises dominate the means and efficiency of capital transferral. Much capital is raised internally, but the search for external sources is an ongoing necessity. Today global businesses often look beyond their home country. Because some nations tie loans and grants to specific projects, foreign country and supranational sources are often tactically interesting.

Financial capital

"Financial capital" is the term used to describe money in its various forms that stimulates free enterprise. But financial capital begets two other kinds of capital: "real capital" which is the equipment and buildings that are the means of production, and "social capital" which is the infrastructure; roads, transportation, communications, and education which make growth possible.

At the risk of sounding elementary, recall that the availability of financial capital depends on return versus risk, and it comes in two forms: debt (bank loans, etc.) and equity (ownership). Although not limitless, for the right return there is actually a great deal of capital available and in many forms, not necessarily currency.

Sources of financial capital

Today the sources are global. At one time enterprises were limited to local lenders and other money markets, but today, financial markets all over the world are convenient. Capital is fully mobile and moves to the beat of the drum of interest rates and return on investment. A business leader in Bangkok, Thailand can pick up the telephone and tap into global financial capital markets wherever it makes best business sense.

The sources of financial capital come in many forms, some of which are: savers, cheap loans, subsidies, stock markets, venture capitalists, duty-free imports, free remittance of profits and dividends after taxes, personal tax exemptions, research and development (R&D) allowances, international lending banks, supranational lending banks, regional development banks and foreign aid.

Savers

Savers are not an extinct breed. Much of the world's wealth is still held in the hands of ordinary people who have led frugal lives and saved a portion of their wages for the rainy day.

What do savers look for? The "cost of capital" is the going market lending (borrowing) interest rate from a nation's best banks. Many people who have excess financial capital want to do better than the cost of capital. If the bank in their country, which is generally a very conservative place to invest, is offering a 7 percent return, many would risk a portion of their savings for a 10 or 12 percent return in another country, even though the investment carried more risk; therefore, for the right project financial capital is readily available. Even gifts and grants are available for the right project.

Stock markets

Stock markets are now worldwide. Financial markets are no longer just in London and New York. Stock markets are open 24 hours a day all over the world: Tokyo, Hong Kong, Singapore, Paris, London, New York, San Francisco. Even Taiwan is moving in the direction of becoming a major financial capital.

Example of Capital Availability: In 1990, the Inter-American Development Bank approved $3.8 billion in lending for Latin America and the Caribbean, exceeding the previous years lending by $1.2 billion. That lending included $300 million each for Mexico, Columbia, and Venezuela. About half of the bank's 1990 lending went to transport and communications, energy, agriculture and social infrastructure. All of this money represented opportunity for private enterprise projects.

Venture capitalists (VCs)

These are the organizations that build a pool of funds from those who are willing to take bigger risks for major returns. Those that provide the funds are those who generally have excess financial capital, enough that a loss might not put them in the pauper's house. Venture capitalists are now operating in almost every country and they are looking for projects that have high potential. VCs often work hand-in-hand with the industrial policies of governments to focus capital into those projects which have high national priority and in some way have a measure of government protection.

> Sirs:
>
>   The Indian who sold Manhattan for $24.00 was a sharp salesman. If he had put his $24 away at 6% compounded semiannually, it would now be $9.5 billion and could buy most of the improved land back.
>
>   S. Branch Walker
>   Stamford, Conn.
>   (*Life* magazine August 31, 1959)

International lending banks

It is no secret that Japanese banks are among the largest in the world. International banking and lending organizations such as Sumitomo or Daichi banks are not limited to local funds, they have offices around the globe which tap local as well as international investors, then make those funds available to borrowers in every land.

Supranational lending banks

Seeing the need to create trade and stimulate growth, the nations of the global economic system in concert have developed a number of supranational lending banks. These exist at the world level as well as at the regional level.

World Bank

The World Bank Group, born in 1944 at the same conference held at Bretton Woods, New Hampshire as the International Monetary Fund (IMF) (discussed later), is the most prominent supranational source of long-term lending and policy advice for developing countries. It promotes economic development and works to raise living standards by investing in productive projects and promoting the adoption of sustainable economic policies. It comprises four institutions:

1 the International Bank for Reconstruction and Development (IBRD), better known as the World Bank;
2 the International Development Association (IDA);
3 the International Finance Corporation (IFC);
4 the Multilateral Investment Guarantee Agency (MIGA).

The World Bank or IBRD makes "hard loans," that is, at market rates of interest for up to 35 years. These loans must be guaranteed by the borrowing government and repaid in convertible currency. To obtain its funds, the IBRD sells bonds on the international capital markets, and by selling its loan portfolios to private investors. Loans are principally used for social capital purposes, that is for infrastructure: agriculture, roads, electric power, water supply, transportation, communications, and education. Figure 10.1, taken from *The Journal of Commerce*, is an

---

Figure 10.1 Example of World Bank loans

IMF Approves Loan for Poland

WASHINGTON – The International Monetary Fund Thursday approved a $2.5 billion financial package for Poland, as IMF officials predicted improving Eastern European economic prospects in 1992.

The IMF loan to Poland, most of it to be disbursed over three years, brings to $8.4 billion the total loans the IMF has committed to five Eastern European countries since Jan. 1.

Hungary has been allocated $2.5 billion, Czechoslovakia $1.8 billion, Romania $1 billion and Bulgaria $634 million.

Disbursements from these commitments will total $5 billion this year, nearly one-third of the total aid Eastern Europe is expected to receive in 1991 from international agencies and Western creditor nations, IMF officials said.

Most of the commitments are to help the East European governments carry out such economic reforms as price decontrol, relaxing import restrictions, tighter fiscal and monetary management and the privatization of state-owned enterprises.

Source: "IMF Approves loan for Poland," *The Journal of Commerce*, April 19, 1991.

example of opportunity available to the global business that keeps tuned to the publication of information related to availability of capital.

The International Development Association (IDA) is the "soft" or no-interest agency for the many developing countries that cannot qualify for World Bank loans. IDA extends credits for periods of up to 50 years repayable, except for a modest service charge, in easy terms after a 10-year grace period. Unlike the World Bank, the IDA does not generate its own capital. It is dependent on member countries for replenishment.

The International Finance Corporation (IFC) participates in private sector industrial projects. It does not make loans to governments, but rather is a lender or investor in equity along with private investors. The IFC gains its funds from member country subscriptions to its capital stock, from sale of its own investment portfolio to private investors, and from its right to borrow from the World Bank up to four times its own unimpaired capital and surplus.

Multilateral Investment Guarantee Agency (MIGA), which began operation in June 1988, insures private foreign investment in developing countries against non-commercial risks such as expropriation, civil strife, and inconvertibility.

United Nations Development Program (UNDP)

The United Nations Development Program (UNDP) is intended to assist in identification, investigation, and presentation to financial agencies those projects in developing nations that make good investment sense.

Regional development banks

In addition to the World Bank Group, nations of specific regions of the world have formed other development banks intended to serve unique development needs.

Inter-American Development Bank (IDB)
Membership in the Inter-American Development Bank (IDB) is made up of the United States and all Latin American countries except Cuba. The IDB offers three categories of funds: "hard loans" those at ordinary capital market rates; "soft-currency window" those loans which have easy terms; and a Social Program Trust Fund (SPTF) to finance low-income housing and other social projects.

Asian Development Bank (ADB)
Established in 1966, the Asian Development Bank (ADB) has 19 Asian members, 11 European members plus the United States and Canada.

African Development Bank (AFDB)

The African Development Bank (AFDB), limited to a membership of only independent African countries, authorizes financial capital for "real" or "social" capital needs.

European Bank for Reconstruction and Development (EBRD)

The European Economic Community (EEC) has formed a new supranational institution named the European Bank for Reconstruction and Development (EBRD). This multinational organization has the goal of promoting democracy, pluralism, and the rule of law in assisting the changing Central and Eastern European nations, which divorced themselves from communism during the peaceful revolution of 1989. Its charter will require at least 60 percent of its resources to be devoted to private sector projects. Thirty of the thirty-nine member nations sent their presidents to inaugurate its birth in April 1991. According to its first president Jacques Attali, its goal is to reunite "the two halves of Europe." To be headquartered in London, the bank will promote business training, advise governments on shifting to market economies, help rebuild infrastructures, take part in creating a banking system and capital markets, assist in privatizing state-owned companies, encourage small business and help restore the environment.

Foreign aid

Many industrialized nations, including Japan, South Korea, Taiwan and Germany, have increased their foreign assistance programs. They dispense funds to less-developed countries through special agencies much like The United States Agency for International Development (USAID). This agency was chartered in 1961 to administer economic and technical programs through grants and loans for private and public sector development projects. In recent times most American capital dispensing assistance funds have emphasized privatization and the stimulation of industrial programs.

Financial capital schemes

Often governments offer financial capital opportunities that amount to equivalencies, which is money that is not immediately bankable, but when considered on the accounting records it affects the bottom-line just as if it were debt or equity capital. It can come in many forms: loans, subsidies, duty-free imports, tax holidays, allowances or even tax exemptions.

Low interest loans

Usually in conjunction with investment projects or production sharing, loans may be offered at as little as two or three percentage point interest rates and extended periods of pay-off.

Subsidies

These include subsidies for factory construction as well as for training the labor needed to produce the goods. Generous depreciation allowances (acceleration), rent-free land, investment tax credits, double deductions for export promotion expenses, and reduced tax liability (tax holidays) are included in this category.

Duty-free imports

To encourage added-value assembly projects, foreign materials that need to be included in the product are often allowed to be entered duty-free.

Free remittance of profits and dividends after taxes

Global businesses want control over their profits and often go only where control is permitted.

Personal tax exemptions

As a scheme to induce transfer of technology and know-how, many nations forgo taxes on foreign employees involved in export-oriented projects.

Research and development (R&D) allowances

In addition to investment and depreciation allowances, some countries offer several other incentive schemes to stimulate higher quality industries and to promote research and development. Included are double deductions for research and development (R&D) expenditures, extension of allowances on R&D oriented buildings, and tax exemptions on income used for R&D purposes.

Real estate deals

Often the local government will arrange to provide land to encourage a company to bring its business. The land deal amounts to financial capital when one looks at the bottom line.

Financial capital problems

Expansion of capital flows and investment across borders is not without problems. The following is a list of considerations, whether recipient or offerer of financial capital.

Ability to repay

Streams of cash flows are the major contributor to the survivability of the enterprise. Cash must be available and predictable to support debt capital. Sales that contribute to return on investment (ROI) must support equity capital.

Political risk

As discussed more completely in an earlier chapter, the various forms of political risk must be taken seriously when selecting investments. Even the aura of mistrust caused by potential political problems pose major obstacles to the global investor.

Exchange rates and/or inconvertibility

Gains and losses caused by the relative values of currencies are also a major consideration.

Exchange rate restrictions

Some nations ration foreign currencies and protect it from market forces by restricting rates of exchange.

Inflation

Nothing diffuses the results of a good capital investment faster and should receive more attention than inflationary considerations.

Access to local capital

Just as some nations protect their currencies from the market, others attempt to ration local capital, opting for infusions from global businesses.

Limits on ownership

Nationalistic thinking often overcomes the need to stimulate growth. Some nations, still harboring fears of foreign business domination, limit ownership of investments.

Taxation

The implications of taxes on capital returns remains a major consideration in investment decisions.

Repatriation of profits

In some ways this may be unimportant, that is, in cases where local
expansion is the strategy. But when the use of profits is to stimulate
growth of the firm and to offset losses in other business units, restrictions on repatriation of profits is a major investment consideration.

Human capital

The other kind of capital is "human capital." In the global economic
system human capital is thought of as a product. Of course, the concept
conjures images of slaves—women and children working "on-the-
cheap" to add labor content to the assembly or manufacturing process—
but the truth is that educated, trainable labor is even more marketable
than cheap labor and government strategies include its growing use for
add-value industries.

It wasn't that long ago that the United States needed to import immigrants
from Ireland, Italy, Russia or Asia to toil in the textile mills of New England.
Taiwan at one time was a source of that low-tech labor. Now the hunt in
America is for high-tech computer programmers and analysts, while the
search in Taiwan is to import a shortage of low-tech laborers. What
happened? Times change. A severe shortage of computer workers in America
and an up-turn in the price of local labor in Taiwan has employers searching for the right talent in a world where labor is mobile.

Human capital is the intelligence and know-how of the people who do
the labor of the enterprise. The development of human capital, more
than any other factor, accounts for the differences among nations. It is
the reason nations like South Korea, Japan, and Taiwan expend huge
sums on the education of their youth. These nations know, in the long-
run, that it is human capital that separates second class nations from
those that compete in the global economic system.

Production sharing

Nations and regions develop schemes to promote the factor endowment
which they have in greatest abundance. The exportation of human
capital as a factor of production has become a major add-value scheme

among those nations that have large populations. On the other hand there are other forms of value that can be added. In nations such as the United States, Japan, and many European countries the added-value of financial capital and know-how are just as exportable as human capital as part of the production sharing process.

Know-how

In addition to the incentives of capital and technology many, nations offer incentive schemes to induce needed management and training skills. An example is the hiring of Russian scientists to work on an American project to develop energy from the fission process. Another method used to induce know-how is to subsidize the education and training of students in a foreign country.

"A Rose by any other name . . ."

The term "production sharing" means manufacturing or assembly in another country or region, not the home base of the parent company, in order to take comparative advantage of production factors, principally to lower cost. Other names commonly used for this process are:

- Captive plants
- Co-production
- Export platforms
- Global factories
- In-bond programs
- Off-border production
- Non-captive plants
- Value-added processing
- Complementary assembly facilities
- Export factories
- Export processing zones
- Global production zones
- *Maquiladoras*
- Off-shore production
- Twin-plants

The theory of production sharing is not new. Adam Smith spoke of the absolute advantage that one country might have over another in international trade due to its natural resources. David Ricardo went further to develop the idea that nations might not only have an absolute advantage, but a relative one as well, product by product. The Swedish economists Eli Heckscher and Bertil Ohlin suggested that the real comparative advantage was in the mix of "endowment factors" (land, labor, capital, etc.) leading to price differences among products.

Today we see that some nations are better off in certain endowment factors than others. Some have distinct advantages in the education of their people leading to a higher level of technology. Others have an abundance of labor leading to lower costs of value-added physical content in the production process.

Value adding

Production sharing or value-added processing is as old as business itself. The Egyptians did it at various locations in Africa, the Romans did it when they went to the Middle East, and the British did it in India. Even the United States, while setting about to rebuild a war-torn world after World War II, encouraged production sharing. Facilities quickly sprang up offering lower labor costs. During the period of its early post-war growth, Japan was best known as one great big offshore assembly factory. Today the Japanese and many other industrialized foreign manufacturers have left their shores and are sharing production in the United States (for know-how) and Mexico (for labor) in order to exploit North American comparative advantages and to be closer to the U.S. market.

The ultimate goal of production sharing is to get the right inputs for the right output. The United States, as an example, has: capital; highly skilled (but relatively expensive) labor; high-technology innovation; sophisticated communications networks, and an excellent east–west transportation system linked with superb seaports.

Advantages

The name of the production sharing game for manufacturers is to transfer those processes that contain high physical content off-shore. Thus, value is added to the product at less cost using lower labor rates and highly trainable foreign work-forces. Off-shore production provides five advantages to the global business:

1 Production/assembly plants can be nearer the export market.
2 Lower costs of production make products more competitive in the domestic marketplace.
3 Products can be offered at more competitive prices for the export market.
4 A firm can add plant capacity without a large capital expenditure.
5 Value can be added to the product at less cost.

Competing in the global age of interdependence requires taking the output of production and vaulting that product into the international market place. But if price isn't competitive and quality isn't world class, nothing happens.

Many firms have products that are no longer at the cutting edge of technology. Facing flat domestic sales they are interested in expanding overseas, but to sustain their competitiveness cost adjustments are required.

Often the major cost driver is physical content. Some American firms move toward automation as a substitute for high labor costs, but many more have neither a product that lends itself to robotics nor the capital to invest.

Most, if not all, of the countries that offer production sharing are classified as developing or least-developed nations. Because the advantages for these countries are jobs, technology transfer, economic development, and foreign exchange income, attracting production-sharing opportunities has become very competitive.

Some say production sharing is the fastest growing industry in the world today. Mexico, closest to the vast U.S. domestic market, is the fastest growing of these off-shore production-sharing areas and has the greatest market share, followed by Singapore, Taiwan, Hong Kong, India, and Malaysia.

India's new international Tech Park is an excellent example of the competition in production sharing. It brings to India what Research Triangle Park offers North Carolina in the U.S.A., a country where industrial parks are ubiquitous, an opportunity for sophisticated companies to work in a creative setting.

ITP is located in a 14-storey circular office building and a smaller 12-storey rectangular building in a 68-acre park, surrounded by a largely undeveloped suburb of Bangalore; the complex will have its own residential area, with water, electricity, telecommunications, medical clinic with facilities for outpatient surgery, a food court, a health club and shuttle bus to ferry workers to and from the city.

Even the countries of the ex-Soviet Union are moving into the production-sharing business. Free economic zones have been authorized for areas ranging from Armenia and Estonia to the Port of Nakhodka in the Far East.

Typical foreign investment incentives for these production sharing zones include: duty-free export and import; a reduction in tax and lease payment discounts; liberal labor policies governed by the local zones; and free market prices.

Considerations

There are five major factors that must be considered when making the production sharing decision:

- Suitability: What is the suitability of the product for production sharing?
- Location: What are the relative advantages of the various production-sharing locations?
- Method: What method of production sharing? Invest (long term) or shelter (short term)?

- Costs: What are the comparative fully burdened costs at each location?
- Control: How much control of the production process?

Methods

Nations with an abundance of lower-cost labor market their production sharing programs as "investment" opportunities, but investment is not the only method. Private companies have ingeniously developed processes to shelter the risk for foreign companies by contracting through intermediaries to rent space, employees, or sub-contract for piece-rate assembly/production. In some cases labor is even transportable to the user nation. As an example, Japan imports labor from the Philippines and Malaysia, and the United States imports from Mexico and the Caribbean.

Risk sheltering

Some countries which offer on-site production sharing have unstable political systems and a history of nationalizing industries on a whim. Thus, the savings brought about by investment is often outweighed by reasons to shelter the risk.

Two sub-methods have sprung up over the years which allow firms to avoid the risk of overseas investment, yet take advantage of lower labor rate opportunities.

Subcontracting
Driven by local investors who offer specialized assembly and manufacturing processes on a piece-rate basis; this method has grown at a natural pace. The contractee can have the entire product manufactured or provide the molds, raw materials, and/or semi-assembled parts, and the contractor returns the product to the U.S. having supplied only the labor.

Subleasing
This method, principally used for the Mexican Maquiladora Program, differs from subcontracting by offering space and employee rental computed at an average hourly rate instead of a per unit basis. With this method, the contractee usually provides the materials, machinery, equipment, and the management.

Control

Global factories can be characterized as "captive" or "non-captive." A captive facility would be one that is dedicated and controlled for the assembly or production for a single parent company. A non-captive plant is typically owned by a native of the country where it may be located and operated to serve many foreign companies on a contractual basis.

Think of investment as a movement toward autarky (self sufficiency), with the plant at an overseas location. On the other hand, sub-contracting is a movement away from vertical integration. Each has its advantages and disadvantages.

Table 10.1 provides a comparison of the methods in terms of cost and commitment to the off-shore production country. Figure 10.2 shows pictorially how they function.

Technology

Technology stands alongside financial and human capital as an engine of growth. It is, therefore, a major element for which nations offer incentives to stimulate trade creation.

Everyone wants technology because it affects the mobility of endowment factors, such as the training and education of human capital, resulting in greater productivity. In fact, innovations in transportation and communications have caused much of the explosion of global trade. Technology's importance has grown as improved communications have brought reality to the "have nots."

Technology is often a misunderstood word. Science, inventions, and discoveries are the source of technology, but technology is meaningless if it sits idly in the library or the garage of the inventor. Technology is the skills and techniques (knowledge) used in the production of goods and services, i.e. the "how to" of making something.

Technology must be put into production and it is "technology innovation" that brings new products from that technology. Technology innovations serve us in two ways: first, in the making of wholly new products (not imitations), and second, in new, economic ways to serve and produce old products.

Table 10.1 Comparison chart of production sharing methods

Method	Production Cost	Commitment	Investment Cost	Control
Own/joint	Least	Most	Major	Complete
Sub-cont.	Most	Least	None	Little
Sub-lease	Less	Less	Minor	Some

Figure 10.2 Production sharing methods

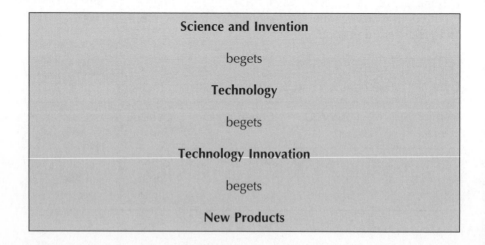

RISK SHELTERING		INVESTMENT
SUB CONTRACT	SUB LEASE	WHOLLY OWNED/JOINT VENTURE
NON-CAPTIVE	NON-CAPTIVE	CAPTIVE

PARENT COMPANY A / B / C

PARENT COMPANY A / C / B

PARENT COMPANY

U.S.A.
FOREIGN

U.S.A.
FOREIGN

SPECIAL CAPABILITY

C A B

COST/PROFIT CENTER OF PARENT

SUB CONTRACTOR OWNS AND OPERATES

SHELTER OPERATOR LEASES SPACE AND EMPLOYEES

VALUE-ADDED CALCULATED AT PER-UNIT RATE

VALUE-ADDED CALCULATED AT BURDENED HOURLY RATE

Science and Invention

begets

Technology

begets

Technology Innovation

begets

New Products

Technology levels

In today's vernacular we think of "high" technology as that which produces aerospace, electronics, biochemicals, and replacement goods (nylon for silk, plastic for rubber/steel).

"Low" technology includes mechanical products, labor-intensive products and those that are at the end of their life cycle.

Need to transfer technology?

There are wide gaps in basic technology development as well as in innovations that create entirely new products and industries. These gaps are caused by a range of problems in less-developed countries and developed countries alike. Because firms in all nations are competing in the global marketplace the need for transfer is increasing.

Education levels

Education is not a prerequisite for controlling technology development and transfer because there are inventors all over the world discovering things, many of whom have little more than a high-school education. However, as the level of technology rises so does the need for higher education. Those nations with weak educational programs often suffer in competition with those which require universal training and have a large output of scientists.

Research and development (R&D)

The function of research and development in the organization of a firm is generally well understood among the business community; however, it is often the first to go when there are budgetary problems. Strategies which do not include this function are doomed to wither from the inability to respond to future customer and country market demands.

Brain drain

Higher education often brings higher personal expectations on the part of young mathematicians, engineers, and scientists. Some nations have experienced the flight of their best brains to other countries. Brain power can be viewed as a product and its market is just as active as it is for other products. Therefore, those who yearn to be better off can be lured by a range of offerings, such as better living conditions, bigger titles suitable to their perceived importance, and more salary.

Basic science

The university gains the centerpiece of our thoughts when we think of basic science. Great universities court great scientists and place high value on their work. Yet not all basic science is developed in the university. Institutes have been formed in many nations which are publicly and privately funded to attract bright people to produce basic science. These organizations also serve as magnets in an attempt to reduce brain drain.

Demand creation

The marketplace is placing its own demand for creation and technology innovation. As more and more firms switch from competitor orientation to customer orientation, marketeers are bringing back to the enterprise ideas that drive the R&D function. Such companies thrive on demand creation and offer high incentives to employees who bring new ideas for research and possible production.

R&D mechanisms

The high cost of research and development (R&D) is another factor in the search for technology. Many companies, as well as nations, cannot afford this as an internal function. To meet the demands of the market-place, R&D is becoming an industry of cooperatives wherein firms take an equity interest in the cooperative giving them some say in direction of research.

Capital for conversion of ideas to product

Entrepreneurs are the first to argue that it is not easy to bring ideas to the market. Yet, in every country there are organizations to assist global businesses to do just that. In the private sector, venture capitalists await the well-thought-out project that has high expectations for profit. The public sector of most nations have schemes to stimulate the conversion of ideas as well. Often these take the form of low-interest loans or guarantees.

Technology as an industry

Today enterprises from one country are competing with other firms from all over the world in the same industry.

The development of technology has become a major industrial sector in its own right. This change is mostly manifested in "quality." As businesses begin competing across borders, the reality of the quality world-class products pushes the global company to assess its production capability and often search for new technology.

Search capability

The search for new technology or opportunities to transfer proven technology is central to national as well as enterprise growth. Intelligence (processed information) is so important in this regard that it is now considered to be the sixth factor of production.

Entrepreneurship

It is the entrepreneur who brings much of the world's technology to the market. Big business places high premium on the development of the entrepreneur within the firm. Yet it is the independent person in the smaller firm who seems to create the most magic. Because of that, most incentive programs focus on the entrepreneurial spirit.

How technology is transferred

Contrary to general opinion, opportunities to obtain technology abound for the global market.

Public domain

Much of basic science is published in journals and technical publications by the professors and scientists of universities. Search and conversion from these public domain sources is a continuing process in all nations. In short, much of the world's technology is already in libraries waiting for the entrepreneur's innovation or imitation.

Joint venture

The alliance or partnering of producers with those that have needed technology is a two-way street. Many nations offer significant financial and non-financial incentives to stimulate joint ventures for technology transfer.

Subsidiary

The subsidiary within another national market is an alternative for the transfer of technology. Obviously this method increases exposure for the firm but carries with it increased control.

Licensing agreements

Licensing of technology to a firm in another country market is often the fastest and least expensive way to enter. Depending on variables such as distribution networks already in place and market readiness for the product, incentives offered to the transferee by recipient nations can result in early streams of income.

Management contracts

Inducements to develop contracts to manage the introduction of technology is a growing method of transfer and go hand-in-hand with trade creation inducements to license across borders.

Official (government) technical assistance programs

Many nations have established technology banks and other assistance programs to connect available technology to private sector development.

United Nations Industrial Development Organization (UNIDO)

This organization was established by the United Nations General Assembly in 1966 to promote and accelerate the industrialization of developing countries and to coordinate the industrial development activities of the United Nations system. UNIDO has a Technology Programme to promote the transfer of technology to developing countries. The findings of research projects and colloquia, conducted under UNIDO auspices, offer opportunities to developing countries to adapt to technological change in such fields as micro-electronics and genetic engineering. It continues to be a first-look organization by any enterprise seeking opportunities to convert technology.

Industrial and Technical Bank (INTIB).

In 1979 the Industrial and Technical Bank (INTIB) was created as a special department of UNIDO. Through its Technology Information Exchange System (TIES) it maintains data on technical processes, patents and licensing agreements for the expansion of private sector firms in developing countries.

World Intellectual Property Organization (WIPO)

The World Intellectual Property Organization's Permanent Committee for Development Co-operation encourages the transfer of technology from the highly industrialized to the developing countries. Their Technical Exchange and Joint Patents Program also fosters inventive and innovative activity in developing countries. Global businesses in qualified countries should include this program in their strategies.

Issues of technology transfer as a strategy

The inclusion of technology transfer among the trade creation incentives of a nation is important. However, the process is not without problems. Some of the issues are listed below.

Management skills

Notwithstanding the urgent need for technology, some nations do not have the developed management skills to support the innovation.

Bargaining power

The transfer of technology involves negotiations between the host enterprise and the owner of the technology. Both make valuable contributions to the introduction of the innovation into the marketplace. Perceptions of who has the greater bargaining power cause difficulties in negotiations.

Risk

There are risks on both sides of the transfer equation. The enterprise that owns the technology risks diffusion and loss of competitive advantage. The risks to the buyer, on the other hand, are that returns will not support the high cost of transfer.

High cost

Typically transfer of technology includes up-front fees, and royalties, but also the financial capitalization of new equipment to support its introduction into the market.

Cultural

Careful assessment of cultural readiness or interest is also a major implication when the technology is new and/or "high-tech" to a society.

Government intervention

It is not unusual that governments cause delays when screening transfers of technology. The intent of this central control in some nations is to avoid duplication.

Worker training

Levels of trainable workers vary from nation to nation depending on education, technical schools, and experience. Often the transfer must include worker training as a condition of the contract.

Dependency

The argument of less-developed nations depending on developed nations raises political issues far beyond the intent of the private sector.

Military technology

The use of technology for military purposes is controlled by most nations. Conflicts with authorities occur when the transfer is construed to have military implications.

Protection of intellectual property

The transfer of technology must include considerations on the part of the host nation for the protection of the intellectual property rights.

Summary

The major elements of trade creation are financial capital, human capital, and technology. Nations use various schemes to induce these trade creation elements.

Sources of financial capital include savers, global enterprises, stock markets, venture capitalists (VCs), international lending banks, the United Nations, the World Bank, regional lending banks, and foreign aid. The transfer of financial capital across borders is accompanied by a significant set of problems.

Human capital is the source of intelligence and know-how of people as well as less costly labor. Production sharing is the base term of a long list of other names that connotes the concept of taking advantage of comparative production factors in another nation to add value.

Technology is the result of science, discoveries and inventions. Technology innovation is the thing that brings new products from technology.

Although much of technology is transferred through the public domain, joint ventures, establishing subsidiaries, licensing agreements, and government programs are some of the ways technology is transferred.

The intent of the next chapter is to explain for the reader trade barriers and how governments use them as part of the torquing process.

CHAPTER ELEVEN

Trade barriers

The only limits, as always, are those of vision.

James Broughton

Barriers or protectionism is the other factor of the torquing process used by governments in the guise of stimulating economic development. What governments give in terms of trade creation (discussed in the preceding chapter), they can take away with barriers to free trade, all in the name of economic development. In real terms trade barriers are distortions to free trade—they add cost to products, deter cross-border economic flows and, in some cases, keep foreign enterprises out of the market all together.

This chapter discusses the "visible" and "invisible" *commercial* barriers that cause these market distortions in the name of national welfare, as well as the various *political* weapons that frequently halt trade altogether.

Distortions

Distortion is a significant bias in product sales for the businesses of one country over another that are not the result of the free market competitive process. An example might be the permissible entry of goods into North America and Canada, but the refusal of similar entry into a South American country.

The need for transparency

Many of the non-tariff distortions to trade are hidden, that is, only the locals know about them and they only know by word-of-mouth. Transparency means an enterprise from, say, Yemen can compete on favorable terms in the United States and a French firm can be confident that Japanese rules are forthright and open because all businesses have access to the written laws or codes.

Governments attempt to steer their economy by applying a torque-like combination of barriers and incentives in order to improve general welfare. But the global enterprise would like to play by a set of fair trade rules—they feel they can do business across borders so long as the rules are transparent and do not cause excessive market distortions.

Free trade (see glossary for fuller definition) is a goal that is often blocked by governments which do not adhere to competitive international trade theory and are pressured by local industries or driven by the self-interest, or economic development needs of their sovereign nation.

Fair trade, on the other hand, can have mean several things. It can mean operating under the same set of rules, or it can be used to justify protectionism by imposing reciprocal rules on businesses from another nation in retaliation for not negotiating an agreeable rule, i.e. the term "level playing field".

Barriers as a commercial weapon

Every nation surrounds itself with a boundary called the "customs territory". This line on a map is often, but not always, synchronous with the nation's frontier geography and is made operable at each port of entry (air, land, or sea) by persons who decide not only what goods will enter, but whether a sum of money in the form of a tax should be collected prior to entry. At the risk of sounding elementary or trivial, smugglers are those who circumvent the ports of entry to bring unlawful goods into the country

Visible (transparent) barriers

The visible barriers are those that are transparent to the global enterprise when it does business across borders, that is, they are written for every trader to see and are applicable to all. There are two forms of visible barriers: tariffs and quotas.

Tariffs

Tariffs (synonymous with "duty") are by definition a tax at the border collected on an *ad valorem* (percentage) of the transaction value based as shown on the invoice at the time of crossing. In the vast majority of cases a tariff is collected on incoming (imports) goods, but theoretically they may be collected on outgoing (exports) as well. For instance, the former Soviet Union placed heavy taxes on outgoing goods, ostensibly to control certain special materials.

Some say the word tariff comes from the Arabic term for inventory, which is *ta'rif*. On the other hand the French word, *tarif*, as well as the Spanish word *tarifa* means price list or rate book. Folklore tells us that the word originated about 700 A.D. Near Gibraltar there is a village named Tarifa. Supposedly a small band of pirates operating from there had as their prey every merchant ship passing through the narrow channel. Each ship captain had to pay a handsome sum of money before the vessel could proceed through the channel. Over time, seamen began calling the money they were forced to pay a "tariff".

Some nations use the money collected as a means for gathering income to operate their central government. For instance the United States enacted its U.S. Tariff Act of July 4, 1789 as an 8.5 percent duty in order to finance the newly created government. Later, in the early 1900s, the nation shifted to an income tax as its primary means of supporting the federal government.

In 1891 the United States collected $216 million in import duties, which was 55 percent of national revenue. In 1985 the collection was $13 billion, but that amounted to only 1.8 percent of national revenue for that year.

Developing countries have historically used customs duties to provide a major share of government revenues. For some, duties provide as much as 60 percent of national revenue, and for most the range is between 20 and 50 percent. Typically, extremely high tariff charges have been encountered on products not produced or unlikely to be produced.

Called protectionism, tariffs are often collected as a deterrent to competition in order to shield home industries. In most countries, tariffs serve both purposes and are a preferential method under the General Agreement on Tariffs and Trade (GATT) because they are more visible and apt to be more fair than other barriers. Some countries go so far as specifying certain tariff schedule duties as "protective," others as "revenue" duties.

In as much as all countries use a border tariff the method has become very transparent, that is each nation has adopted a method, usually a loose-leaf book, which shows their schedule of duties. Most countries have even joined the Customs Cooperation Council (CCC) to standardize the nomenclature/numbering structure making it even easier to do business across borders.

For decades, the international trading community was confronted with problems caused by differing classification and numbering systems covering the movement of goods. The Customs Cooperation Council (CCC) was formerly known as the Brussels Tariff Nomenclature (BTN). In 1970, with the assistance of forty-eight countries and more than a dozen private and public organizations, a thirteen-year process developed a system capable of meeting the principal requirements of customs authorities, statisticians, carriers, and producers. The result, beginning in 1983, was the adoption of a harmonized commodity description and coding system by most of the nations of the world. Thus, tariffs have become even more transparent.

Historically, there have been conditions when average tariffs worldwide exceed 40–50 percent. America's Smoot-Hawley Act of 1930 had duties of 50 percent. Tariffs imposed by Western nations on goods from communist countries were often 40 percent or more.

Tariffs vary from product to product in the percentage value applied to the invoice, depending on the international trade theory adopted by each nation. Table 11.1, based on data prior to the Uruguay round of GATT, shows a selected group of nations and their tariff rates (not exhaustive).

Table 11.1 Nations and their tariff rates

Nation	Tariff rate (*ad valorem*)
Argentina	General 0–38%, 55% on autos, and 10 to 90% infomatics
Australia	Average 15%
Brazil	Average 45%, sometimes over 200%
Canada	Average 9 to 10%. For the U.S.A. it will reduce to 0% over the next 10 years.
Chile	Average 50%
China	Average 9.2%
Columbia	Average 51.6%
European Community	Variable Levies (VL's) designed to raise import prices to EU price levels.
Finland	Average 1.5 to 4.1%
India	Average 137.6%
Indonesia	0% on needed raw materials to as high as 100% on luxuries.
South Korea	Average 20%, agriculture 30–50%
Malaysia	Average 15%
Mexico	20 to 30%
New Zealand	25% on many goods, but 40 to 85% on goods competing with domestic
Pakistan	Average 67%
Philippines	Average 29.17%
Taiwan	Average 20% and ranging up to 57.5%
Thailand	Average 23.5%, with 40% on consumer goods
Venezuela	Average 45% with some as high as 70%
OECD members and the United States of America	Average less than 5%

Quotas (quantitative restrictions)

Because they are listed in the harmonized schedule quantitative restrictions (QRs) or quotas are also a very transparent means of controlling the entry of products at the border. Quotas include complete bans on the import or export of specific commodities, as well as import and export quotas which limit the volume. They differ from duties in that they affect the quantity of goods permitted to enter the customs territory. Typically, they are divided into two types: absolute and tariff-rate. Table 11.2 shows examples.

Absolute

Absolute quotas limit the quantity of goods that enter in a specific period. Some are global while others are allocated to specific countries.

Typically, because absolute quotas are filled at or shortly after beginning the quota period, they are usually opened at specific time on the first work day of the quota so all importers have the same opportunity

Table 11.2 Examples of quotas

Commodity	Absolute	Tariff rate
Textiles	Cotton Silk blends Fibers of cotton Wool Man-made fiber Vegetables	
Steel	Stainless steel bar Tungsten	
Food	Ale, Stout, Beer Chocolate, Sugars Peanuts, Candy Apple and Pear juice White wines	Tuna fish
Dairy Products	Butter, Cheese Animal feeds Milk, Cream Ice cream	
Other consumables	Watches Watch movements	Whisk brooms

for simultaneous presentation of their entries. If a quantity of quota merchandise offered at entry exceeds the quota, the commodity is released on a pro rata basis (i.e. the ratio between the quota quantity and the total quantity offered for entry). If not filled at the opening, quotas are filled on a "first-come, first-served" basis. Imports in excess of the quota are typically warehoused for entry during the next quota period.

Tariff rate quotas

Tariff rate quotas permit a specified quantity of imported merchandise to be entered at a reduced rate of customs duty during the quota period. There is no limitation to the amount of the quota product that may be entered at any time, but quantities entered during the quota period in excess of the quota for that period are subject to higher duty rates.

Impact on enterprise

Tariff barriers distort trade depending on the duty applied to specific merchandise. The effect on enterprise may range from negligible to a total halt in product trade. Because they cannot be considered prima facie "unfair," they are, under the rules of the General Agreement on Tariffs and Trade (GATT) permitted. Tariffs are an accepted method of protection under GATT. A very high tariff may not violate international rules unless a country has made a "bound" commitment not to exceed a specific rate. On the other hand, where measures are inconsistent with international rules, they are actionable under U.S. trade law and through GATT (see Chapter 13).

Invisibles (non-transparent)

At least tariffs and quotas are visible. They can be seen, on paper, and their impact on the enterprise can be predicted. But it is the invisibles (sometimes called non-tariff) that can keep the firm from doing business all together, and they affect not only goods, but services, investment, and property rights. The United States classifies the invisibles into ten categories:

1 rules of origin;
2 import licenses (automatic/non-automatic);
3 customs barriers (other than tariff and quotas);
4 standards, testing, labeling, and certification;
5 government procurement;
6 export subsidies;
7 lack of intellectual property protection;
8 services barriers;

9 investment barriers;
10 other barriers
    (a) structural impediments;
    (b) trade only through state trading companies;
    (c) violation of anti-trust;
    (d) false advertisement;
    (e) uncompetitive pricing/dumping;
    (f) public health;
    (g) excise taxes (not taxed at borders).

Rules of origin

Countries require imported articles produced abroad to be conspicuously legible, indelible, and permanently marked with country of origin. There are three purposes for these markings:

1 To provide transparency to the ultimate user, the name and country of manufacture and/or modification. "User" being defined as the consumer or the last person to receive the product in its form as it crosses the border.
2 To substantiate tariff requirements.
3 To prevent exporters from circumventing bloc borders.

Import licenses

Import licensing is the process of requiring a permit or documentation, other than that required for customs purposes, as a prior condition for importing goods. They are used by governments to keep track of the nature and quantity of imports and to administer restrictions, such as quotas. Developing countries often use them to monitor and control the use of convertible currency.

Such licensing may have acceptable uses, but trade is frequently made more difficult by many countries as a result of inappropriate use. For example, applications for licenses are often ambiguous, complicated, and require documents which are completely unrelated to the function of the license. Sometimes documents must be submitted with multiple copies which serve to tie up administrative employees in unnecessary paper work, resulting in needless delays. In addition, licensing officials sometimes cannot be located or require submission of documents at certain hours or days before the vessel carrying the goods is due to depart, causing carrier scheduling problems.

Prior to the Tokyo Round of the GATT, trade restrictive measures such as embargoes and quotas were covered by rules, but most aspects of import licensing were not. The GATT Licensing Code made effective on

January 1, 1980 sets forth general provisions on procedures in terms of automatic and nonautomatic import licensing.

Automatic

In the context of the GATT agreement, automatic import licensing means that government approval of a license application will be freely granted. These usually are methods employed to collect statistical data or other information regarding imports when no other appropriate procedure is available. The intent of the Code is only to prevent trade-restrictive effects, and encourage their discontinuance as soon as their underlying purpose can be achieved in a more appropriate way.

Nonautomatic

Nonautomatic licensing refers to import licensing used in the administration of quotas and other import restrictions. The aim of the Code is to eliminate any trade restrictive effects those licenses may have which are incidental to the imposition of the restrictions themselves. This is principally done through the Code which requires transparency and distribution of information well in advance of the opening and closing dates of quotas.

Customs barriers

The valuation of goods as they pass through customs has been inconsistent among nations. Prior to the Tokyo Round, the most common method was the Brussels Convention on Valuation (or Brussels Definition of Value (BDV)) drawn up by the Customs Cooperation Council (CCC) in 1950. Several nations, including the United States, maintained their own independent valuation system which was considered by trading partners as a trade barrier.

Tokyo Round negotiators developed a uniform customs valuation called the Customs Valuation Code, the goals of which are: ensuring fairness and simplicity, conforming to commercial reality, outlawing arbitrary or fictitious customs values, and giving importers and exporters predictability in assessing the amount of duty owed on imported goods.

Standards, testing, labeling, and certification

A standard is a technical specification approved by a recognized standards body which sets out a product's characteristics in terms of dimensions, safety requirements, or performance. The standard can also specify testing requirements and methods, labeling, and the procedures for administering the specifications.

Needless to say, many government regulations in this category are legitimate. They protect plant, animal and human life, and prevent consumer fraud. But trade can be distorted when the standards become disguised discriminatory trade restrictions.

The importance of the differences between nations standards, testing, and approval procedures had long been talked about it, but little had been done about their impact on international trade until the Tokyo Round of the Multilateral Trade Negotiations (MTN). On January 1, 1980, a Standards Code, negotiated and accepted by GATT was entered into force. The Code is composed of four different types of provisions: general principles, open procedures, information and assistance, and dispute settlement procedures.

The Code's most important aim was to eliminate unnecessary trade barriers by encouraging the use of appropriate international standards and of standards based on performance instead of design criteria. It obligates countries to treat imported products no less favorably than domestic products.

Signatories are required to use open (transparent) procedures when developing new or amended standards and rules of certification systems.

It requires access through an "inquiry point", the purpose of which is to provide information to other signatories regarding technical regulations, standards, and certification systems. This section of the Code makes provision for special and differential treatment for developing countries, since they may need specific advice on establishing national standardization bodies and certification institutes.

A primary intent of the Code was, for the first time, to establish international rules between governments regulating procedures by which standards and certification systems are prepared, adopted and applied, and by which products are tested for conformity with standards.

Finally, the code establishes a Committee on Technical Barriers to Trade, which meets periodically to oversee implementation and administration of the agreement, as well as to discuss any new issues or problems which should arise.

On October 23, 1990 the government of Mexico gave two weeks' notice of new labeling requirements for textiles imported into that country. Under one provision of the procedures labels must name both the American exporter and the Mexican importer, a requirement most traders find almost impossible to meet since most shipments go to a number of different importers. U.S. exporters charged that the new requirements were an ill-concealed attempt to stop a surge in imports from the United States after Mexico lowered textile tariffs and eased licensing rules the previous year.

Government procurement

With the increase of "privatization", less and less of the world's manufacturing is done under the auspices of a government; however, the buying of goods is another thing. Governments remain among the world's largest purchasers of goods. By discriminating against global businesses, "Buy national" policies obviously constitute a significant distortion to international trade and constitute a considerable non-tariff barrier.

Prior to the Tokyo Round Agreement on Government Procurement, GATT rules requiring "national treatment" (i.e. prohibiting discrimination against imports) did not apply to "procurement by government agencies of products purchased for government purposes" (GATT 1969).

Under the Agreement, signatories undertake not to discriminate against or among the products of other signatories in purchases of goods by government entities (e.g. ministries and departments) listed in an annex to the Agreement. In 1987 the Code covered contracts for product purchases above the level of 150,000 special drawing rights (SDRs) (an amount equal to $171,000).

The Agreement includes:

- Detailed requirements for open and fair government purchasing procedures.
- Strong dispute settlement procedures.
- Exchange of data on purchases covered by the Agreement.
- Provision for special and differential treatment for developing countries.
- Regular meetings of the signatories to discuss the operation of the Agreement.
- Within three years, expansion of the coverage (including service contracts).

The Agreement does not cover national security items, state and local government purchases or federally funded grant programs. Services such as construction contracts are covered only to the extent incidental to procurement of goods.

Export subsidies

In general terms, a subsidy is a bounty or grant (usually provided by a government) that confers a financial benefit on the production, manufacturing, or distribution of a good or service. In this case the subsidy is a direct government payment or other economic benefit contingent upon export.

All governments maintain subsidy programs of one form or another. Some of the typical forms are:

- direct cash grants;
- credits against taxes;
- concessionary loans;
- infrastructure services.

Some subsidies are granted to foster the elimination of regional economic disparities (called domestic or internal subsidies, but most have the objective to stimulate exports of goods or services. Thus, the subsidy affords a competitive advantage to nationally produced products in one country over the unsubsidized production of another. The result is a distortion to international trade.

Recognizing that subsidies can cause or threaten real economic injury to competing industries in other countries, the defense used by many countries is to impose what is called "countervailing duties" at the border.

The International Subsidies Agreement negotiated and accepted during the Tokyo Round acts as the basic set of rules governing both subsidies and countervailing measures.

The Code, which went into force for the signatories on January 1, 1980, flatly prohibits subsidies on industrial and mineral products, regulates the use of export subsidies on agricultural products and primary fishery and forest products, and sets out broad guidelines for the use of domestic subsidies.

Countervailing duties are to be imposed in any amount no greater than the net subsidy borne by a product and then only where subsidized imports cause or threaten material injury to an industry in the importing country. The Code provides for dispute settlement and special retaliatory countermeasures against the trade of the country that has broken the agreed rules.

Lack of intellectual property protection

Intellectual property are innovations and creations. The protection of intellectual property fosters creativity, development of technology, and expertise, and encourages investment in research as well as new facilities to exploit the results of successful research.

The forms of intellectual property protection include patents, copyrights, trademarks, trade dress, trade secrets, and semiconductor mask works.

In practical terms, the underlying purpose of protection is to encourage inventors (through payment of royalties, etc.) to bring their creations out of the garage or back rooms so the rest of the world can benefit. However, piracy and counterfeiting occur because copying has become easier, far less expensive and risky than developing and building a market for a new product.

Many countries do not have laws that enable authors, inventors, or trademark owners to acquire, exercise, or effectively enforce rights to prevent others from pirating their creative works.

Even in those countries where there are adequate laws, effective enforcement may not occur. Inadequate penalties or lack of governmental commitment to enforce laws encourages pirates and counterfeiters to take advantage of resources without sharing the development cost.

Services barriers

The service industries of many countries far outpace manufacturing industries in terms of employment and sales volume. Yet a wide range of government measures (barriers) exist that limit the ability of such businesses to go global. These non-tariff obstacles have become increasingly distortive to international commerce. In recent years trade barriers against the globalization of such services as banking, insurance, telecommunications, transportation, data processing, construction and engineering have received great attention in the international business community.

Investment barriers

Some governments refuse to grant investment by global businesses on the same basis as domestic investment. When this happens the trade effects are a dampening or distortion effect comparable to those created by quantitative restrictions. By denying investment, host-country producers and consumers lose the benefits of additional production as well as product and service exports.

On the other hand, incentives which link the attraction of investment to performance in terms of product content can also distort trade by artificially increasing the supply of the affected products in world markets and displace more efficient home market production and exports. Similarly, local content requirements displace home or third country imports and have the same effect as a quota.

Other barriers

The list of non-tariff barriers must include problems considered routine by the home country, but significant to the global competitive process.

Structural impediments

Structural impediments include a number of government measures and, in some cases, historical ways of doing business which are so inconsistent with modern management that they contribute to significant cross-border distortions. One Japanese businessman observed, "You Americans perceive our retail and wholesale layering is intended to keep you out of our market. But it is the way we have done business for hundreds of years."

Nevertheless, layering of archaic distribution systems and other trade organizations, such as preshipment inspection firms, only add to the inefficiency of the market. According to the U.S. Department of Commerce, preshipment firms operate in 25 countries in Africa, Asia, Latin America and Central America. These firms are under contract to the government and essentially act as the country's customs service by standing between the companies involved to manage scarce foreign exchange, eliminate customs fraud, and capital flight.

Global businesses see these types of structures as inefficient methods propped by trade associations and governments to sustain employment or protect balance of payments problems at the expense of modernization. Artificial distribution systems are non-transparent barriers to market access, add to the cost of all products, not just imports, and have a direct impact on the consumer's pocketbook.

Trade only through state trading companies

Bureaucracies *per se* are not always a barrier to trade. Many serve as filters of business ensuring stronger competitive processes. However, in the case of state trading companies, used extensively in non-market countries, they are for market-oriented enterprise like a wall. Time is money and these kinds of organizations are corruptive of not only of time but also efficiency.

Violation of anti-trust

Anti-trust laws are not uniform throughout the world resulting in some local businesses achieving essentially monopoly positions in their national market.

False advertisements

Again laws about false advertising are not uniform worldwide, often allowing local businesses to declare to consumers sometimes outlandish product qualities.

Uncompetitive pricing/dumping

Dumping is the practice of placing products in a market at prices much below fair market value (often below domestic manufacturing costs) in order to gain market superiority or entry.

Public health

Public health issues become barriers to markets when a nation adopts unique or non-uniform laws.

Excise taxes (not taxed at borders)

It is not unusual that local, regional, or states adopt taxes that, while often not intended, impose a barrier to the foreign business attempting to compete in that market.

Trade as a political weapon

Rightly or wrongly the disruption of international trade is among the bag of tricks one nation can use against another to win the political chess game. From least disruption to most disruption to trade these include:

1 threats;
2 orderly market agreements (OMA);
3 extended negotiations;
4 foreign exchange controls (FEC);
5 cancellation of licenses;
6 sanctions;
7 boycott;
8 embargo;
9 expulsion;
10 *coup d'etat*;
11 revolution;
12 expropriation;
13 terrorism;
14 blockade;
15 war.

Although not on the list, the threat of or the actual carrying out of a strike by private sector unions can have the same devastating effects on international trade.

Threats

Least disruptive of general international trade among two nations, yet very effective in terms of the product in question, are threats by one nation to another related to a specific trade practice. An example might be an industrial nation threatening to cut-off general systems of preferences (GSP) of a less-developed nation if certain perceived unfair trade practices are not stopped. On the other side of the coin, a less-developed nation might threaten to expropriate an industrialized nation's businesses for some trade-related inequity.

Orderly market arrangements

Alternately called voluntary restraint agreements (VRA) are political pressures to protect a nation's industry without resorting to tariff barriers.

Extended negotiations

This is among the least disruptive to general business and is usually focused on one company or industry. It can come about as a result of a law suit or even an ethical disagreement. Extended negotiations essentially act as an embargo for the goods of the firm involved and sometimes require intercession by another government on behalf of the global business.

Foreign exchange controls

Exchange controls stem from a shortage of foreign exchange held by a country. They are a form of currency rationing. Under the controls, a domestic company earning freely convertible foreign exchange through exporting is required to sell this exchange to the control agency, usually a central bank. Except for state trading companies, exchange controls are the most complete method of regulating international trade. In practice, control of exchange amounts to a government monopoly of all dealings related to foreign currency and means that the exchange is in scarce supply.

A company wishing to import goods must buy exchange from the control agency rather than in a free market. The government only rations its currency for those supplies that it favors for the good of its economy. Generally, hard currency is released for needed raw materials, or capital equipment but expenditures for luxuries are avoided.

Cancellation of import/export licenses

In those countries that require licenses, that license can be visualized as if it were a controlled good and can be used as a weapon against the global business.

Sanctions

Countries that do not behave according to the norms of the greater global society may be sanctioned by one or another supranational organization or even a group of nations. The sanctions might consist of a simple warning within certain boundaries. If the behavior is not changed by a certain time limited boycotts or embargoes would automatically become effective. On the other hand, the sanctions might be curtailment of some traditional export which would be lifted when and if the behavior changed.

Boycott

Boycott is the refusal to do business with a person, corporation, or country. International economic boycotts are used by one country against the trade of another. Such is the case of the Arab boycott of the goods of Israel.

Historical Note: The word boycott comes from the name of Captain Charles Boycott, an Englishman of the 1800s. As land agent for Lord Erne, he was so harsh with his Irish tenants that the people living nearby refused to have anything to do with Boycott or his family.

Embargo

Embargo is an order to stop the movement of persons or property into or out of a country. There are several types of embargo. A hostile embargo is one which a government uses in times of peace to exert pressure on another government for political or economic reasons. It may include the seizing of goods or detaining of persons in or out of ports of entry. This type of embargo is usually a prelude to war and if war breaks out the property is seized as a prize. If it does not break out, the property is usually returned to its rightful owner. Hostile embargoes were condemned by the 1907 Hague Convention.

Civil embargoes are those used by a country to internally restrain its own people and property. The intent of this type is to keep needed supplies in a country or prevent vital supplies from being shipped to a warring country.

Freight embargoes are internal constraints used as emergency measures because of bad weather, strikes, or unusual traffic conditions, sometimes issued by transportation companies or regulatory agencies. Control of military arms is a form of embargo.

Expulsion

For the global business expulsion would be the ultimate economic sanction brought about by a sovereign nation against a specific company. This act could be caused by an unethical or immoral behavior or could accompany expropriation.

Coup d'etat

The violent overthrow or alteration of a government by a small group is the definition of *coup d'etat*. Its effect on international trade varies, depending on the nature of the causes for change. The causes are often power struggles based on differences in national economics policies; therefore, the *coup d'etat* can change the entire approach to international trade.

Revolution

The internal strife caused by a revolution typically sets a nation's international trade efforts backwards and the result is a reversal of any economic development progress it may have gained during peaceful times.

Expropriation

Expropriation is the act of the state taking or modifying the property rights of an individual in the exercise of its sovereignty. A global business might experience expropriation following a revolution or *coup d' etat*.

Terrorism

In modern times the world has been exposed to a series of terrorist acts which amount to political actions by groups without portfolio. These acts have had a pronounced effect on world trade. People are concerned about travel and their personal safety as well as the implications when the terrorist acts are against production and assembly plants of certain firms.

Blockade

Like the embargo, there can be "hostile" or "pacific" blockades. The first can only be declared by a nation that has the power to enforce it. That is a naval force so large that it can guard a given port in such a manner that a merchant ship cannot "run the blockade." International case law requires that countries declare a blockade formally and must notify neutral nations.

A pacific blockade, like the one President John F. Kennedy ordered in 1962 to halt shipments of missiles to Cuba, applies only to ships of the nation being blockaded.

War

War is the ultimate political action and it causes the greatest setback to international trade. Routine business stops while the nations involved concentrate on war-making. It is not unusual that a nation is reversed so much in its economic development and international trade that generations and decades will suffer during the period to regain the levels it had gained before the war.

Transformation of goods

The bonded warehouse, free (U.S.A. uses the term foreign) trade zone (FTZ) and free trade area (FTA), such as the Mexican Maquiladora, are the forms of free zones which have been adopted worldwide to permit international businesses the opportunity to transform goods and or comply with various forms of national preferential barriers prior to entry into a country's customs territory. When using any of the three

Figure 11.1 Transformation tactics

methods goods are permitted to enter the zone free of tariff or other compliances and remain in the zone for various lengths of time until they are entered for consumption. While in the zone, transformation of the content of the goods may take place such that the entry tariff may change from the original to meet preferential opportunities. Figure 11.1 shows pictorially how a global strategist might use any one of the methods to meet NAFTA content requirements.

Summary

Barriers to international trade are the other part (besides incentives) of the torquing process nations use to stimulate economic development. Barriers tend to distort the free market of goods and services across borders.

Transparency makes the barriers visible to all enterprise, regardless of country, and leads to fair trade.

Visible barriers are of two kinds: tariff and quotas. The Customs Cooperation Council (CCC) has standardized the tariff nomenclature and numbering system under the Harmonized Tariff Schedule. Quantitative restrictions are also listed in the Harmonized Tariff Schedule, therefore, they are visible and transparent.

Invisible (non-tariff) barriers are those that are not written for all to see. The United States classifies non-tariff barriers in ten categories.

Nations use various trade restrictions as political weapons upon other nations to impose their political will. Political weapons range from the least disruptive—threats of trade distortion—to the most disruptive—war.

The next chapter is the first of Part Four which discusses actions the greater global society is taking to bring harmony to the global business system.

In search of harmony

■ CHAPTER TWELVE ■

Monetary harmonization

> The man of yesterday has died in that of today, that of today dies in that
> of tomorrow.
>
> *Plutarch (De E apud Delphos 18)*

This part of the book is not about the resolution of international
commercial transaction disputes. Those are matters of everyday enterprise which do require resolution, but are handled in the courts or
through arbitration. For the resolution of commercial disputes there
are three primary bodies of international commercial law: common,
code, and Islamic (*Shari'a*). There are also many subordinate bodies of
law practiced in smaller states. A clause which specifies which body of
law and in which country a commercial dispute would be adjudicated
should always be clearly delineated in a commercial contract. Most
international business persons believe it is even better to specify an
arbitration body such as the International Chamber of Commerce. Seeking such a settlement through arbitration is less expensive than the
courts.

Part Four is about how the world is struggling to establish a set of
rules to resolve barrier disputes brought about by interstate controls
which cause distortions to the market, and consists of three chapters
which, when viewed as a whole, explain the global harmonization
system.

■ Chapter 12: Monetary Harmonization
■ Chapter 13: Trade Harmonization
■ Chapter 14: Economic Integration

This chapter deals with monetary harmonization and looks at its two
parts: inside the world monetary system and outside the monetary
system.

Introduction

Laissez-faire, invisible hand, free market—good ideas, in theory, but
international trade is not free, it is regulated.

Why?

One reason it is regulated is the unscrupulous few sometimes take advantage of the ethical many. On the other hand global trade is inseparably linked to growth economics, and every nation attempts to manage economic growth and therefore cross-border trade. As a result there are a constantly expanding number of innovative schemes that cause distortions to global markets.

All nations have interstate controls which distort the free market and these laws, regulations, procedures, practices, and currencies differ among the states making it difficult for enterprise to operate on a cross-border basis.

Harmonization is the process of defining, then peacefully negotiating a common set of rules (fair trade) and procedures so that international trade can be progressive. Interstate controls cause conflict and confusion when they restrain free trade and this leads the world in the direction of protectionism, economic depression, and war; therefore there is a constant need for harmonization.

In practice, the harmonization process turns out to be a debate between free traders versus managed traders and nationalists versus globalists. How much torque (see Chapter Nine) is to be allowed and by whom?

Many people believe the key to peace is contented people—they don't fight. Therefore, for some the concept of a supranational harmonization system offers hope for continued growth of global business. As an example there have been attempts, over time, particularly by intellectuals, to establish strong global supranational organizations to administer the harmonization of global social and political processes in addition to international trade. Some, like the League of Nations, have failed. Others, such as the United Nations, and the World Trade Organization (formerly the General Agreement on Tariff and Trade (GATT)) still exist with the hope that sovereign nations might see fit to make them work.

To depict world monetary harmonization as a "system" stretches the definition of the word system. As Figure 12.1 shows, harmonization is not linked in any formal way. Rather, the system is more an umbrella of gentlemen's agreements to which all nations abide in order that global business can take place. The system is a collection of supranational organizations that are evolving and improving over time, which provide standards for "fair trade" among global businesses as well as account for differences in national growth development activity.

Because there will always be some trade distortions, individual organizations or methods under the umbrella can, at best, only reduce or dampen the major distortions.

Figure 12.1 Monetary harmonizing system

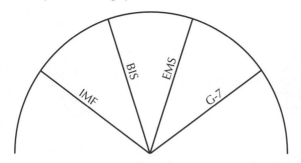

Inside the monetary system

All other things being equal, global businesses would prefer that world-wide currency conditions be as if they were doing business in one country, no fuss, no bother. If they had their way there would be only one world currency and if that were so competition would be based only on the commercial factors of a product such as quality, price, service, etc.

However, each nation has its own national banking system, creates its own money, and manipulates their currency according to the internal welfare needs of that nation. That means every national currency has a relative price to every other currency in the world—so many dollars equal so many yen, and so many pounds equal so many marks. Relative prices of currencies are in almost continuous movement, seldom perfectly stable. Many currencies are convertible to another, some are not. Figure 12.2 is an illustration of the importance of currency in trade and economic development.

Historically, business has been done across borders despite currency instability, and just as historically businesses have recommended to government leaders and the best of the world's economic advisers that they need to improve the international monetary system so more business can take place.

Before Bretton Woods

The purpose of the World Monetary System is to provide a method to overlay the various nation-state currencies and attempt to bring harmony to money, the lubricant of trade, and thus allow the global business system to grow. Short of having a single world currency, the community of nations have experimented with various schemes to stabilize exchange rates.

During some periods of history the experiments have been disastrous.

Figure 12.2 Currency trade

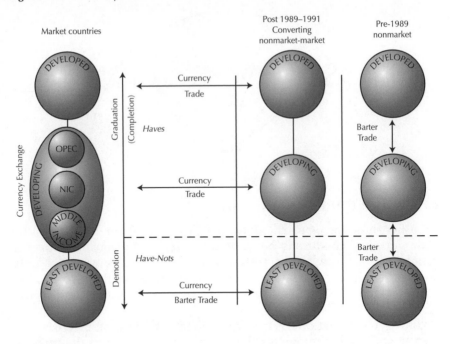

The period before World War II was an ugly time in terms of money. No one quite knows how or why the medium of gold became the international standard for converting currencies. Over time it just evolved into a general practice.

After World War I, from 1918 into the mid 1920s, there was little cooperation among nations with regard to currency stability. To protect the jobs of returning soldiers, and in an attempt to give a competitive edge to a country's factory products, many currencies were devalued. It got so bad that countries like France wouldn't accept another currency—they wanted only gold. Soon the "watchword" among governments was "Beggar thy neighbor" (self interest) and protectionism. The result was world depression and total interruption of global trade. By 1934, things were so bad that only the U.S. dollar could be exchanged for gold. Before long the ugliness turned into World War II and instead of money, the medium of exchange became guns, powder, and bullets.

International monetary system

Toward the end of the war, in 1944, with "military victory" poised, a group of the most brilliant economists and government leaders from forty-four nations met for a conference at the fashionable Bretton Woods

Resort, in the White Mountains of New Hampshire to ensure "economic victory" as well. These wise people were determined to learn from the mistakes of World War I. They wanted to create a monetary system that would prevent countries from changing exchange rates for competitive advantage.

Members of the Bretton Woods conference wanted stable currencies so businesses could trade across borders with confidence. Therefore, they invented a quasi-international bank called the International Monetary Fund (IMF) to monitor and discipline the system and provide temporary loans to countries with balance of payments problems.

International Monetary Fund (IMF)

Although not established until 1946, the IMF was the international financial institution proposed at the Bretton Woods Conference. Its purpose was to stabilize the international monetary system as a sound basis for the orderly expansion of international trade. Specifically, among other things, the fund was to monitor the exchange rate policies of member countries, lend them foreign exchange resources to support their adjustment policies when they experienced balance of payments difficulties, and provide them with financial assistance through a special "compensatory financing facility" when they experienced temporary shortfalls in commodity export earnings. The Bretton Woods members decided on five important articles of agreement by which the IMF would operate:

1 promote international monetary cooperation;
2 facilitate the growth of trade;
3 promote exchange rate stability;
4 establish a system of multilateral payments;
5 create a reserve base for deficit countries.

All of this was in the best interests of the global business system and John Maynard Keynes, who was representing Great Britain, went so far as to suggest a new "world" currency to be used for international settlements. He wanted to call it the "Bancor."

Keynes' idea was not adopted, but, for that time, an almost equally attractive solution was embraced. The key to the system was the central banks of each nation which were to adjust their rates by buying and selling currencies to remain within stable bands. The United States dollar became the equivalent of a universally accepted currency, freely convertible to gold with all other currencies fixed within a one percent band to the dollar. For purposes of adjustment of balance of payments it was agreed that each country could adjust their rates in relation to the dollar as much as ten percent in the first year.

Once again there was currency stability, and it survived until 1971.

Bank for International Settlements (BIS)

Located in Basel, Switzerland, the Bank for International Settlements (BIS) was originally created in 1930 to handle the World War I reparations from Germany. Over time the bank has become the congenial, confidential meeting place for the central bankers of the major industrial countries. In effect it serves as the place where harmony is brought to the global economic system by preserving the identity and amounts (from traders) of short-term currency and gold transfers among the shareholders of the bank who are the governors of the 29 major central banks of the world.

The bank also serves as a meeting place for the board of directors who are the governors of the central banks of Europe and the Group of Eleven: Belgium, Britain, Canada, France, Holland, Italy, Japan, Sweden, Switzerland, Germany, and the United States.

The BIS has also served as a source of so called "bridge" loans for cash-short nations until IMF and private bank loans could be arranged.

Eurodollars

De facto, the United States dollar became the world currency. Loans to Europe were made in dollars and goods were purchased in dollars. By the early 1960s there was a glut of dollars deposited in banks outside the United States. Multinational corporations, which routinely move large sums of surplus funds between countries to finance off-shore operations, found the Eurodollars deposits attractive. Instead of holding their surpluses in American banks they moved them to the European market. This in effect created a new money supply. U.S. banks lost control of a large portion of their dollar supply, but solidified the dollar as the cornerstone of the international monetary system. Today more than half of all U.S. dollars are outside national control and explains the world's interest in the health of the American economy, especially the country's rate of inflation.

After 1971

The problem with the Bretton Woods monetary system was that the United States essentially became the world's banker, and that spelled eventual doom for an otherwise reasonable solution. Eventually the perception that the U.S. was gaining a wind-fall profit (called *seigniorage*) as well as political power by this unofficial banker role caused first France and then other nations to convert their dollar holdings into gold. By the late 1960s, a system that had worked for more than 25 years came unraveled.

The collapse of the Bretton Woods System began when the dollar lost its stability against gold and began to experience erratic movements. In August 1971, when there were sharp declines and America's gold reserves began to fall rapidly, the United States suspended convertibility of the dollar to gold. This left the major foreign currencies floating against the dollar, but it was not a "clean" float because central banks intervened.

This caused the largest industrial countries, nicknamed by journalists the "Group of Ten," to meet and search for a new solution. The result was the Smithsonian Agreement, which recommended to, and later was adopted by, the IMF that the dollar be devalued to $38 dollars per ounce and all other currencies develop parity against the dollar.

Several methods were adopted to keep currencies within a stability band. Central banks would intervene to buy or sell their own currency using the official rule that has become known as the "tunnel", that is, a band no greater than $2^1/_4$ percent either side of the dollar, or a total band *vis-à-vis* the dollar of $4^1/_2$ percent. The stronger European Economic Community (ECC) countries elected to keep their band narrower, in a range of no more than $1^1/_8$ percent either side, or a total band of $2^1/_2$ percent and that has become known as the "snake." Some nations within the EEC went even further to maintain their band difference less than $1^1/_8$ percent and they called that the "worm." Finally, some nations intervened to "peg" their currency so that it moved exactly with the dollar. The peg within the worm within the snake within the tunnel became that became international monetary system. Figure 12.3 shows this in graphic terms.

Petrodollars

By 1973 the dollar was under heavy pressure. A devaluation from $38 to $42.22 per once of gold caused most major currencies to begin an unofficial float against the market. The system of floating exchange rates became severely challenged by the oil cartel of the Middle East. Outraged by American support of Israel during the Yom Kippur War, the Organization of Petroleum Exporting Countries (OPEC) placed an embargo on oil sales to the United States and the Netherlands. After the embargo was relaxed, OPEC raised the price from $1.30 a barrel in 1970 to $10.72 in 1975. This rapid increase in oil prices worked to the advantage of the U.S. dollar in terms of value because the price hike spurred one of the most massive transfers of wealth in world history, from oil

---

Figure 12.3 The international monetary system

| U.S. $ | < tunnel $2^1/_2$ | < snake $1^1/_8$ | < worm less than $1^1/_8$ | < peg |

users to oil suppliers. It pushed the OPEC members into the paradoxical problem of investing their windfall profits in United States and European banks. Those banks now bloated with dollars began, as quickly as they could, loaning the money to Third World countries who were desperate for economic development capital. This began the process which is now called "petrodollar recycling," which led to a debt crisis among many of the developing nations. Figure 12.4 shows graphically the unpleasant story. Needless to say, the inflation shocks of the jarring rise in oil prices caused a severe disruption in the relative prices of currencies and the world monetary system once again scrambled for stability.

1976 Jamaica

After the petrodollars began their cycle to and from the developing nations, stability again returned and in 1976, at a meeting in Jamaica, gold was officially demonetized and flexible (floating) exchange rates approved.

European Monetary System (EMS)

The goal of achieving a "single currency area" for Europe was first discussed at the 1969 Hague Summit, but it wasn't until 1979 at the Bremen Summit that it became a serious idea and it will not be until about the year 2000 that it will become a reality. In 1979, with central

Figure 12.4 Petrodollar recycling

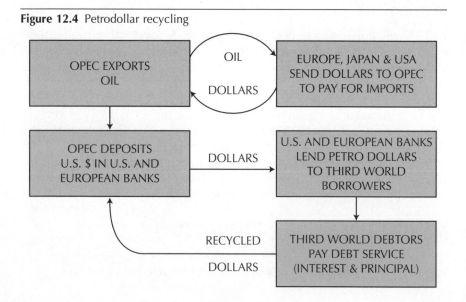

banks already intervening to manage their own floats, the European Common Market countries, without Britain, decided to create a new form of currency to be used for "settlements."

The European Currency Unit (ECU) (called "ecu" after an ancient coin used during the Middle Ages in France) was actually an equivalency of a basket of six European currencies. Participating countries were to maintain exchange rates within $2\frac{1}{4}$ percent on either side of ecu par. Thus, for practical purposes, the world had two monetary systems: The European Monetary system became a monetary system within the World Monetary System.

Single-currency area

As a result of the 1992 Maastricht Treaty the European Monetary Union will become a "single-currency area" early in the twenty-first century, with the euro replacing member currencies and the European Monetary Authority (central bank) monitoring the process. Success depends on nations of the European Union achieving the five joining criteria: price stability, low long-term interest rates, exchange rate stability, sustainable low government budget deficits and a low ratio of public debt. Initially, eleven nations met the criteria. They became the original "Euroland" and make up a population market of almost 300 million and accounts for about 20 percent of world product. Britain, a qualifying but skeptical nation, and Spain, Portugal and Greece, which did not initially meet Maastricht criteria, remained outside.

Currency boards

A currency board is a small group appointed by the government who manage a nation's fiat currency independently of the central bank. Political control is surrendered to the currency board and the money is automatically pegged to an external standard, usually the U.S. dollar. With this system a country's money supply is fully backed by foreign reserves (either currencies or gold) so that redemptions are automatically translated into a reduction of local money supplies. Investors have a predictable government policy to steer by, instead of having to guess the content of secret councils at the central bank who often just print more money and inflate away people's wealth. It is a stimulant for interstate controls that bring in foreign currency and a first call on the use of those foreign reserves to back the linked local currency instead of paying for imports or debt service.

Most notable of those countries which have currency boards is Hong Kong. Set up in 1983, the former British colony's Hong Kong dollars are pegged to the U.S. dollar. Other countries that tie their money through currency boards are China, Argentina, and Lithuania.

Where are we?

Figure 12.5 shows the road we have come, from gold to economic coordinated, currency intervention, and the beginning of single-currency areas.

G-5 and the road to world economic coordination

In September of 1985, a meeting was held at the Plaza Hotel in New York of what was then called by the pundits the "Gang (Group) of Five" or G-5: United States, France, Great Britain, Japan, and West Germany. At this meeting, called at the initiative of then United States Secretary of the Treasury, James Baker, it was agreed to return to an informal system of managed float. This meant *intervention* (buying and selling currencies) by central banks in foreign exchange markets, but in coordination with the other members of the major industrial nations. Further, the group would hold periodic economic summits to coordinate economic policy. It was at this conference that it was agreed, in order to bolster the United States' trade deficit, to devalue the dollar against the yen.

G-7 and the 1986 Tokyo summit

At the 1986 Tokyo economic summit, now the G-7 with the addition of Canada and Italy, a suggestion was made to develop a better method of coordinating economic policies and, in turn, exchange rates. The *Tokyo Economic Declaration* asked the G-7 finance ministers to "review their individual economic objectives and forecasts collectively at least once a year."

1987 Louvre Accord

As a follow-up, a formal commitment was reached among the G-7 nations at the Louvre Accord in February 1987 to formulate a mechanism of agreed-upon parameters (target zones) for exchange rates. Using

---

Figure 12.5 The world monetary system route

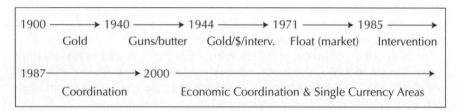

these indicators, finance ministers began reviewing their economic objectives and sharing their ideas. This was the beginning of world economic coordination.

1998 London

It was in February 1998, shortly after the Asian financial crisis that the G-7 (with Russia making eight as an associate member) met in London to embark on an overhaul of global economic management. The G-7 called on the IMF to develop a code of conduct for stricter supervision of banks and other financial institutions and faster reporting of liabilities. The intent was that in the future, in order to give public warning, a greater openness and collaboration would be required of all nations. At its meeting in Washington, DC in April 1998 the IMF did adopt, among other initiatives, such a code which will bring more openness to the world's financial system.

Outside the monetary system

Only the market economies are members of the World Monetary System. Communist nations stand outside; therefore, their currencies are artificially valued. Even businesses within a nation that is a member sometimes find themselves with insufficient convertible currencies and instability.

Hedging

No one wants currency to be a barrier to the global economic system. Invisible product costs caused by instability only inhibit world trade. Currencies that are not convertible to other currencies stand in the way of global trade. Take away the risk and uncertainty by resolving unpredictable movement and the global economic system grows.

Despite the efforts by world bankers, currencies still have some instability, so business people sometimes take the matter into their own hands. This method is called "hedging" against the unspeakable chance that the relative value of a currency might significantly change against a firm during a transaction. This way around instability does add cost, not value to products and can become a factor to industrial noncompetitiveness. Nevertheless, by using the forward markets, a contract can be drawn up such that a specified relative value of one currency to another can be "locked" until a future date. Business people often match these locked rates against future receivable, thereby minimizing exposure to variable changes.

Most major international banks can handle this kind of contract, it is done at a daily rate of as much as $50 billion.

This market in futures is quoted daily in most major newspapers of the world. Figure 12.6 shows two examples taken from the *Wall Street Journal* in 1985 and 1998. They compare the "spot" rates (today's quotation ordinarily good for two days) as they have changed over time for most convertible currencies of the world, and the 30-, 90-, and 120-day forward rates for the major currencies.

Blocked funds

The capture and control of foreign convertible currency is called blocked funds. The currency thus captured are designed to purchase high priority imports for national development purposes, and to repay loans.

Figure 12.6 Currency quotations

CURRENCY TRADING

EXCHANGE RATES
Wednesday, March 4, 1998

The New York foreign exchange selling rates below apply to trading among banks in amounts of $1 million and more, as quoted at 4 p.m. Eastern time by Dow Jones and other sources. Retail transactions provide fewer units of foreign currency per dollar.

Country	U.S. $ equiv. Wed	U.S. $ equiv. Tue	Currency per U.S. $ Wed	Currency per U.S. $ Tue
Argentina (Peso)	1.0001	1.0001	.9999	.9999
Australia (Dollar)	.6739	.6787	1.4839	1.4734
Austria (Schilling)	.07820	.07850	12.788	12.739
Bahrain (Dinar)	2.6518	2.6518	.3771	.3771
Belgium (Franc)	.02663	.02679	37.545	37.325
Brazil (Real)	.8842	.8849	1.1310	1.1300
Britain (Pound)	1.6467	1.6515	.6073	.6055
1-month forward	1.6441	1.6490	.6082	.6064
3-months forward	1.6391	1.6438	.6101	.6083
6-months forward	1.6319	1.6366	.6128	.6110
Canada (Dollar)	.7033	.7030	1.4218	1.4225
1-month forward	.7039	.7035	1.4207	1.4214
3-months forward	.7046	.7043	1.4192	1.4198
6-months forward	.7056	.7053	1.4173	1.4178
Chile (Peso)	.002208	.002218	452.85	450.95
China (Renminbi)	.1208	.1208	8.2790	8.2789
Colombia (Peso)	.0007395	.0007413	1352.21	1349.04
Czech. Rep. (Koruna)				
Commercial rate	.02936	.02951	34.073	33.882
Denmark (Krone)	.1443	.1449	6.9310	6.9010
Ecuador (Sucre)				
Floating rate	.0002198	.0002198	4550.00	4550.00
Finland (Markka)	.1811	.1821	5.5210	5.4911
France (Franc)	.1639	.1647	6.1020	6.0699
1-month forward	.1642	.1651	6.0909	6.0584
3-months forward	.1648	.1656	6.0692	6.0374
6-months forward	.1639	.1665	6.1024	6.0059
Germany (Mark)	.5499	.5523	1.8185	1.8105
1-month forward	.5509	.5534	1.8151	1.8071
3-months forward	.5529	.5553	1.8088	1.8007
6-months forward	.5556	.5582	1.7997	1.7915
Greece (Drachma)	.003482	.003494	287.18	286.22
Hong Kong (Dollar)	.1291	.1292	7.7430	7.7425
Hungary (Forint)	.004784	.004787	209.02	209.12
India (Rupee)	.02533	.02532	39.475	39.500
Indonesia (Rupiah)	.0001031	.0001093	9700.00	9150.00
Ireland (Punt)	1.3657	1.3719	.7322	.7289
Israel (Shekel)	.2797	.2799	3.5751	3.5722
Italy (Lira)	.0005587	.0005615	1790.00	1781.00
Japan (Yen)	.007895	.007920	126.67	126.27
1-month forward	.007929	.007954	126.12	125.72
3-months forward	.007997	.008025	125.05	124.62
6-months forward	.008101	.008128	123.45	123.04
Jordan (Dinar)	1.4134	1.4134	.7075	.7075
Kuwait (Dinar)	3.2776	3.2776	.3051	.3051
Lebanon (Pound)	.0006565	.0006565	1523.25	1523.25
Malaysia (Ringgit)	.2625	.2631	3.8100	3.8010
Malta (Lira)	2.5126	2.5221	.3980	.3965
Mexico (Peso)				
Floating rate	.1165	.1171	8.5830	8.5380
Netherland (Guilder)	.4879	.4899	2.0496	2.0412
New Zealand (Dollar)	.5825	.5859	1.7167	1.7068
Norway (Krone)	.1323	.1323	7.5583	7.5568
Pakistan (Rupee)	.02296	.02296	43.560	43.560
Peru (new Sol)	.3577	.3577	2.7959	2.7959
Philippines (Peso)	.02509	.02519	39.850	39.695
Poland (Zloty)	.2872	.2862	3.4825	3.4935
Portugal (Escudo)	.005374	.005396	186.09	185.31
Russia (Ruble) (a)	.1646	.1646	6.0770	6.0750
Saudi Arabia (Riyal)	.2666	.2666	3.7505	3.7506
Singapore (Dollar)	.6103	.6111	1.6385	1.6365
Slovak Rep. (Koruna)	.02875	.02891	34.777	34.590
South Africa (Rand)	.2028	.2027	4.9300	4.9340
South Korea (Won)	.0006394	.0006427	1564.00	1556.00
Spain (Peseta)	.006488	.006515	154.13	153.50
Sweden (Krona)	.1251	.1254	7.9932	7.9715
Switzerland (Franc)	.6756	.6809	1.4802	1.4687
1-month forward	.6782	.6838	1.4744	1.4625
3-months forward	.6836	.6889	1.4629	1.4515
6-months forward	.6910	.6969	1.4471	1.4350
Taiwan (Dollar)	.03126	.03121	31.992	32.036
Thailand (Baht)	.02240	.02281	44.650	43.850
Turkey (Lira)	.00000433	.00000433	231145.00	230775.00
United Arab (Dirham)	.2725	.2723	3.6700	3.6730
Uruguay (New Peso)				
Financial	.1003	.1003	9.9750	9.9750
Venezuela (Bolivar)	.001928	.001929	518.65	518.33
SDR	1.3498	1.3496	.7408	.7409
ECU	1.0884	1.0931		

Special Drawing Rights (SDR) are based on exchange rates for the U.S., German, British, French, and Japanese currencies. Source: International Monetary Fund.

European Currency Unit (ECU) is based on a basket of community currencies.

a-Fixing. Moscow Interbank Currency Exchange. Ruble newly-denominated Jan. 1998.

The Wall Street Journal daily foreign exchange data for 1996 and 1997 may be purchased through the Readers' Reference Service (413) 592-3600.

FOREIGN EXCHANGE

Tuesday, May 7, 1985

The New York foreign exchange selling rates below apply to trading among banks in amounts of $1 million and more, as quoted at 3 p.m. Eastern time by Bankers Trust Co. Retail transactions provide fewer units of foreign currency per dollar.

Country	U.S. $ equiv. Tues.	U.S. $ equiv. Mon.	Currency per U.S. $ Tues.	Currency per U.S. $ Mon.
Argentina (Peso)	.002252	.002252	444.00	444.00
Australia (Dollar)	.6716	.6615	1.4889	1.4814
Austria (Schilling)	.04470	.04399	22.35	22.795
Belgium (Franc)				
Commercial rate	.01574	.01499	63.50	65.35
Financial rate	.01564	.01507	63.90	65.00
Brazil (Cruzeiro)	.0002024	.0002024	4940.00	4940.00
Britain (Pound)	1.2200	1.1820	.8200	.8291
30-Day Forward	1.2155	1.1773	.8227	.8324
90-Day Forward	1.2079	1.1698	.8279	.8378
180-Day Forward	1.1988	1.1602	.8342	.8447
Canada (Dollar)	.7245	.7083	1.3802	1.3803
30-Day Forward	.7236	.7074	1.3819	1.3854
90-Day Forward	.7217	.7055	1.3856	1.3891
180-Day Forward	.7185	.7024	1.3917	1.3952
Chile (Official rate)	.006674	.006674	149.84	149.84
China (Yuan)	.3498	.3435	2.859	2.8522
Colombia (Peso)	.007560	.007560	132.27	132.27
Denmark (Krone)	.06750	.0844	14.275	11.61
Ecuador (Sucre)				
Official rate	.01489	.01489	67.18	67.18
Floating rate	.008849	.008849	113.00	113.00
Finland (Markka)	.0875	.1474	6.5860	6.65
France (Franc)	.1034	.0993	9.67	9.8475
30-Day Forward	.1022	.0993	9.6863	9.8638
90-Day Forward	.1029	.0903	9.718	9.895
180-Day Forward	.1025	.0986	9.759	9.9365
Greece (Drachma)	.007142	.007190	140.00	136.30
Hong Kong (Dollar)	.1285	.1285	7.7820	7.7820
India (Rupee)	.07949	.0777	12.58	12.60
Indonesia (Rupiah)	.000900	.00090	1111.00	1111.00
Ireland (Punt)	.98	.9730	1.02	1.0277
Israel (Shekel)	.001050	.001050	952.03	952.03
Italy (Lira)	.0004943	.000476	2023.00	2058.00
Japan (Yen)	.003954	.003846	252.90	254.80
30-Day Forward	.003961	.003833	252.42	254.22
90-Day Forward	.003976	.003846	251.54	253.45
180-Day Forward	.00400	.003905	249.94	250.93
Lebanon (Pound)	.05755	.05755	17.375	17.375
Malaysia (Ringgit)	.4052	.4016	2.4680	2.49
Mexico (Peso)				
Floating rate	.004149	.004065	241.00	246.00
Netherlands (Guilder)	.2776	.2672	3.5760	3.6670
New Zealand (Dollar)	.4540	.4550	2.203	2.1978
Norway (Krone)	.1099	.1063	9.10	9.220
Pakistan (Rupee)	.06309	.0639	15.85	15.85
Peru (Sol)	.0001104	.0001104	9056.59	9056.59
Philippines (Peso)	.05408	.05408	18.49	18.49
Portugal (Escudo)	.3711	.3711	2.6950	2.6950
Saudi Arabia (Riyal)	.2770	.2770	3.6090	3.6090
Singapore (Dollar)	.4513	.4474	2.2160	2.2350
South Africa (Rand)	.4993	.4950	2.002	2.020
South Korea (Won)	.001154	.001154	866.40	866.40
Spain (Peseta)	.005615	.005594	178.10	178.75
Sweden (Krona)	.1055	.1088	9.1350	9.19
Switzerland (Franc)	.3757	.3672	2.6615	2.7130
30-Day Forward	.3768	.3623	2.6540	2.705
90-Day Forward	.3788	.3642	2.6397	2.6908
180-Day Forward	.3825	.3675	2.6145	2.667
Taiwan (Dollar)	.02508	.02508	39.87	39.87
Uruguay (New Peso)				
Financial	.01102	.01102	90.75	90.75
Venezuela (Bolivar)				
Official rate	.1333	.1333	7.50	7.50
Floating rate	.07943	.07943	12.59	12.59
W. Germany (Mark)	.3160	.3033	3.1650	3.2310
30-Day Forward	.3167	.3038	3.1574	3.2261
90-Day Forward	.3182	.3045	3.143	3.2185
180-Day Forward	.3205	.3054	3.1205	3.208
SDR	0.979662	0.976173	1.02076	1.02441
ECU	0.702132	0.690176		

Special Drawing Rights are based on exchange rates for the U.S., West German, British, French and Japanese currencies. Source: International Monetary Fund.

ECU is based on a basket of community currencies.

Source: European Community Commission.

Source: *Wall Street Journal* (March 4 1998 and May 7 1995)

Businesses are caught in the middle, because in the name of economic development competition has been stifled and the consumer short changed.

Countertrade and offsets

The availability of convertible currency in some countries continues to be a barrier to trade. As a result a variety of commercial compensation arrangements have been developed which are intended to reduce (offset) the need for money. Some of these are mandated by governments for budgetary and balance of payments reasons, while others are just creative methods of doing business. Regardless of their origin counter-trade practices have as their objectives to:

- reduce or offset the budgetary or balance of payments effect of major import transactions;
- create employment;
- stimulate exports;
- stimulate technology transfer;
- accomplish creative marketing;
- deal with controlled (non-market) economies.

Actually "countertrade" is the umbrella term for a variety of these unconventional reciprocal trading arrangements and includes:

- *Counterpurchases* obligate the supplier to purchase from the buyer goods and services unrelated to the goods and services sold.
- *Reverse countertrade* contracts require the importer to export goods equivalent in value to a specified percentage of the value of the imported goods—an obligation that can be sold to an exporter in a third country.
- *Buyback arrangements* obligate the foreign supplier of plant, machinery, or technology to buy from the importer a portion of the resultant production during a two to twenty-five-year period.
- *Clearing agreements* are between two countries that agree to purchase specific amounts of each other's products over a long-term specific period of time, using a designated "clearing currency" or barter in the transactions.
- *Switch arrangements* permit the sale of the unpaid balance of a clearing account to be sold to a third party, usually at a discount, that may be used for producing goods in the country holding the balance.
- *Swaps* are schemes through which products from different locations are traded to save transportation costs.
- *Barter* directly exchanges goods between two parties deemed to be of approximately equivalent value without any flow of money taking place.

- *Offsets* are generally used for long-term sales to help recover the hard currency drain resulting from the purchase. These can be directly or indirectly related to the product in question. For direct transactions, local producers joint venture with the vendor. Indirect offsets involve the vendor in buying unrelated goods or investing in an unrelated business.
- *Combinations* of all of the above are among the "bag of tricks," a creative global business can still do business when all else seems improbable.

Although, theoretically, international trade in an environment of countertrade could approximate the free market, it is more likely they introduce distortions and increase costs. In addition, despite the long list of arrangements available, the need to do business in lieu of using currency causes many smaller firms, without the necessary experience, to avoid doing business altogether.

Summary

Resolution of barrier disputes differs from commercial dispute resolution in that barrier arguments are about a nation's use of interstate controls. Commercial problems, on the other hand, are about firms seeking resolution of contractual squabbles through the courts or arbitration.

Because international business is linked to economic development trade is very regulated. Harmonization is the process of defining, then peacefully negotiating, a common set of rules for fair trade such that international trade can be progressive.

Currency is the lubricant of cross-border trade. Because each nation creates its own money and manipulates their currency according to its own needs and to avoid the mistakes of the post-World War I period, the World Monetary System was fashioned to bring harmony to world monetary processes.

The Group of Seven plus Russia manage the world's economy through a process of annual meetings and continuous communications and coordination.

Countertrade remains a method of doing business for those nations outside the monetary system or have insufficient convertible currency .

The next chapter explains the world's harmonization efforts for international trade.

CHAPTER THIRTEEN

Trade harmonization

If trade could be encouraged, then our destinies would be bound together. We could not afford to go to war with each other.

Henry Kissinger

This chapter continues the explanation of the global harmonization system. In addition to the monetary harmonization system, Figure 13.1 shows the umbrella of processes which attempt to bring harmony to trade as well as currency. Economic integration or bloc forming is another part of the harmonization system but is explained separately in Chapter 14. This chapter includes discussions of all the major methods and organizations: bilateral negotiations, most favored nation treatment, multilateral trade negotiations, fast track, the World Trade Organization (formerly General Agreement on Tariffs and Trade (GATT)), United Nations, Customs Cooperative Council (CCC), intellectual property rights, orderly marketing agreements (OMAs), multi-fiber agreements (MFA), national remedy systems, and lobbying. Figures 13.2 and 13.3 show the pre- and post-1989 trading systems.

Bilateral negotiations

A commercial treaty, in technical terms called a friendship, commerce and navigation (FCN) treaty, is one way to establish trade relations and negotiate harmony in cases where there are trade distortions between two nations. There are many FCN treaties in effect among nations today and the procedure whereby two countries negotiate a detailed agreement to lower duties and other restrictions is still commonly used for specific interstate problems. This method was almost exclusively used during the period when the paradigm of mercantilism dominated the intellectual influence of nations. During this very protectionist period, when countries looking to accumulate gold did everything to foster exports and minimize their imports, nations negotiated on a case-by-case basis. But this technique proved to be laboriously slow.

The era of free trade, brought about by the thinking of Adam Smith,

Figure 13.1 Trade harmonizing system

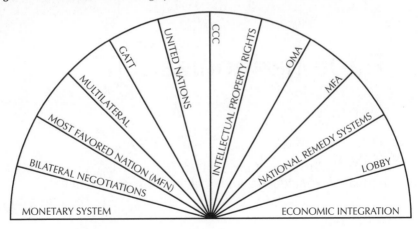

Figure 13.2 Pre-1989 world trading system

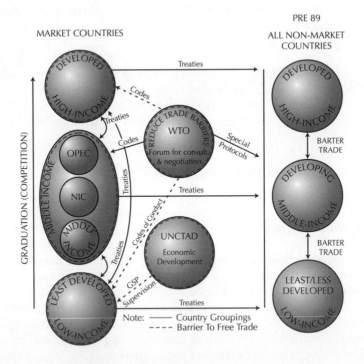

Note: Grouping labels do not imply superiority or inferiority; just higher or lower income, more or less industry.

Figure 13.3 Post-1989 world trading system

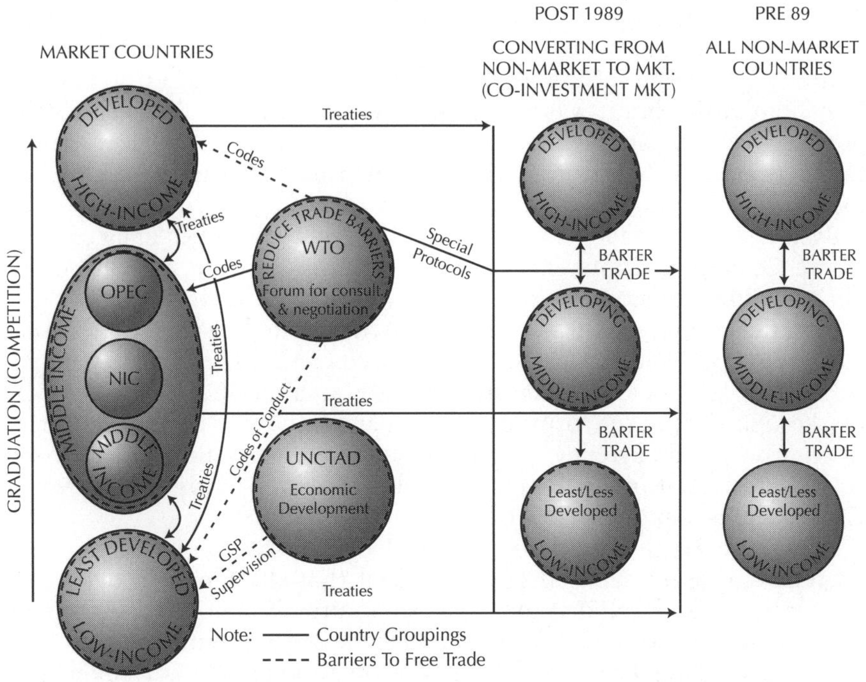

POST 1989   PRE 89

MARKET COUNTRIES   CONVERTING FROM NON-MARKET TO MKT. (CO-INVESTMENT MKT)   ALL NON-MARKET COUNTRIES

GRADUATION (COMPETITION)

DEVELOPED HIGH-INCOME

Treaties

Codes

Treaties

OPEC

NIC

MIDDLE INCOME

REDUCE TRADE BARRIERS
WTO
Forum for consult. & negotiation

Codes

Special Protocols

Treaties

Codes of Conduct

UNCTAD
Economic Development

Treaties

GSP Supervision

LEAST DEVELOPED LOW-INCOME

Treaties

DEVELOPED HIGH-INCOME

BARTER TRADE

DEVELOPING MIDDLE-INCOME

BARTER TRADE

Least/Less Developed LOW-INCOME

DEVELOPED HIGH-INCOME

BARTER TRADE

DEVELOPING MIDDLE-INCOME

BARTER TRADE

Least/Less Developed LOW-INCOME

Note: ——— Country Groupings
- - - - Barriers To Free Trade

Note: Grouping labels do not imply superiority or inferiority; just higher or lower income, more or less industry.

then Ricardo, sent men and nations looking for better ways to resolve trade distortions and for enterprises to do business in other countries.

Most Favored Nation Treatment (MFNT)

The Cobden Treaty of 1860 turned out to be a monument to free trade. Britain, France and several other European countries negotiated the lowering of tariffs and stated that trade would be conducted on a non-discriminatory basis. In fact, an alternate name for MFNT is "non-discriminatory tariff treatment."

Instead of negotiating country by country, the benefits of any bilateral tariff reduction were extended to all of the most favored countries. Although there are discussions that this principal, now called most favored nation treatment (MFNT) was used as early as the 1700s, the Cobden Treaty was the first to contain such a clause. This principal simply means that one nation is to treat a second nation as favorably as it treats any third nation upon which it has bestowed MFNT.

During the late 1800s the United States was the most protected country in the world. In fact, much of the growth of the era known as the Industrial Revolution was gained by protecting infant industries. After World War I there was a slight recession, and jobs for returning soldiers influenced a series of protectionist measures. In the United States the Forney-McCumber Tariff Act of 1922 did not bring particularly high tariffs, but it was very protective because it could be applied to precisely the industries where higher imports and external competition was expected in the future. Other nations threw up barriers and before long "beggar-thy-neighbor" became the order of the day.

By 1928, world leaders knew something had to be done. They called a World Economic Conference to moderate the growing protectionism, but that conference proved to be a failure. In the aftermath of the conference things got worse when, in the United States, the Smoot-Hawley Act of 1930 was passed. It produced tariffs as high as 53 percent.

Every nation defended an increasingly smaller share of the world market. Barriers in the form of higher quantitative and non-quantitative restrictions, and currency controls resulted in disequilibrium of world commercial relations and that contributed significantly to the world Great Depression of the 1930s.

When President Roosevelt's "New Deal" came to power in 1932, Secretary of State, Cordell Hull, realized that the Smoot-Hawley Act not only choked imports but it also indirectly inhibited American exports. By enacting the Reciprocal Trade Agreements Act of 1934, the United States became the first nation to gradually surrender high tariffs. Other nations followed suit. The Act used the principle of most favored nation treatment (MFNT) and allowed President Roosevelt to reduce tariffs without ratification of the United States Senate. Between 1934 and 1946, thirty-two bilateral conventions were negotiated. For the United States the result was trade increased twice as much with treaty countries as with non-treaty countries.

Multilateral Trade Negotiations (MTN)

World War II was a period of economic as well as military struggle. Following that ugliness, the leaders of the victorious nations realized that cooperation was essential to maintain peace. But before harmony could be achieved, more effective ways than bilateral negotiations would have to be established. The bilateral method just took too long. By negotiating item by item, minor points became the subject of protracted argument, which gave manufacturers' lobbyists more time to bring pressure to bear on negotiators.

Multilateral trade agreements are an improvement over bilateral in that a large number of countries can simultaneously agree to a set of rules for the liberalization of trade. However, this method requires nations to surrender some sovereignty and subject themselves to international procedures.

After the war, aid to the distressed lands of Europe, in the form of the Marshall Plan, had to be administered in some proportionate way and, according to the plan, the countries were left to settle among themselves the fairest method. Europe's method to manage the Marshall Plan was the Organization for European Economic Cooperation (OEEC). Early after its founding in 1948, the OEEC determined that unless a liberalization of European trade restrictions took place businesses in the OEEC countries could not overcome distortions unfavorable to growth. Using multilateral negotiations procedures they established a method where, in the first year, 50 percent of imports from other member nations were freed from quotas. In the second year 60 percent of all items became free of quotas. Round after round of multilateral negotiations gradually eliminated the quotas until the reductions reached the 90 percent level. When the process began to hurt, international forums heard the complaints. Escape clauses were authorized, but if they were invoked by any country, that country had to consent to a hearing to examine its economic situation. The OEEC set a standard for good sense in trade matters, and by 1961 when the United States, Canada and Japan joined it changed its name to the Organization for Economic Cooperation and Development (OECD) and its focus shifted from trade to development aid.

Before the General Agreement on Tariffs and Trade (GATT)

In 1945, even before the OEEC was founded and after a series of consultations with the British, the United States put forth a proposal for an international trade organization entitled "Proposal for Expansion of World Trade and Employment." The proposal sought to address a number of factors inhibiting trade: government restrictions, private cartels, erratic commodity markets, unemployment, and irregular production cycles. These ideas were folded into a draft charter, which was amended in successive conferences from 1946 to 1948 in London, New York, Geneva, and Havana.

Having stepped forward to promote this new organization called the International Trade Organization (ITO), this initiative had historical importance for the United States in that it served as a declaration that a protectionist past had been replaced by a new liberalism.

Meeting at Havana, Cuba in 1948, a charter was drawn for a supranational organization similar to the World Bank. Protectionists from almost every included nation hammered away at the charter until it was so weakened beyond effectiveness that the congress of the nation that proposed it in the first place failed to ratify. The United States Senate declared it a pitiful remnant of the original idea.

General Agreement on Tariffs and Trade (GATT)

The General Agreement on Tariffs and Trade (GATT) came into being in 1947 and except for the Communist bloc, was joined by 23 founding nations because its original purpose as an organization was simply to keep the records of various tariff negotiations. Like an accounting system it was needed so that one concession was not undercut by another. By 1994 the organization had 101 contracting parties representing over four-fifths of world trade.

GATT was never intended to become the ITO or even a supranational organization; however, many of the policy provisions of Havana were incorporated into the founding GATT document. The Interim Commission of the ITO became the GATT Secretariat with headquarters in Geneva, Switzerland, and the United States joined by getting around Senate ratification through the use of an Executive Agreement (no approval needed).

De facto, GATT became the supranational organization ITO was intended to be and in many ways became more effective than other supranationals so constituted. Ironically, as a result of the Uruguay Round the World Trade Organization was established and produced the same results in 1995 as might have been achieved in 1947.

GATT's place in international business

GATT became the major harmonizing institution for international trade. It was the keeper of the rules and a forum to argue and to settle disputes.

"Fair trade," which can be viewed in a protectionist sense, can also be viewed in a positive sense as a set of rules and a council of peers, both of which GATT provided. The guiding principals or "rules of the trade game" were:

- Most favored nation treatment (MFNT) or reciprocity is the cornerstone.
- The exceptions to MFNT are regional unions which do not have to offer treatment agreed to internally to the whole world.
- Tariffs are not forbidden, but increases of existing tariffs are. Once a tariff is fixed by "binding" or lowering then binding, it cannot be raised, only lowered.
- Except in agriculture, quotas are forbidden.
- Maximum levels of tariffs are fixed.
- Settlements are to be negotiated by consultation and conciliation.
- Must meet the needs of developing nations. Essentially this means assisting countries to ignite the growth development process through additional "torquing."

- Contracting parties must agree to abide by principals of GATT.
- Countries that break the rules are called to order.
- Disputes are to be brought before a GATT panel.
- Provides for appeals and escape clauses.
- Appeals (a temporary departure) may be made for Balance of payments problems and in some cases under the "infant industry argument."
- Escape clauses (more permanent departure) may be asked for: economic development; balance of payments; national currencies; infant industry arguments; retaliation; technical transfer; industrial policy.

Market access

Barriers caused by national interstate control schemes result in distortions to the market and prevent access by foreign business. The aim of the harmonization process is "tariffication," that is, replace all other forms of protection, such as quotas or outright bans, with tariffs to harmonize trade rules and hopefully ease market access.

Rounds

Members of GATT met in regular annual session as well as at periodic tariff conferences. These conferences, called "rounds," were extended negotiating sessions to bargain tariff and non-tariff barriers. A Council of Representatives dealt with matters between sessions and prepared the agenda for each session.

The first eight rounds concentrated on reducing tariff rates using the most favored nation treatment (MFNT) or reciprocal agreements method. Table 13.1 shows the results.

Tokyo Round (1973–79)

It should be noted that the success of GATT had as much to do with the disappointing results of the Dillon Round as any other factor. The United States Trade Expansion Act of 1962 was initiated as a direct result of those less than aggressive consequences. The act granted the U.S. President sweeping powers to deal with the EU and third countries. It authorized abolishment of certain import duties, lowering of certain others by half, and if they are already lower than five percent, abolish them altogether. This Act served as a challenge to other members of GATT to achieve better outcomes at future rounds.

The Kennedy Round did produce improvement, but it was not until the passage of the U.S. Trade Act of 1974 which included a "fast track" procedure for Congressional approval that real gains were made. In

Table 13.1 Multilateral trade negotiations under GATT

Date	Name	Outcome
1947	Geneva	45,000 tariff concessions representing half of world trade.
1949	Annacy	Modest tariff reductions.
1950–51	Torquay	Twenty-five percent tariff reduction in relation to 1948 level.
1955–56	Geneva	Modest tariff reductions.
1960–62	Dillon	Modest tariff reductions.
1962–67	Kennedy	Average tariff reduction of 35 percent for industrial products; only modest reductions for agricultural products. Concentrated on tariffs, but for the first time also discussed non-tariffs.
1973–79	Tokyo	Average tariff reductions of 34 percent for industrial products.
1986–93	Uruguay	Significant tariff and non-tariff reductions and establishment of the WTO.

Source: *Focus*, GATT Newsletter

addition to fast track, this act gave the President negotiating authorities for participation in the Tokyo Round.

The outcome of this round was more tariff cuts, but more importantly six Tokyo Round Trade Agreements or "Codes of Conduct" and one "special rule," were reached on non-tariff issues.

Uruguay Round (1986–1995)

The Uruguay Round, launched in Punta del Este, Uruguay, in September 1986 set the agenda for the most ambitious and complex round of multilateral trade negotiations thus far under the auspices of GATT.

Representatives of 74 countries agreed to continue the work of the seven previous rounds, by taking up the issues left unresolved, undertaking to improve rules already implemented, and to extend the rules of GATT to aspects of international trade that remained largely outside the discipline of GATT. Figure 13.4 shows the structure of the Uruguay Round with the Trade Negotiating Committee (TNC) overseeing three sub-groups called the Surveillance Body, Group of Negotiations on Goods (GNG) and the Group of Negotiations on Services (GNS).

The Surveillance Body oversaw the standstill and rollback of trade restrictions to other measures that distort trade.

Figure 13.4 Uruguay Round structure

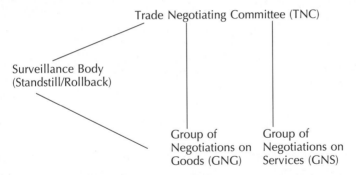

Source: Uruguay Round Update, February 1991, Department of Commerce.

Fourteen negotiating groups were set up under the GNG. They included:

1 reduction and elimination of tariffs;
2 non-tariffs measures (NTMs);
3 natural resources-based products (NRBOs): forestry, fishing, non-ferrous metals, etc;
4 textiles and clothing;
5 agriculture;
6 tropical products;
7 GATT articles (balance of payments; rights of countries in tariff negotiations, FTA, etc;
8 MTN agreements and arrangements (Tokyo Round Codes);
9 safeguards;
10 subsidies and countervailing measures;
11 intellectual property rights;
12 trade-related investment measures;
13 dispute settlement;
14 functioning of GATT system (FOGS).

Outcome of the Uruguay Round

After being mired in emotional disputes about agriculture and subsidies with no results in eight years, the membership that had grown to 117 while negotiating the round, finally reported out on December 15, 1993 and went into force on July 1, 1995 with the results as listed below.

Market access for goods

Tariffs were eliminated in major industrial markets and significantly reduced or eliminated in many developing markets, in the following areas:

- construction;
- agricultural equipment;
- medical equipment;
- steel;
- beer;
- distilled spirits;
- pharmaceuticals;
- paper;
- toys;
- furniture.

Deep cuts ranging from 50–100 percent on important electronics items (e.g. semiconductors, computer parts, semiconductor manufacturing equipment).

Harmonization of tariffs by developed and major developing countries in the chemical sector at very low rates (0, 5.5 and 6.5 percent).

In general, most tariff reductions to be implemented in equal annual increments over five years. Some tariffs, particularly in sectors where duties would fall to zero, such as pharmaceuticals, would be eliminated when the agreement entered into force. Other tariffs, particularly in sensitive sectors, would be phased-in over a period of up to ten years.

Agriculture

The Uruguay Round agreement on agriculture strengthened long-term rules for agriculture trade and assured the reduction of specific policies that distorted agriculture trade.

Textiles and clothing

The Agreement on Textiles and Clothing contains an agreed schedule for the gradual phase-out of quotas established pursuant to the multi-fiber Arrangement (MFA) over a ten-year transition period, after which textile and clothing trade would be fully integrated into GATT and subject to the same disciplines as other sectors. The Agreement provided for expanded trade, improved market access and improved safeguard mechanisms.

Safeguards

The Agreement incorporates many concepts that ensure that all countries will use comparable rules and procedures when taking safeguard actions.

Antidumping

The key provisions of the new antidumping agreement achieves transparency and improves fairness of antidumping regimes.

Subsidies and countervailing measures

The new agreement establishes clearer rules and stronger disciplines in the subsidies area while also making certain subsidies non-actionable, provided they are subject to conditions designed to limit distortive effects.

Trade-related investment measures

The agreement prohibits local content and trade balancing requirements. This prohibition will apply, whether the measures are mandatory or are required, in return for an incentive/advantage. A transition period of five years would be afforded for developing countries to eliminate existing prohibited measures, but only if they notify the GATT regarding each specific measure. Only two years is provided for developed countries. Investment issues are also dealt with in the General Agreement on Trade in Services.

Import licensing procedures

The agreement more precisely defines automatic and non-automatic licensing.

Customs valuation

The negotiations resulted in three amendments to the Valuation Code which will:

- further clarify the rights and obligations of both importing and exporting countries in cases of suspected fraud;
- instruct the Customs Valuation Committee to accord sympathetic consideration to requests to retain officially established minimum values under paragraph three of the Protocol to the Agreement on Implementation of Article VII of the GATT;
- encourage developing countries, with the assistance of the Brussels-based Customs Cooperation Council, to undertake studies in areas of concern relating to the valuation of goods imported by sole agents, sole distributors and sole concessionaires.

Preshipment inspection

This part of the Agreement regulates the activities of Preshipment Inspection ("PSI") companies and reduces or eliminates the impediments to international trade for exporters resulting from the use of such companies by developing countries to supplement or replace national customs services. It also sets up a dispute settlement mechanism to resolve disputes quickly between PSI companies and exporters.

Rules of origin

The Agreement establishes a three-year work program to harmonize rules of origin among the GATT contracting parties. The results of this work program would be annexed as an integral part of the Agreement. The Agreement establishes a GATT Committee on Rules of Origin and a Customs Cooperation Council Technical Committee on Rules of Origin. These committees were to develop, within three years, detailed definitions on which to base harmonized rules of origin.

Technical barriers to trade (TBT)

The new Agreement improved the rules respecting standards, technical regulations and conformity assessment procedures. Furthermore, every country that is a member of the new World Trade Organization will be required to adhere to the new TBT Agreement.

Sanitary and phytosanitary measures

The Agreement on the Application of Sanitary and Phyosanitary ("S&P") measures established rules and disciplines for the development and application of S&P measures—i.e. measures taken to protect human, animal or plant life or health in the areas of food safety and agriculture. These new rules and disciplines will guard against the use of unjustified S&P measures against agricultural exports. At the same time, animal and plant health measures and food safety requirements are protected.

Services

The General Agreement on Trade in Services (GATS) was the first multilateral, legally enforceable agreement covering trade and investment in the services sectors. The GATS also provides a specific legal basis for future negotiations aimed at eliminating barriers that discriminate against foreign services providers and deny them market access.

Trade-related intellectual property rights (TRIPS)

The TRIPS agreement establishes improved standards for the protection of a full range of intellectual property rights and the enforcement of those standards both internally and at the border. The intellectual property rights covered by the agreement are: copyrights, patents, trademarks, industrial designs, trade secrets, integrated circuits (semiconductor chips) and geographical indications. The TRIPS text is covered by the Dispute Settlement Understanding, thus ensuring application of the improved dispute settlement procedures, including the possibility of imposing trade sanctions, such as increasing tariffs, if another member violates TRIPS obligations.

The agreement also includes strong enforcement provisions that are critical to obtaining effective enforcement of the agreed standards. Members must also enforce copyrights and trademarks at their borders against counterfeiting and piracy.

Dispute settlement

The Dispute Settlement Understanding (DSU) creates new procedures for settlement of disputes arising under any of the Uruguay Round agreements. It significantly improves the existing system by providing strict time limits for each step in the dispute-settlement process. The effectiveness of the system is also improved through provisions guaranteeing a right to a panel, adoption of panel reports unless there is a consensus to reject the report, appellate review of the legal aspects of a report on request, time limits on when a member must bring its laws into conformity with panel rulings and recommendations, and authorization of retaliation in the event that a member has not brought its laws into conformity with its obligations within that set period of time. There would be a single system that would apply the strengthened rules and procedures to all disputes with only minor exceptions. A single panel would now be able to address all issues raised under any of the covered agreements. Public access to information about disputes is increased.

GATT articles

The balance of payments (BOP) reform text increases disciplines and transparency over the use of BOP measures. The text provides that when a country experiences serious balance of payments problems, it will impose the least trade distortive trade measures (e.g. import surcharges instead of quantitative restrictions) for the shortest period of time possible. It contains a commitment for the least-developed countries to announce a plan for the liberalization of such measures. It also provides for more rigorous GATT surveillance of BOP-related trade restrictions, and guarantees full rights for GATT members to use GATT dispute-settlement procedures to challenge any matter arising from the application of BOP measures.

Trade Policy Review Mechanism (TPRM)

The final act confirms an April 1989 agreement by ministers establishing the Trade Policy Review Mechanism (TPRM), which would examine, on a regular basis, national trade policies and other economic policies having a bearing on the international trading environment.

The text makes permanent an agreement to conduct annual reviews of the operation of the trading system. The text reconfirmed existing notification requirements and called for the establishment of a central registry of notifications that are made under various agreements (e.g., standards, subsidies).

Ministerial decisions and declarations

The Ministerial Decisions and Declarations state the views and objectives of the Uruguay Round participants on a number of issues relating to the operation of the global trading system, provide for the continuation of the improvements to the dispute-settlement system that became effective in 1989, and deal with other matters concerning the operation of the dispute-settlement system.

Government procurement

This new agreement expanded coverage to significant new areas of procurement and improved the disciplines applicable to government procurement. In addition to the current members of the Agreement (European Union, Japan, Canada, the Nordic countries, Hong Kong, Switzerland, Austria and Israel), South Korea has agreed to join.

In contrast to the existing agreement, which covered only central government procurement of goods, the new Agreement included procurement of services and construction and some coverage of sub-central governments and government-owned utilities. The United States and the EU, in particular, have agreed to seek expansion of their bilateral coverage packages to subcentral and the new Agreement contains provisions that would improve enforcement of the Agreement's disciplines, as well as provisions anticipating future changes in procurement practices, such as streamlining procurement and electronic contracting.

World Trade Organization (WTO)

The Uruguay Agreement established the World Trade Organization (WTO) which, unlike the GATT, now has a stature commensurate with that of the Bretton Woods financial institutions, the World Bank and International Monetary Fund. As shown in Figure 13.5, the WTO encompasses the current GATT structure and extends it to new disciplines that have not been adequately covered in the past. It facilitates the implementation of the trade agreements reached in the Uruguay Round by bringing them under one institutional umbrella, requiring full participation of all countries in the new trading system and providing a permanent forum to address new issues facing the international trading system.

Figure 13.5 World Trade Organization

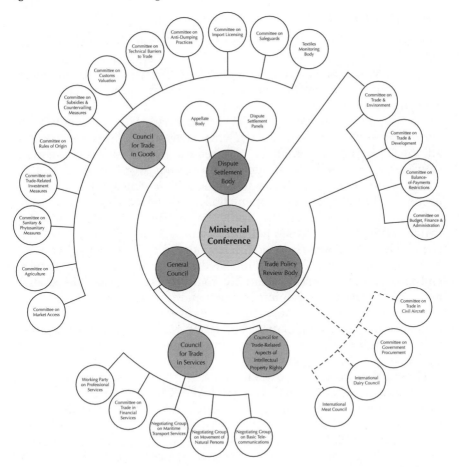

The objective of the WTO is to promote the use of multilateral rules and disciplines and limit the resort to unilateral measures for solutions of conflicts. By bringing together disciplines on government practices affecting trade in goods and services and the protection of intellectual property rights under one institutional umbrella, the WTO Agreement also facilitates the "cross-retaliation" mechanism of the integrated dispute settlement understanding.

In addition, the WTO helps to resolve the "free rider" problem in the world trading system. The WTO system is available only to countries that are contracting parties to the GATT, agree to adhere to all of the Uruguay Round Agreements, and submit schedules of market access commitments for industrial goods, agricultural goods and services. This eliminates the shortcomings of the former system in which, for example, only a handful of countries voluntarily adhered to disciplines on subsidies under the 1979 Tokyo Round agreement.

The structure of the WTO

The structure of the WTO is dominated by its highest authority, the Ministerial Conference, composed of representatives of all WTO members, which is required to meet at least every two years and which can take decisions on all matters under any of the multilateral trade agreements.

The day-to-day work of the WTO, however, falls to a number of subsidiary bodies, principally the General Council (also composed of all WTO members) which is required to report to the Ministerial Conference. As well as conducting its regular work on behalf of the Ministerial Conference, the General Council convenes in two particular forms—as the Dispute Settlement Body, to oversee the dispute settlement procedures and as the Trade Policy Review Body to conduct regular reviews of the trade policies of individual WTO members.

The General Council delegates responsibility to three other major bodies—namely the Councils for Trade in Goods, Trade in Services and Trade-Related Aspects of Intellectual Property Rights. The Council for Goods oversees the implementation and functioning of all the agreements covering trade in goods, though many such agreements have their own specific overseeing bodies. The latter two Councils have responsibility for their respective WTO agreements and may establish their own subsidiary bodies, as necessary.

Three other bodies were established by the Ministerial Conference and report to the General Council. The Committee on Trade and Development is concerned with issues relating to the developing countries and, especially, to the "least-developed" among them. The Committee on Balance of Payments is responsible for consultations between WTO members and countries which take trade-restrictive measures, under Articles XII and XVIII of GATT, in order to cope with balance-of-payments difficulties. Finally, issues relating to WTO's financing and budget are dealt with by a Committee on Budget, Finance and Administration.

Each of the four plurilateral agreements of the WTO—those on civil aircraft, government procurement, dairy products and bovine meat—establish their own management bodies which are required to report to the General Council.

Representation in the WTO and economic groupings

The work of the WTO is undertaken by representatives of member governments but its roots lie in the everyday activity of industry and commerce. Trade policies and negotiating positions are formulated in capitals, usually with a substantial advisory input from private firms, business organizations, farmers as well as consumer and other interest groups. Most countries have a diplomatic mission in Geneva, sometimes headed by a special ambassador to the WTO, whose officials attend meetings of the many negotiating and administrative bodies at WTO headquarters. Sometimes expert representatives are sent directly from capitals to put forward their governments' views on specific questions.

As a result of regional economic integration—in the form of customs unions and free-trade areas—and looser political and geographic arrangements, some groups of countries act together in the WTO with a single spokesperson in meetings and negotiations.

The largest and most comprehensive grouping is the European Union and its 15 member states. The EU is a customs union with a single external trade policy and tariff. While the member states coordinate their position in Brussels and Geneva, the European Commission alone speaks for the EU at almost all WTO meetings. The EU is a WTO member in its own right, as are each of its member states.

A lesser degree of economic integration has so far been achieved by the countries which are GATT members of the Association of South East Asian Nations (ASEAN)—Malaysia, Indonesia, Singapore, the Philippines, Thailand and Brunei Darussalam. Nevertheless, they have many common trade interests and are frequently able to coordinate positions and to speak with a single voice.

Among other groupings which occasionally present unified statements are the Latin American Economic System (SELA) and the African, Caribbean and Pacific Group (ACP). More recent efforts at regional economic integration—for instance, NAFTA (Canada, US and Mexico) and MERCOSUR (Brazil, Argentina, Paraguay and Uruguay)—have not yet reached the point where their constituents frequently have a single spokesperson on WTO issues.

A well-known alliance in the Uruguay Round—bringing together a similarity of trade interests rather than a regional identity—was the Cairns Group which comprised, and still comprises, agricultural exporting nations from developed, developing and Central European countries.

How the WTO makes decisions

The WTO continues a long tradition in GATT of seeking to make decisions not by voting but by consensus. This procedure allows members to ensure their interests are properly considered even though, on occasion, they may decide to join a consensus in the overall interests of the multilateral trading system. Where consensus is not possible, the WTO Agreement allows voting. In such circumstances, decisions are taken by a majority of the votes cast and on the basis of "one country, one vote".

There are four specific voting situations envisaged in the WTO Agreement. First, a majority of three-quarters of WTO members can vote to adopt an *interpretation* of any of the multilateral trade agreements. Second, and by the same majority, the Ministerial Conference may decide to waive an *obligation* imposed on a particular member by a multilateral agreement. Third, decisions to *amend* provisions of the multilateral agreements can be adopted through approval either by all members or by a two-thirds majority, depending on the nature of the provision concerned. However, such amendments only take effect for those WTO members who accept them. Finally, a decision to *admit a new member* is taken by a two-thirds majority in the Ministerial Conference.

The WTO secretariat and budget

The WTO secretariat is located in Geneva. It has around 450 staff and is headed by its Director-General, and four Deputy Directors-General. Its responsibilities include the servicing of WTO delegate bodies with respect to negotiations and the implementation of agreements. It has a particular responsibility to provide technical support to developing countries, and especially the least-developed countries. WTO economists and statisticians provide trade performance and trade policy analyses while its legal staff assist in the resolution of trade disputes involving the interpretation of WTO rules and precedents. Other secretariat work is concerned with accession negotiations for new members and providing advice to governments considering membership.

The WTO budget is around US $83 million (105 million Swiss francs) with individual contributions calculated on the basis of shares in the total trade conducted by WTO members. Part of the WTO budget also goes to the International Trade Center.

How countries join the WTO

Most WTO members were previously GATT members who signed the Final Act of the Uruguay Round and concluded their market access negotiations on goods and services by the Marrakesh meeting in 1994. A few countries which joined GATT later in 1994 signed the Final Act and concluded negotiations on their goods and services schedules, and became WTO members. Other countries that had participated in the Uruguay Round negotiations concluded their domestic ratification procedures only during the course of 1995, and became members thereafter.

Aside from these arrangements which relate to "original" WTO membership, any other state or customs territory having full autonomy in the conduct of its trade policies may accede to the WTO on terms agreed with WTO members.

In the first stage of the accession procedures the applicant government is required to provide the WTO with a memorandum covering all aspects of its trade and economic policies that have a bearing on WTO agreements. This memorandum becomes the basis for a detailed examination of the accession request in a working party.

Alongside the working party's efforts, the applicant government engages in bilateral negotiations with interested member governments to establish its concessions and commitments on goods and its commitments on services. This bilateral process, among other things, determines the specific benefits for WTO members in permitting the applicant to accede. Once both the examination of the applicant's trade regime and market access negotiations are complete, the working party draws up basic terms of accession.

Finally, the results of the working party's deliberations contained in its report, a draft protocol of accession, and the agreed schedules resulting from the bilateral negotiations are presented to the General Council or the Ministerial Conference for adoption. If a two-thirds majority of WTO members vote in favor the applicant is free to sign the protocol and to accede to the Organization; when necessary, this is after ratification in its national parliament or legislature.

Figure 13.6 is the author's pictorial which attempts to provide the reader with a way to visualize WTO as it overlays the global business system, its members, and its trading blocks.

The United Nations in trade harmonization

The WTO ministerial recognizes its responsibilities to the less-developed nations; however, the rapid expansion in the world economy following World War II gave rise in the 1960s to the need for a

Figure 13.6 World Trade Organization overlay

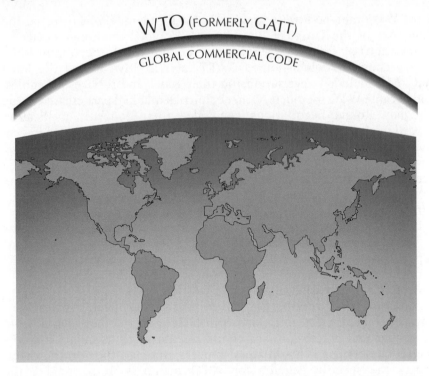

multilateral organization to assist developing countries in their efforts to industrialize and to participate in world trade. The General Assembly in 1964 convened, in Geneva, the United Nations Conference on Trade and Development (UNCTAD-1). It decided later that same year to maintain the Conference as one of its permanent organs.

UNCTAD

Initially, the intent of UNCTAD was to analyze the practices of international trade and to enhance economic development wherever possible. It has since broadened its scope to include the formulation of international trade policies, harmonization through mediation of multilateral trade agreements, and coordination of trade and development policies of governments and regional economic groups.

To promote international trade harmony its 168 members, with its full time secretariat, have come together at conferences held every four years (with exceptions) the sequence of which have been: 1964, Geneva; 1968, New Delhi; 1972, Santiago; 1976, Nairobi; 1979, Manila, and

1983, Belgrade. The Trade and Development Board holds twice-yearly sessions in Geneva.

The Board's members are selected from: the "Group of 77" developing counties; free market economy countries; centrally planned economy countries; and China.

The objectives of the Board are reflected in its subsidiaries: the Committee on Commodities; the Committee on Manufactures; the Committee on Invisibles and Financing related to Trade; the Committee on Shipping; the Committee on Preferences; the Committee on Transfer of Technology; the Committee on Economic Cooperation among Developing Countries.

Commodities

One of the primary responsibilities of UNCTAD is the stabilization of commodity prices by financing global stock operations during periods of acute shortage to surplus. The Conference also seeks to stabilize the world economy through promoting the negotiation of commodity agreements for sugar, tin, cocoa, rubber, jute, olive oil and wheat.

Manufactures

UNCTAD attempts to stabilize exports of manufactured goods through its generalized system of preferences, established during its 1968 session in New Delhi. The system is based on the principle that developing nations should not allow developed countries the same degree of market access as the developed should allow the developing.

Least-developed countries

In 1979, UNCTAD launched a New Program of Action for least-developed nations. The main objectives were: to promote the structural changes needed to overcome their extreme economic difficulties; to provide full, adequate and internationally accepted minimum living standards for the poor; to identify and support major investment opportunities and priorities; and to mitigate as far as possible the adverse effects of natural disasters.

Economic cooperation and transfer of technology

Enhancement of self-help is another objective of UNCTAD. By collecting information on trade barriers among developing countries, and developing a global system of trade preferences patterned after the generalized system of preferences, it is hoped there will be a harmonizing process whereby the developing world will be given preferential treatment and financial and technical assistance.

UNIDO

The United Nations Industrial Development Organization (UNIDO) was established by the General Assembly in 1967 to promote and accelerate the industrialization of developing countries and to coordinate the industrial development of the United Nation's System. It became a specialized agency of the United Nations on 21 June 1985.

The principal organ of UNIDO is the Industrial Development Board whose members are Members of the United Nations or of the intergovernmental agencies associated with the United Nations.

The Board meets annually to act on the reports of a Permanent Committee and to formulate principles and policies.

General Conferences of UNIDO review the background to international economic problems and look for ways to alleviate obstacles to industrial development. There have been four conferences: in 1972, New York; 1975, Lima; 1980, New Delhi; and 1984, Vienna.

The harmonizing functions of UNIDO have been to propose a number of measures, aimed at: an end to protectionism through trade liberalization; a balanced approach to external financing of industry through a mixture of investment, commercial bank lending and official development assistance; a reversal of the net outflow of capital from the developing world.

Customs Cooperative Council (CCC)

In a joint declaration made in Paris on 12 September 1947, thirteen governments of the Committee for European Economic Cooperation formed a study group to consider the issue of forming a Customs Union based on the principles of GATT. The work of the study group, hosted by the Benelux countries in Brussels, was eventually suspended; however, the Customs Committee, assigned the specific task of making a comparative study of Customs techniques, pursued their work.

This was the origin of the Brussels Tariff Nomenclature (BTN) which met on 15 December 1950 to sign three conventions: The convention on Nomenclature for the Classification of Goods in Customs Tariffs; the convention on the Valuation of Goods for Customs Purposes; and the convention establishing a Customs Cooperation Council (CCC).

The purpose of the CCC was to implement the two specialized conventions into a single organization and "to secure the highest degree of harmony and uniformity in Customs systems and especially to study the problems inherent in the development and improvement of Customs technique and Customs legislation in connection therewith."

The inaugural session of the Council was held in Brussels on January 26 1953, under the chairmanship of the Belgian Minister of Trade with 17 member countries. From its limited European origins, the CCC has developed into an influential organization of worldwide scope and influence. Membership now exceeds 100 and it administers 15 international conventions and some 50 recommendations dealing with various customs matters.

Usually meeting in Brussels on an annual basis, it has also met in other locations such as: Vienna, 1971; Kyoto, 1973; Buenos Aires, 1975; Nairobi, 1977; Canberra, 1979; Varna, 1981; Seoul, 1984; Ottawa, 1987; and Williamsburg, 1989.

The Council has a General Secretariat which consists of 111 staff members who conduct their business in two official languages: English and French. However, it works mainly through six technical committees: Permanent Technical Committee; Enforcement Committee; Valuation Committee; Technical Committee on Customs Valuation; Nomenclature Committee, and Harmonization System Committee; plus the Annual Training Seminar.

Significant accomplishments

The primary accomplishment of the CCC has been the development of a harmonized commodity description and coding system. This multipurpose nomenclature system has some 5000 article descriptions included in book form of 21 sections and 97 chapters.

Beginning in 1970, the Harmonized System Committee made a comprehensive study of the system to meet the needs of four groups of practitioners: customs authorities, statisticians, carriers, and producers. The result of 12 years work by experts from 60 countries was adopted by the Council in 1983 and made effective on January 1 1988.

Forty-six parties initially contracted to what is now called the Harmonized Convention. This convention has subsequently been integrated into GATT framework, and adopted as the United Nations' economic classification, and the Standard International Trade Classification (SITC Revision 3).

Another accomplishment has been the implementation of agreement between the GATT Secretariat and the Customs Valuation Committee to ensure technical uniformity and interpretation of customs matters. The Permanent Customs Technical Committee (PTC) has produced the KYOTO Convention which is an international convention on the simplification and harmonization of customs procedures, including standardization of the ATA Carnet and adoption of ADP information support systems.

Very significant has been the work of the Customs Enforcement Committee. The NAIROBI Convention provided for the prevention, investigation, and repression of customs offenses. This committee co-operates with the UN and ICPO/ Interpol, IATA, IAPH, ICS, FIATA, IECC, and the IFPI. In conjunction with the work of the Enforcement Committee, the Technical Cooperation and Training Committee expressed in its Seoul Declaration a program of customs cooperation, including annual training programs and seminars.

CCC's future

The CCC has accepted the challenges of the new century and intends to: encourage harmonization and simplification of customs; develop improved control and enforcement; improve human resources, organization and management of customs administration; and cooperate with the WTO to improve the rules of origin.

Intellectual property protection

Every nation has, or should have, a code or set of standards for the protection of intellectual property rights. These include: patents, copyrights, trade marks, and trade secrets.

Intellectual property, the result of individual creativity, does human-kind little good if it remains in the garage or kitchen of the creator. Yet it would if creativity never reaped a deserved reward. The purpose of intellectual property protection is to promote innovation and intellect-ual creativity and encourage the spread of technology.

Registration

Over time nations have developed treaties and foreign conventions for registration of intellectual property. The Paris Convention, as an example, guarantees citizens of other countries the same rights in patent and trademark matters as is given its own citizens. Ninety-three countries belong to this convention.

Negotiated in June 1970 in Washington, DC and taking effect on January 24 1978 with 41 member countries, the Patent Cooperation Treaty has centralized filing procedures and a standardized application format.

The Madrid Arrangement for International Registration of Trade-marks has 22 members. The European Patent Convention has 16 European area members while the Community Patent Convention has nine EEC countries.

The World Intellectual Property Organization (WIPO) is a specialized agency of the U.N. which administers the Paris Union, otherwise known as the "Bern Union," another collective registration organization.

The problem

The problem is not registration. The problem is *protection*. There has been little or no world enforcement of intellectual property rights. Unethical entrepreneurs from all too many countries think nothing of taking the creative work of others and turning it in to profit for themselves without providing for the originator. As a result, there has been a slower dissemination of technology—creators hide their work for as long as possible and consumers suffer.

Some nations do not have effective protection under national laws, and bilateral negotiations take too long. Trade distortions have been caused due to absence of dispute-settlement mechanisms, particularly about how to deal with imports of products that infringe intellectual property.

An example of the intellectual property enforcement problem is one that arose in China in 1998, wherein a knockoff of the drug Prozac, which helps people who suffer from depression, was sold without the permission of the American firm Eli Lilly & Co. Patents which protect Prozac elsewhere in the world until 2003, are not so protected under Chinese law. A loophole in their law permitted Chinese drug manufacturers to copy a patented medicine; therefore, the problem became a major trade issue between the two countries.

WTO solution

The World Intellectual Property Organization (WIPO) has not been an effective agent for protection, and other international conventions have been deficient. Therefore WTO has undertaken, as a result of the Uruguay Round, to establish new rules for the protection of intellectual property. The elements of the WTO proposal are:

1 standards for all nations;
2 enforcement;
3 dispute settlement;
4 transparency/notification;

Orderly marketing agreements (OMA)

Orderly marketing agreements (arrangements) were developed whereby importing countries would set up "trigger levels" to control, by quotas, the volume of goods entering a country. Alternately called voluntary restraint agreements (VRAs), these are self-imposed quotas, such as those established for Japanese car exports to the United States.

OMAs tend to restrict international competition by preserving national markets for local manufacturers; however, they are even used within the United States for fruit, vegetables and nuts, and certain meat products.

Multi-fiber arrangement (MFA)

The multi-fiber arrangement (MFA) is the largest of the orderly marketing arrangements (OMA) and serves the textile/apparel industry. This very labor-intensive, highly market-competitive industry employs mostly women and is everywhere.

The original treaty, called the Long-term Arrangement Regarding International Trade in Cotton Textiles (LTA), involved 33 countries and was first negotiated and extended twice under the aegis of GATT in 1962.

By the late 1960s man-made fiber textiles had gown so fast that in 1973 representatives of 50 nations, under GATT's aegis, formalized the MFA into a four-year agreement. MFA came into force on January 1, 1974 for a four-year period, but has been extended in four-year increments, the latest, called MFA—IV, extended the treaty by another five years through July 1991.

Description of MFA

MFA is a framework for regulating international trade in textiles and apparel to obtain "orderly marketing" and to avoid "market disruption" in importing countries.

MFA includes coverage to include all known fibers, including: cotton, wool, and man-made fibers; all negotiable fibers and silk blends. It provides a basis for countries to negotiate bilateral agreements or impose restraint on disruptive imports. It also provides standards for determining market disruptions, minimum levels of restraints, and annual growth of imports.

The Textile Surveillance Body (TSB) supervises the Arrangement and examines disputes. The United States, Japan, and the ECC are its permanent members. Although textile issues are discussed apart from other trade issues, MFA signatures retain their GATT rights. The United States, as an example, has negotiated bilateral agreements with 29 signatory countries and 10 non-signatores. The TSB seeks a broader definition of "circumvention" to include transshipments and false declaration, and has increased cooperation requirements to detect and prove circumvention.

National trade remedy systems

Neither the WTO nor any other of the formal harmonization processes have provided for resolution of all trade disputes. At best these methods can address only the major distortions. Interstate controls interfere with ability to compete on a global basis. They cause distortions of the market, all of which cannot be solved by multinational negotiations. Therefore, nation-states have developed internal methods by which businesses bring their trade problems to the attention of government representatives.

The United States has developed a complex method which includes informing the International Trade Administration of the U.S. Department of Commerce, the U.S. Trade Representative (USTR), and the International Trade Commission (ITC) of which specific U.S. laws obtain to an industrial dispute. If investigated and found unfair, the offending nation can be placed on what is commonly called the "Super 301: Watch list." Many nations have developed similar procedures.

Lobbying

In addition to the formalized procedures described above there is another growing trade remedy method. Like it or not, this method, used by individual enterprises, business groups and industry associations, calls for the hiring of local lobbyists to represent one country to influence the government officials of another country.

Fast track

To avoid a repeat of the watering down by national parliaments of major trade negotiations as experienced in 1948 after the ITO negotiations, many countries have established what are fast-track procedures. Fast track means that a treaty negotiated by a nation's trade representatives can be only be voted up (ratified) or down (not ratified). In other words a parliament cannot, after the fact, change what has already been agreed to by the national negotiators. This permits a level of confidence by negotiators that that which has been agreed to will in fact become the law.

Summary

The system of harmonization of trade distortions caused by inevitable competition in the free market condition is complex. Individual businesses and governments stretch free enterprise for their own self interest, causing a need for regulation mechanisms.

When bilateral negotiations became too time consuming the most favored nation (MFN), a reciprocal nondiscriminatory tariff treatment process, became the norm. It extends benefits of tariff reduction to all favored nations.

The World Trade Organization, formerly the General Agreement on

Tariffs and Trade (GATT), is headquartered in Brussels. It holds gatherings (called Rounds) of national trade negotiators, during which representatives attempt to bring harmony to an otherwise controlled global trading system.

UNCTAD is a United Nations subordinate organization designed to promote and harmonize trade among the developed and underdeveloped nations. The mission of the Customs Cooperative Council (CCC) is to bring harmony and uniformity to the world's customs systems. Bringing harmony to the registration and protection of the results of the creative process is the function of the Intellectual Property Protection system.

Orderly marketing agreements (OMA) and the multifiber arrangement (MFA) are intended to resolve textile quota disagreements.

Notwithstanding the world's efforts to bring harmony, nations have developed their own internal methods to allow enterprise to bring to the attention of government market distortions. Enterprises and groups of enterprises from foreign nations lobby the governments of other nations to harmonize interstate controls.

The next chapter explains economic integration and its place in the harmonization system.

CHAPTER FOURTEEN

Regional harmonization: economic integration

The move toward a regional headquarters in North America (to take advantage of the U.S.—Canada—[Mexico] Free Trade Agreement) is fast becoming an essential part of almost every successful company's transition to global competitor status.

Kenichi Ohmae (Former Head of McKensey & Company's office in Tokyo.)

Negotiated economic integration to stimulate the exchange of economic wealth within regions and blocs is another method nations use to harmonize international trade and investment for the global business system.

There is strong evidence that total trade tends to increase within a region of trading nations due to reduction of interstate controls. Enterprises are thus artificially encouraged to expand their operations into other markets within the region. Economic integration tends to have an overall positive effect on trade by providing increased understanding within trading blocs and more cooperation among nations. On the other hand, most forms of regional economic cooperation are highly preferential and, in the views of some, serve as barriers to outsiders and in opposition to multilateral trade concepts.

This chapter discusses the various forms of cooperation between nations to improve exchange of economic wealth. They range from a very simple bilateral agreement to the highest level of cooperation: the formation of an economic union.

Economic integration is not new. The United States of America was one of the earliest when, in 1776, visionary leadership established an economic union of the original 13 states wherein the concept of the four fundamental freedoms, *people, goods, services* and *money*, was to move freely across state boundaries. Today that union has expanded to 50 states and over time that form of economic cooperation has proved to be of great value to the growth of North America.

Hierarchy of economic integration

Because of the trade-development linkage, other unions of trading nations became popular during the twentieth century. The various labels include: bloc forming; regional integration; free trade zones; free trade agreements; free trade associations; free trade areas; customs unions; common markets; economic unions; and political unions.

Care must be used when discussing these terms because each implies more or less control and/or loss of sovereignty. All forms of integration require very careful point-by-point interstate negotiations. Figure 14.1 shows the hierarchy of these integration forms.

Figure 14.1 Hierarchy of economic integration

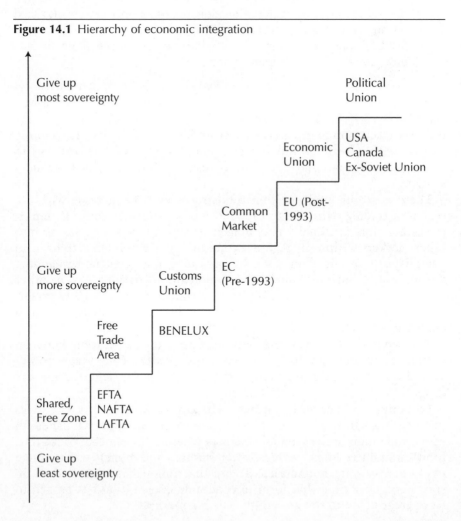

Free trade zones (FTZ)

Free trade zones (FTZ) were the earliest form of economic cooperation among nations. These are rather small areas of property (a
warehouse or fenced field) designated within the customs territory
of a nation, wherein goods might be stored without paying tariff
until the goods are entered into the customs territory for consumption. No tariff is paid if the goods are re-exported. These are
typically fenced warehouses or even areas surrounding factories
which are under the enforcement of the customs service. Goods
brought to the zone may be manipulated or otherwise changed prior
to entry. Figure 14.2 shows the theory of the FTZ physically within
a customs territory, yet considered to be outside. Figure 14.3 shows
that an FTZ could be shared by two nations and, therefore, be a
form of economic integration.

Figure 14.2 Free trade zone

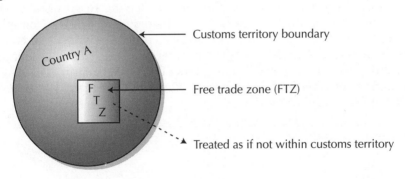

Figure 14.3 Shared free trade zone

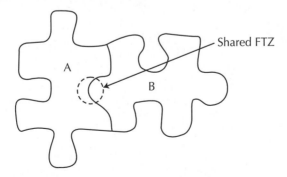

Free trade area/agreement (two or more countries)

Free trade areas may be bilaterally or multilaterally negotiated. The contents of the agreement can and do include the harmonization of many conditions that range from customs procedures, to rules of origin, to the range of products to be included (industrial, agricultural, complete exchange).

Typically the nations involved agree to reduce or abolish mutual import duties and other restrictions (which could include some non-tariff barriers (NT)), often defining a time period during which duties are gradually changed. A common internal tariff (CIT) system tends to improve the uniformity and transparency of existing interstate controls.

Free trade agreements do not go so far as to harmonize the economic policies of the negotiating nations. Nor is there a negotiated common external tariff (CXT). Each member country retains its own tariff and quota system on trade with a third country. As a result outside exporters sometimes scheme to send their goods by way of the country with least tariff for their particular good or service; therefore, these agreements can be defective unless rules of origin are carefully enforced. This leads to complaints from exporters and shippers of "having to go back to the grave" for information on parts or an ingredient's origin. Examples include: European Free Trade Association (EFTA), North American Free Trade Agreement (NAFTA) Latin American Free Trade Association (LAFTA), Australian, New Zealand Free Trade Association (ANZAC), and Caribbean Free Trade Association (CARIFTA). Figure 14.4 shows a FTA composed of four nations.

Figure 14.4 FTA example

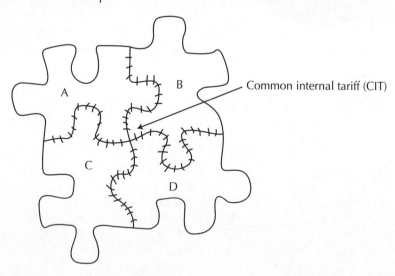

Customs union

A customs union abolishes most protectionism inside the union and sets up a common external tariff (CXT) system with regard to outside countries. It would include common non-tariffs (CNT) as well. A union is a sophisticated level of economic integration, but it does not go so far as to harmonize the economic policy within the negotiated region. Examples include: Belgium, the Netherlands and Luxembourg (BENELUX) and the Economic Community of West African States (ECOWAS). Figure 14.5 shows a customs union with its common external tariff.

Common market

While having the same trade policy as a customs union, a common market also allows the free transfer of the factor endowments: capital, technology, management/know-how, labor, and intelligence, as well as products between member nations. Under certain crisis situations, such as massive unemployment or foreign exchange shortages, an individual nation may temporarily erect barriers to the free flow between itself and the other members. Examples are: European Economic Community (EEC), Central American Common Market (CACM), Association of South East Asian Nations (ASEAN), and Andean Common Market (ANCOM).

Figure 14.5 Customs union

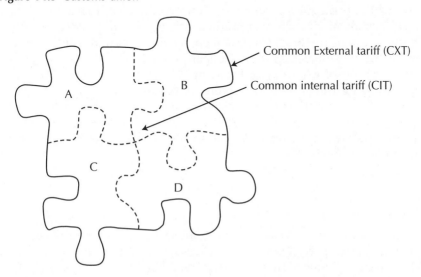

Economic union

This is an even greater degree of economic integration than the common market, because of the effects of harmonization of national economic policies. The major characteristic of this stage of economic integration is the surrendering of sovereignty beyond the CIT and CXT of the customs union to allow a supranational government (above the national governments) to be responsible for economic policy. As in the United States the economic union has a single monetary system, central bank, and a common industrial/economic policy. This is a difficult stage to attain. Unlike the U.S.A., which essentially achieved this stage from its birth, blocs such as the European Union (EU) must attempt to harmonize laws and rules that have been in place for long periods.

Political union

The ultimate form of multinational integration is only achieved after a supranational body is promoted to unite the political environment of an earlier stage of economic integration. It requires the subordination of a national entity to that of the union's entity.

The former Union of Soviet Socialist Republics (U.S.S.R.), although disintegrated as a bloc in 1991, had been since its founding in 1922 the world's largest economic and political union. The Council of Mutual Economic Assistance (COMECON or CMEA), which included the USSR, Bulgaria, Czechoslovakia, East Germany, Hungary, Mongolia, Poland, Rumania, Cuba, and Vietnam, was formed in 1949. This Moscow-based Eastern bloc organization was an example of a coordinating group to facilitate trade among the Communist nations. In early 1991, with the disintegration of the bloc, the group changed its name to the Organization for International Economic Cooperation (OIEC).

The election of a European Parliament within the EU was the first step toward forming a European political union.

Table 14.1 summarizes these cooperative forms and shows the escalation of these integrative forms with the concomitant loss of sovereignty. Table 14.2 shows a summary of the forms of economic integration in place in the early 1990s.

Issues and implications

Economic integration requires harmonization of interstate controls among regional participants but brings with it political as well as welfare issues. Some of those are discussed below.

Table 14.1 Summary chart of economic integration

Stage of integration	CIT	CXT	CNT	Surrender sovereign	Common econ. policies	Free move of cap./tech or labor
Free Trade Zones	no	no	no	no	no	no
Free Trade Areas	yes	no	could	some	no	no
Customs Union	yes	yes	could	more	no	no
Common Market	yes	yes	yes	same	no	yes
Economic Union	yes	yes	yes	much	yes	yes
Political Union	yes	yes	yes	most	yes	yes

Table 14.2 Summary of forms of economic integration

Free trade area	Customs union	Common market	Economic union	Political union
EFTA	BENELUX	EEC	USA	Former-SOVIET UNION (COMECON)
LAFTA	ECOWAS	CACM	EC	USA
ANZAC		ASEAN		
CARIFTA		ANCOM		
NAFTA				

Sovereignty versus integration

The success of economic integration is predicated on the extent the people will allow the political managers of their government to transfer sovereignty to economic unions. Nationalism plays a large part in the success of economic integration.

Borders

Borders may be the last barrier of the global business system. Governments have increasingly recognized that their role is to smooth the way for free enterprise, not stand in its way. Those who argue for elimination of borders acknowledge it is doubtful there will be rapid change; however, they say, when it happens be certain it will be the global enterprise that will lead the way to, if not eliminate, at least reduce the impact of sovereignty on the well being of humankind.

At this juncture of time, those against elimination of borders dominate global thinking. They argue the free movement of people, capital, and goods would be disruptive. They say people would migrate to specific locations leaving the planet with pockets of wealth and empty pockets of poverty. The other side argues that Adam Smith's "invisible hand" would soon turn the pockets of poverty into pools of wealth never thought of as possible.

Insider

A major issue for the global enterprise is the importance of taking an insider position within the trading bloc. In order to find an export outlet for goods within, many manufacturers believe the best positioning is to own or co-own a plant inside so as to take advantage of beneficial rules of origin and be perceived as a local player.

Inward free trade

Blocs tend to expand markets for companies within by lowering barriers and encouraging intratrade.

Outward isolation

Focus on trade within the bloc tends to drain efforts to extend markets across the trade region's border.

Trade diversion

Because of preferential treatment, trading unions tend to shift trade from lower-cost producers outside the union to higher cost producers inside the union.

Trade creation

Because of trade creation implications which increase competition by regional players, trade unions induce a shift from higher-cost producers within to lower-cost producers within the union.

Unequal results

Nations with relatively equal economic strength tend to gain equal value from integration. Weaker nations tend to gain more from the collective reduction of barriers and the resultant increase in trade.

Pros and cons of economic integration

Economic integration is not without debate. The following arguments are put forward by those who are in favor:

1 Empirical observations show that total trade within an economic union increases. The reduction of interstate controls within a union allows a series of benefits which outweigh any negative effects.
2 Market extension: the elimination of barriers increases market opportunities.
3 Economies of scale: the integration of marketing allows amortization of costs over a larger market base.
4 Increased competition: consumers benefit from the introduction of newer and less expensive products.
5 Intensifies innovation: particularly for firms that produce differentiated products.
6 Stimulates capital investment: trade creation possibilities lead businesses to invest in production and marketing facilities within the region in order to get behind any tariff and nontariff walls.

There are, however, several negative implications:

1 The preference effect of members over nonmembers tends to require nonmembers to seek an insider position.
2 Blocs that integrate developed nations with other developed nations, or developing with other developing, reap differing benefits than developed nations with developing nations. Nations of like development make relatively equal gains, while developing nations tend to make greater gains than their developed nation partners.
3 Regional preference mitigate against a rule-based world trade system.

In addition to their overall positive effects on trade, economic integration offers excellent prospects for improved global welfare. They open prospects for increased harmonization; and they become building blocks for cooperation in other areas, such as social and political processes.

The Triad

In his book *The Borderless World*, Kenichi Ohmae speaks of "The Triad." What he refers to is the apparent formation of three major regional trading blocs which some believe will dominate global trade into the next century. The Triad includes:

1 The fifteen nations of the European Union and the overlapping European Free Trade Association (AFTA), plus any additional nations

of that region such as Poland, The Czech Republic and Turkey which may be approved to integrate.

2 The North American Trading Area including Canada, the United States, Mexico and a growing number of South American nations.

3 The ASEAN group which originally included Brunei, Indonesia, Malaysia, Singapore, the Philippines, Thailand, and Vietnam but may include Japan, South Korea, Taiwan and Hong Kong.

Figure 14.6 illustrates these three potential trade blocs.

European Union (EU)

The European Union is a modern example of a customs union (formed a common external tariff (CXT) in 1968) which expanded into an economic union, then further into a potential political union. The level of difficulty to form such a union has been far greater than it was for the United States in that the original 12 European Community (EC) members had well-established ways. Although in 1776, the leaders of the American states did debate "states rights" the nation had not sufficiently matured compared to the problems confronting Europe in the 1980s and 1990s.

History

The struggle to develop a common economic bloc in Europe is not new. The integration has developed in several stages and in various forms. It began in about 1950 when the French economist Jean Monnet, who is called the "Architect of United Europe," authored the idea of a European Community by proposing the European Coal and Steel Community. The Treaty of Paris of 1951, established the Coal and Steel Community between Belgium, France, the Federal German Republic, Italy, Luxembourg, and Holland. Monnet became its first president.

In 1957, the European Economic Community (ECC) was formed when the members of the Coal and Steel Community signed the Treaty of Rome. The more popular term "European Community" (EC) is the organization that resulted from the 1967 Treaty of Fusion: it merged the secretariat (the "Commission") and the intergovernmental executive body (the "Council") of the older European Economic Community (EEC) with those of the European Coal and Steel Community (ECSC) and the European Atomic Energy Community ("EURATOM"), which was established to develop nuclear fuel and power for civilian purposes.

Figure 14.6 The Triad

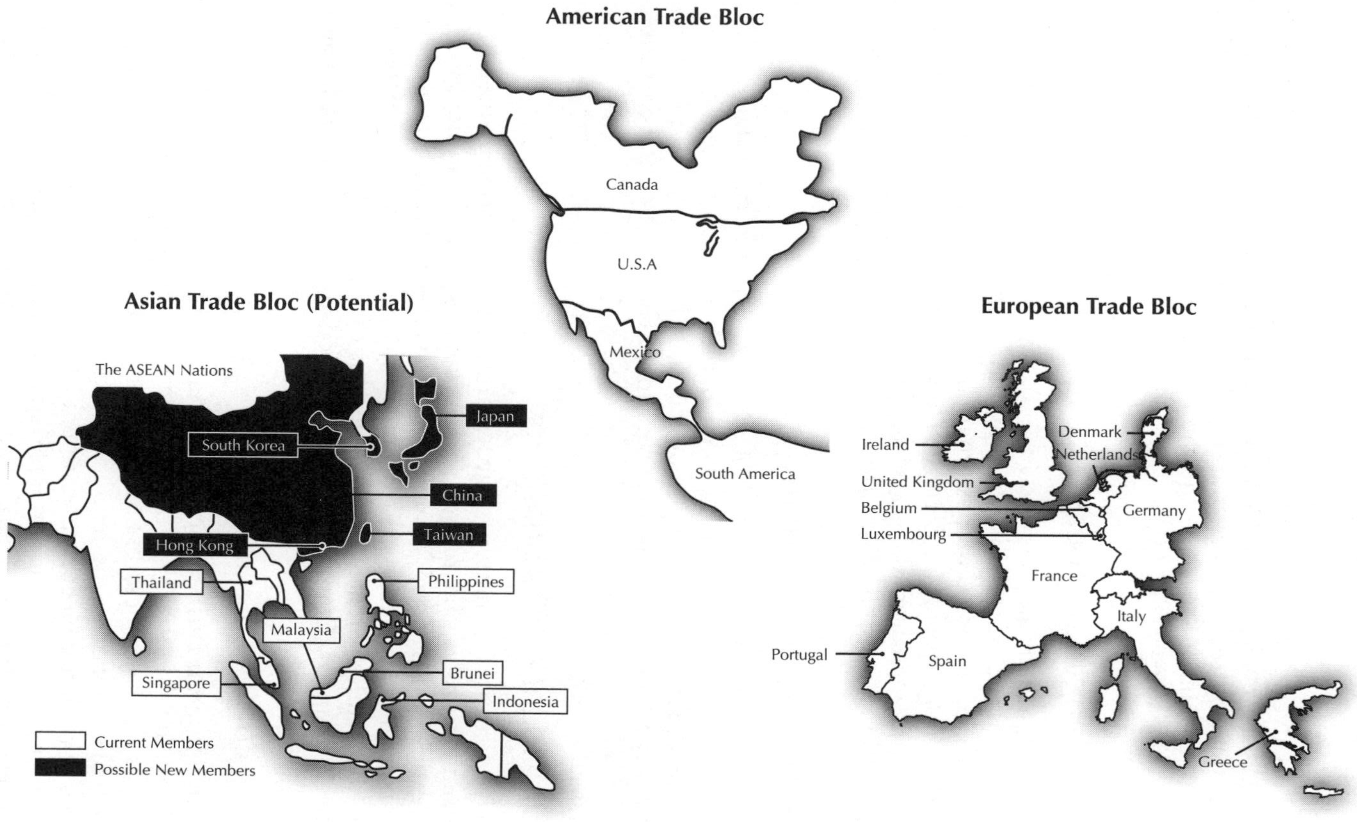

American Trade Bloc

Canada

U.S.A

Mexico

South America

European Trade Bloc

Ireland

United Kingdom

Belgium

Luxembourg

Denmark

Netherlands

Germany

France

Italy

Greece

Spain

Portugal

Asian Trade Bloc (Potential)

The ASEAN Nations

Japan

China

Taiwan

Philippines

Brunei

Indonesia

South Korea

Hong Kong

Thailand

Malaysia

Singapore

☐ Current Members

■ Possible New Members

1985 White paper

The continued maintenance of internal barriers perpetuated the costs and disadvantages of separate national markets and the need for further action was evident. The Commission published a White Paper, titled "Completing the Internal Market," which listed some 282 legislative proposals and a timetable for their adoption. It was endorsed by the Heads of State.

1987 Single European Act

This act, which amends the EEC Treaty, was ratified by the governments and parliaments of all Community countries, confirmed the aim of achieving a single European market by 1992 and the timetable of the 1985 White Paper. It adopted the Community's decision-making procedures and increased the scope for voting by a qualified majority (as opposed to unanimously) within the Council.

1992 Maastricht Treaty

In December 1992 leaders of the 12 EU member states met in Maastricht, the Netherlands. The outcome was a treaty that committed the members to adopt a common currency by January 1 1999 and paved the way for closer political cooperation, even the eventual creation of a political union.

Organizational institutions

What sets the Community apart from more traditional international organizations is the unique institutional structure. In accepting the Treaties of Paris and Rome, member states relinquish a measure of sovereignty to supranational independent institutions representing national and shared interests. The institutions of the Community are the Parliament, Commission, the Council, and the Court of Justice.

The European Parliament

The European Parliament (called "Assembly" in the various treaties) is elected by the citizens of the member states by direct universal suffrage. It provides a democratic forum for debate, has a watchdog function, and also plays a part in the legislative process, particularly in budgeting. In that it does not elect a government, Parliament exercises only symbolically the functions of a true parliament such as exists in a democracy. Instead the functions analogous to government provided for in the treaties are performed by the Council and the Commission. Parliament has powers of supervision only over the Commission and not over the Council. The Commission is supervised by means of its accountability to Parliament and the need to report annually to the latter.

The Council

This is the main decision-making institution. It is made up of the Ministers from each member state with responsibility for the policy area under discussion at a given meeting: foreign affairs, agriculture, transportation, etc.

The Presidency of the Council rotates, changing hands every six months. There is also a General Secretariat, based in Brussels. The Council is responsible for coordinating the general economic policies of the member states. It also adopts Community legislation (regulations, directives, and decisions).

Commission

Since the accession of Greece, Portugal and Spain, the Commission has consisted of 17 members (two members each from France, Germany, Italy, Spain and the United Kingdom and one from each of the other member states, appointed by the governments of the member states for a term of five years). The Commission's functions are:

- Acts as the starting point for every Community action and must present proposals and drafts for Community legislation to the Council. In certain circumstances the Commission has law-making powers.
- Guardians of the Community treaties.
- Defending Community interests by serving as mediator between member states.
- Serves as the executive body, i.e. implementor of the Community budget, competition law and the administration of the protective clauses contained in the treaties and secondary legislation.

Court of Justice

Based in Luxembourg, the Court of Justice comprises 13 judges assisted by six advocates-general, all appointed for a six-year term by common agreement between the member states. The Court has two main functions:

- To check the laws enacted by the Community institutions for compatibility with the Treaties.
- To give its opinion on the correct interpretation or the validity of the Community provisions when requested to do so by a national court.

Objectives

From the beginning, a principal objective of the Community was the establishment of a customs union, other forms of economic integration, and political cooperation among member countries. The Treaty of Rome provided the *four fundamental freedoms* enabling *people*, *goods*, *services* and *money* to move unhindered throughout the EU. This included the gradual elimination of customs duties and other internal trade barriers, the establishment of a common external tariff (CXT), and guarantees of free movement of labor and capital within the Community. The United Kingdom, Denmark and Ireland joined the Community in 1973, Greece in 1981, and Spain and Portugal in 1986. The Community's Council, which is headquartered in Brussels, meets several times a year at the Foreign-Minister level, and occasionally at the Heads-of-State level. Technical experts from Community capitals meet regularly to deal with specialized issues in such areas as agriculture, transportation or trade policy.

Community law

Every social organization has a constitution. By that means the structure of a political system is defined to include the relationship of the various parts to the whole and the objectives and rules common to the organization. The constitution lays down the rules for making binding decisions. The Community constitution, as opposed to its member states, is not a comprehensive document, but arises from the totality of rules and fundamental values by which those in authority regard themselves bound. These rules are found in the founding treaties or in legal instruments produced by the Community institutions, but also partly rest on custom.

How the EU makes laws

It is necessary to be familiar with the procedures by which the Community passes laws in order to understand the details in the various summaries of those laws, directives, and regulations. The following is an outline of those procedures:

- The Commission (which has both executive and administrative roles) initiates and drafts a proposal which it submits to the council.
- The European Parliament (which is elected by the citizens of the Community) and the Economic and Social Committee (which consists of representatives from employer organizations, trade unions and other interest groups) consider and comment on the proposal.
- The Council (whose members represent the governments of the

member states, normally at ministerial level) adopts the proposal which then becomes law. In some cases, this power can be exercised by the Commission.

Potential enlargement of EU

The four fundamental freedoms provide the framework for limitless boundaries of the potential expansion and formation of a new Europe. Over the next decades the Community will welcome new members, the alacrity depending on economic and political reforms in Eastern Europe and the republics of the former Soviet Union. Certainly the European Free Trade Association (EFTA) nations would be the first to formally join. The agreement forming the European Economic Area between the EU and the EFTA countries signified the next step towards the economic integration of all Europe. Applications to join the EU are pending for Turkey (1987), Austria (1989), Sweden (1991), Finland (1992), and Switzerland (1992).

Transatlantic free-trade pact

Discussions between American and the European Union trade representatives to substantially expand U.S.—EU trade and cooperation began in 1998. The potential for a transatlantic free-trade pact is one of the options being considered.

European Free Trade Association (EFTA)

EFTA is a regional grouping established in 1960 by the Stockholm Convention, headquartered in Geneva, now comprising Austria, Iceland, Norway, Sweden, and Switzerland. Finland is an Associate Member. Denmark and the United Kingdom were formerly members, but they withdrew from EFTA when they joined the European Community in 1973. Portugal, also a former member, withdrew from EFTA in 1986 when it joined the EU. EFTA member countries have gradually eliminated tariffs on manufactured goods originating and traded within EFTA. Agricultural products, for the most part, are not included in the EFTA schedule for internal tariff reductions. Each member country maintains its own external tariff schedule and each has concluded a trade agreement with the European Community that provides for the mutual elimination of tariffs for most manufactured goods except for a few sensitive products. As a result, the European Community and EFTA form what is now called the de facto European Economic Area (EEA), nicknamed "Euroland."

Central and Eastern Europe

The EU has also entered into bilateral association agreements with Poland and Hungary, and will negotiate with the Czech and Slovak republics. It is likely that the Community will expand to a customs union of at least 20 countries by early in the next century. A "Greater Europe," stretching from the Atlantic to the Urals will only develop into an organized power if it is built around a stable nucleus capable of speaking and acting as one. Tables 14.3 through 14.6 show the trading potential of an expanded European bloc.

Common currency

Targeting 1999 at the latest, the European Union expects to have a common currency, called the euro. The composition of the euro will be a basket of the 12 currencies dominated by a 30 percent DM share and 20 percent FF share. All other currencies are represented but in shares ranging from as much as 12 percent UK£ to as little as one percent ESC.

Table 14.3 European trading bloc

Country	Population millions	National income bn $	Nation income per head $
European Union (EU)			
Germany	84.1	1,450.0	17,900
France	58.0	1,080.0	18,670
UK	58.6	1,140.0	19,500
Italy	57.5	1,090.0	18,700
Spain	38.8	565.0	14,300
Netherlands	15.6	301.9	19,500
Belgium/Lux.	10.2	197.0	19,500
Denmark	5.2	112.8	21,700
Greece	10.6	101.7	9,500
Portugal	10.0	116.2	11,000
Ireland	3.5	54.6	15,400
Austria	8.0	152.0	19,000
Finland	5.1	92.4	18,200
Sweden	8.9	177.3	20,100
Totals/averages	344.1	6,630.9	Ave: 17,355

Source: *The World Almanac and Book of Facts, 1998,* World Almanac Books, New Jersey, 1998.

Table 14.4 European Free Trade Association (EFTA)

Austria	8.0	152.0	19,000
Finland	5.1	92.4	18,200
Sweden	8.9	177.3	20,100
Switzerland	7.2	158.5	22,400
Norway	4.4	106.2	24,500
Iceland	0.27	5.0	18,800
Totals/averages	33.8	691.0	Ave: 20,500
			Total Ave Europe: 18,298

Source: *The World Almanac and Book of Facts, 1998*, World Almanac Books, New Jersey, 1998.

Table 14.5 Eastern Europe: non-aligned

Country	Population millions	National income bn $	National income per head
Czech Republic	10.3	106.2	10,200
Poland	38.7	226.7	5,800
Romania	21.4	105.7	4,600
Yugoslavia	10.6	20.6	2,000
Hungary	9.9	72.5	7,000
Albania	3.2	4.1	1,210
Slovakia	5.4	0.4	7,200
Bosnia-Herzegovina	2.6	1.0	300
Bulgaria	8.6	43.2	4,920
Totals/averages	110.7	580.0	4,803

Source: *The World Almanac and Book of Facts, 1998*, World Almanac Books, New Jersey, 1998.

National treatment

A White Paper issued in 1985 consolidated the principle of mutual recognition of national laws and regulations. This eliminated the need to create a new uniform body of EC regulations. Harmonization at EC level was only necessary where basic health, safety or the environment were too divergent.

Table 14.6 Eastern Europe: Congress of Independent States (CIS)

Country	Population millions	National income bn $	National income per head
Azerbaijan	7.7	11.5	1,480
Belarus	10.4	49.2	4,700
Estonia	1.4	12.3	7,600
Georgia	5.2	6.2	1,080
Kazakhstan	16.9	46.9	2,700
Kirghizistan	4.5	5.4	1,140
Lithuania	2.0	13.0	6,700
Latvia	2.4	14.7	5,300
Moldovia	4.5	10.4	2,310
Russia	147.9	796.0	5,300
Tadzhakistan	6.0	6.4	1,040
Turkmenistan	4.2	11.5	2,820
Ubekistan	23.8	54.7	2,370
Ukraine	50.7	174.6	3,370
Totals/averages	287.6	1,212.8	3,422

Source: *The World Almanac and Book of Facts, 1998,* World Almanac Books, New Jersey, 1998.

Market access: the single market

That White Paper resulted in the Single European Act (SEA) that contained a series of amendments to the Treaty of Rome which made it easier to negotiate the directives needed to make the single market work. The key innovation in the SEA was to extend the use of majority voting in place of unanimity in the EC's main decision-making body. Without majority voting, it would have been impossible to have passed the more than 280 separate items of legislation required to be enacted to eliminate internal EC frontiers and have the single market ready by the end of 1992.

The measures already adopted are:

- the liberalization of public procurement;
- the harmonization of taxation;
- the liberalization of capital markets;
- standardization, thanks to a new approach to certification and testing, recognition of the equivalence of national standards;
- the abolition of technical barriers (freedom to exercise an activity and recognition of the equivalence of training qualifications) and physical

barriers (elimination of border checks) to the free movement of individuals;
■ the creation of an environment which encourages business cooperation by harmonizing company law and approximating legislation on intellectual and industrial property.

VAT harmonization

Each EC member has a standard value-added tax (VAT) which is assessed on the sale of both domestic and imported products. Table 14.7 shows these tax rates. The VAT is a sales or consumption tax imposed on buyers upon the sale of goods, from the beginning of the production and distribution cycle to the final sale to the consumer.

The Community exporter and importer of any given item is required to file a declaration with their local value-added tax (VAT) authority in their home country. The VAT authorities in the member states are to cooperate closely to ensure that frauds are not being committed. A standard rate of VAT of between 15 percent and 25 percent with a range of exceptions for essential goods—food, medicines, books, transport, etc.

Table 14.7 VAT rates in the 12 member states of the Community

	Standard [1]	Reduced [2]	Increased [3]	Other [4]
Belgium	19.5%	12%		
Denmark	25%			
France	18.6%	5.5%		
Germany	15%	7%		
Greece	18%	8%		
Ireland	21%	10%		0%
Italy	19%	9%	38%	
Luxembourg	15%	6%		
Netherlands	17.5%	6%		
Portugal	16%	5%	30%	
Spain	15%	6%	28%	
United Kingdom	17.5%			0%

Notes:
[1] A standard rate applies to most products. Exceptions are noted in other footnotes, below.
[2] Reduced rates are levied on basic necessities, such as foodstuffs, electricity, heat, lumber, books, etc. but items affected and rates vary between countries.
[3] Increased rates are generally levied on luxury items including perfumes, jewelry, hi-fi and stereo equipment, cameras, cars, etc.
[4] Zero rates of duty are applied by some EC countries on foodstuffs and medicines.

that qualify for a lower rate. Payment of VAT was made in the country where a product or service is finally sold; however, after 1996, it is paid in the country of origin. In other words firms can now buy, sell and invest in any member state without having to go through checks or formalities when crossing intra-community borders. Citizens may obtain goods for their own use in any Community member state and take them across borders without being subject to controls or liable for tax.

For importers from non-community nations the VAT should be applied on the cost, insurance and freight (c.i.f.) value plus the duty charged on the particular good. Thus [c.i.f. + duty (c.i.f. × duty rate)] + [VAT] = total cost to importers.

North American Free Trade Agreement/Area (NAFTA)

The North American Free Trade Agreement/Area (NAFTA) is a treaty that retains each nation's external tariffs, but over a period of 15 years reduces most internal tariffs to zero. Figure 14.7 illustrates this by showing a Common Internal Tariff (CIT) and differing external tariffs. The tactical implications of NAFTA depend on a product-by-product analysis as well as whether the firm is an insider or outsider.

History of NAFTA

The first step in building the American trade bloc was an agreement in 1989 between Canada and the United States negotiated to harmonize interstate controls and achieve a common internal tariff (CIT) over a ten-year period. It began in March 1985, when President Reagan and Prime Minister Mulroney explored ways to reduce and eliminate existing barriers to trade. In September of 1985, Mr. Mulroney requested that the U.S. and Canada examine a free trade agreement (FTA). In December of 1985 the negotiations were put on a "fast track," and by June 1986, the first negotiations were underway. By October of 1987 President Reagan notified the U.S. congress and December of that year the text of treaty had been initialed. Reagan and Mulroney signed the treaty in January 1988.

Key provisions of the Canada/U.S. FTA

The key provisions of the Canada/U.S. Free Trade Agreement (CFTA) were:

■ eliminate all tariffs by 1998;
■ use Rule of Origin to prevent third-country intrusion;
■ eliminate customs user fees and duty drawback by 1994;

Figure 14.7 NAFTA

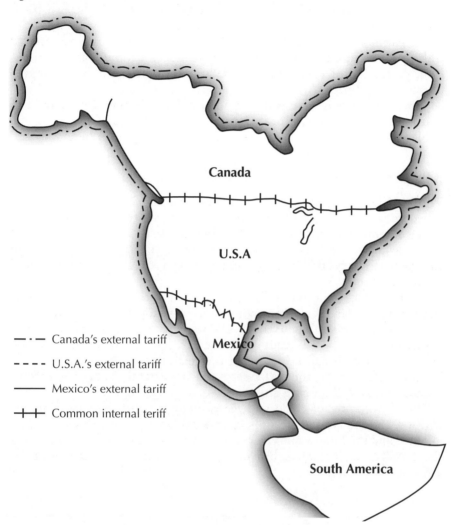

- Canada's external tariff
- U.S.A.'s external tariff
- Mexico's external tariff
- Common internal teriff

Canada

U.S.A

Mexico

South America

- eliminate quotas unless grandfathered;
- prohibit product standards as a trade barrier;
- eliminate agriculture tariffs and subsidies;
- expand the size of government procurement markets;
- no discrimination on laws related to service providers.

In May of 1991, Canada and Mexico requested an examination of a North American Free Trade Agreement (NAFTA) and negotiations began in June of 1991. By August of the following year the text was initialed and President Bush notified Congress in September. The three leaders, Bush, Mulroney, and Salinas signed the document in December of 1992; the following May the U.S. Congress extended the fast-track procedure. The summer of 1993 was a period of renegotiation among the participants as they fulfilled President Clinton's campaign promise to link several non-trade treaties such as labor migration, illegal immigration, protection of the environment, human rights, and democracy to passage of the NAFTA.

Other nations edging toward joining the bloc include: Chile, and the Southern Cone countries of Argentina, Brazil, Paraguay and Uruguay. Tables 14.8 and 14.9 show the potential of the American bloc.

Key provisions of the NAFTA

The NAFTA treaty is over 1000 pages long and its companion tariff schedule is even longer. Obviously, over the years there will be changes to the documents negotiated by the three countries. Those changes will be the result of users (exporters and importers) shoring up loopholes and finding better ways of doing business. However, the basic document will remain the same.

The following treatment follows the format of the actual treaty, but is not the legal document. It provides only a synopsis and is offered for your basic understanding of the NAFTA and its various parts. It is not a substitute for detailed reading of the treaty and its tariff schedule documents which can be found in the nearest government repository library. Reference to the full treaty and its several changes is recommended prior to finalizing any business activity.

The elimination of trade and investment barriers between Canada, Mexico, and the United States is intended to create a strategic economic alliance and the largest and richest bloc in the world. To accomplish this the NAFTA has established a minimal organization for management and administration.

Table 14.8 North American trade bloc

Country	Population millions	National income bn $	National income per head $
Canada	29.1	694	24,400
U.S.A.	268	7,170	27,607
Mexico	97.5	721	7,700
Totals/averages	394.6	8,585	19,902

Source: The World Almanac and Book of Facts, 1998, World Almanac Books, New Jersey, 1998.

Table 14.9 Potential South American trade bloc

Country	Population millions	National income bn $	National income per head $
Argentina	35.7	278.5	8,100
Bolivia	7.6	20	2,530
Brazil	164.5	976.8	6,100
Chile	14.5	113.2	8,000
Columbia	37.4	192.5	5,300
Ecuador	11.7	44.6	4,100
Paraguay	5.6	17	3,200
Peru	24.9	87	3,600
Uruguay	3.2	10.2	3,300
Venezuela	22.4	195.5	9,300
Totals/averages	327.5	1,935.3	5,353

Source: *The World Almanac and Book of Facts, 1998,* World Almanac Books, New Jersey, 1998.

Preamble

Implemented January 1 1994, the NAFTA preamble states the commitment of the three countries to:

- contribute to the harmonious development and expansion of world trade and provide a catalyst to broaden international cooperation;
- create an expanded and secure market for the goods and services produced in their territories;
- enhance competitiveness in global markets;
- protect the environment;
- create new employment, improve working conditions, and living standards in their respective territories;
- promote sustainable development;
- protect and enhance workers' rights and conditions.

Objectives

- eliminate barriers;
- promote conditions of fair competition;
- increase investment opportunities;
- protect intellectual property rights;
- procedures to resolve disputes;
- further trilateral, regional, multilateral cooperation;

- observe: national treatment, MFN, transparency;
- respect rights under GATT and other international agreements.

Potential enlargement of NAFTA

The second summit of the Americas held in Santiago, Chile in April 1998 brought the American hemisphere closer to what Europe has created, a common market. The Free Trade Area of the Americas (FTAA) would potentialy merge NAFTA, Mercosur, the Andean Community, the Central American Common Market and even the Caribbean free-trade association known as CARICOM.

Forming the Asian trade bloc

Japan stands alone as the major trading nation of Asia; however, the Association of South East Asian Nations (ASEAN) has considered expanding to become the APEC trade bloc.

ASEAN to APEC

The Association of South East Asian Nations (ASEAN) was formed in 1975 and included Indonesia, Malaysia, the Philippines, Singapore, and Thailand. ASEAN has considered expanding to include South Korea, Hong Kong, Taiwan, and Japan. Should these countries join, the East Asian bloc would become the largest of the Triad with a total population of about 500 million, compared to the EU with about 320 million and the NAFTA with about 365 million. Another possibly is the East Asia Economic Caucus (EAEC), which is similar to APEC but excludes Canada, New Zealand, Australia and the U.S.A. Should the People's Republic of China (PRC) choose to become a member with its population of over a billion people, the Asian Bloc would become the largest of the Triad with a total population of about two billion compared to the EU with about 350 million and NAFTA with about 400 million.

This bloc is weakened by its geography and economic gaps. Made up mainly of islands strung north and south, the idea of a single bloc is difficult to grasp. The economic gap is even more formidable. For instance, Indonesia's percapita GDP is about $3,500 while Singapore is about $23,000. Table 14.10 shows the membership of this potential bloc and Figure 14.8 shows the disbursement of the ASEAN group.

Minor world trade blocs

Over the past 50 years or so nations have been forming blocs. In terms of trade volume the minor trade blocs are as listed below.

Table 14.10 Potential Asian trade blocs

Country	Population millions	National income bn $	National income per head $
ASEAN (Association of South East Asian Nations)			
Brunei	0.3	3.6	12,000
Indonesia	209	711	3,500
Malaysia	20.3	193.6	9,800
Philippines	76.1	180	2,530
Singapore	3.4	66.1	22,700
Thailand	59.4	416.7	6,900
Vietnam	75.1	87	1,300
Totals/averages	443.6	1,658	6,847
APEC (Asia-Pacific Economic Cooperation)			
ASEAN	443.6	1,658	6,847
Australia	18.4	405.4	22,100
Canada	29.1	694	24,400
China	1,210	2,610	2,500
Japan	125.7	2,680	21,300
Korea (South)	45.9	591	13,000
Korea (North)	24.5	21.5	920
New Zealand	3.6	62.3	18,300
China (Taiwan)	21.6	290.5	13,500
United States	268	7,170	27,607
Totals/averages	1,922.8	16,181.7	11,972
EAEC (East Asia Economic Caucus)			
ASEAN	443.6	1,658	6,847
China	1,210	2,610	2,500
China (Taiwan)	21.6	290.5	13,500
Japan	125.7	2,680	21,300
Korea (South)	45.9	591	13,000
Totals/averages	1,847	7,829.5	8,930

Source: *The World Almanac and Book of Facts, 1998,* World Almanac Books, New Jersey, 1998.

Figure 14.8 Dispersement of potential ASEAN bloc

Latin America Free Trade Agreement (LAFTA)

The Treaty of Montevideo negotiated in 1960, initiated the Latin America Free Trade Agreement which includes Argentina, Bolivia, Brazil, Chile, Peru, Uruguay, Mexico, Paraguay, Columbia, and Ecuador. Intended as a free-trade area to liberalize trade among the participants, it turned out to be weak because the reduction of barriers had many loopholes. In 1981, LAFTA was superseded by the Latin American Integration Association (LAIA) which changed the purpose to become an area of preferences instead of a free-trade area.

Central American Common Market (CACM)

In 1962, the Central American Common Market (CACM) was formed to include Guatemala, Nicaragua, Honduras, Costa Rica, and El Salvador.

Mercorsur

In 1991, the Southern Cone countries of South America began negotiations to frame an agreement for a regional trading bloc, formulated a year later, the trade alliance called Mercorsur which significantly lowered tariffs and includes: Argentina, Brazil, Paraguay and Uruguay.

East Africa Economic Community

East Africa formed their Economic Community in 1967 to include Kenya, Uganda, and Tanzania.

Economic Community of West African States (ECOWAS)

The Economic Community of West African States (ECOWAS) consists of Nigeria, Ghana, Liberia, Ivory Coast (Coast D'Vion), Senegal, Togo, Benin, Upper Volta, Gabon, Cameroon, Mali, Gambia.

Caribbean Free Trade Association (CFTA)

In 1968, the Caribbean Free Trade Association came together and includes Antigua, Barbados, Guyana, and Trinidad.

CARICOM

Established in 1973, the Caribbean Economic Community is made up of 13 English-speaking countries of the region, including Belize in Central America, the Bahamas, and Guyana in South America. Its aim is to strengthen the economies of its members through increased regional trade and a common approach to trade negotiations with third countries. It plans to establish a common market by 1995.

Andean Common Market (ANCOM)

Following in those footsteps of CFTA, the Andean Common Market (ACM) with Peru, Chile, Columbia, Ecuador, Bolivia, and Venezuela was formed in 1969.

Gulf Cooperation Council (GCC)

On the African continent, six Arab Gulf states, Bahrain, Oman, Qatar, Saudi Arabia, and the United Arab Emirates (U.A.E.) formed the Gulf Cooperation Council (GCC) in 1981. The main objective was regional economic integration, but also to develop cooperation in the economic, political, communication, social and cultural fields.

Arab Economic Union (AEU)

The Arab Economic Union, consisting of Libya, Tunis, Mauritania, and Morocco, was formed in the late 1980s for purposes of regional cooperation.

Arab Cooperation Council (A.C.C.)

One of the most recent attempts at integration is the Arab Cooperation Council (A.C.C.). Formed in 1989 it includes Egypt, Jordan, Iraq, and Yemen.

British Commonwealth

The British commonwealth was one of the earliest economic unions.

German Zollverein

Another early attempt was the German Zollverein (Federal Republic of Germany) in 1834.

Benelux

Benelux, made up of the first letters of each of the member country's names: Belgium, The Netherlands, and Luxembourg, is an economic union first formed as a customs union in 1948 with a single (common) external tariff. By 1956, more than 95 percent of trade among the nations was free of all interstate controls. It was not until 1958 that the Benelux Treaty established the economic union, which when it came into effect in 1960 established the world's first completely free labor market. The Benelux Nations eventually created a common foreign trade policy which permitted the free movement of goods, workers, services and capital.

Summary

Regional integration is a form of harmonization and its popularity came about because there is strong evidence that total trade increases within agreed unions due to reduction of interstate controls and nearness of cross-border markets. Thus far two major trading blocs have been formed; however, a triad could come in to being if an Asian bloc is formed. There are at least 12 minor world trade blocs.

Care must be taken when using the various terms of economic integration because each implies more or less control and/or loss of sovereignty. Free trade areas or agreements (FTA) usually result in the negotiation of a common internal tariff (CIT) while a customs union abolishes all protectionism within the union and establishes a common external tariff (CXT).

A common market requires the negotiation of the free transfer of the factor endowments: capital, technology, management (know-how), labor, and intelligence, and an economic union surrenders sovereignty beyond a common market to allow a common economic policy. The ultimate form of economic integration is the political union which subordinates individual nations to a supranational entity.

Appendices

Appendix A
Singapore
A country case study

This country has no natural resources other than its harbor and its people, so in early 1961 the Government established an autonomous body called the Singapore Economic Development Board. This quasi-government organization's task was to spearhead the transformation of the country from a trading nation to a modern diversified economy with emphasis on manufacturing and services. In so doing, their thrust was the development of capital-intensive, highly skilled, export-oriented manufacturing industries.

While the author acknowledges that the following information is out of date, its purpose is to show what a nation did to stimulate the growth of their economy to become one of the greatest success stories of the twentieth century.

Background

Singapore is an island located at the southern tip of the Straits of Malacca, about 137 kilometers north of the Equator. The Republic of Singapore comprises the main island and 57 smaller ones with a total land area of about 600 square miles. It has a population of 2.6 million, half of whom are under the age of 30.

It is second only to Rotterdam in terms of tonnage moved through its port and is by far the busiest port in Asia. Known as the crossroads of the world, it is served by more than 500 shipping lines and is an important stopover in the networks of most international airlines.

Modern Singapore was founded in 1819 by Sir Stamford Raffles as a trading post for the East India company and in 1867, along with Malacca and Penang, became a British colony. Following several organizational changes, during the 1950s and early 1960s, Singapore separated from Malaysia by mutual consent.

By the late 1960s, a rapid inflow of investments by multinational corporations (MNCs) from around the world brought a rapid industrialization which today can support the manufacturing of such sophisticated products as computers, Winchester disk drives, facsimile machines, optics and other precision engineering products.

At the time, under United States Tariff Schedules (harmonized) 9802.00.80503 and 9802.00.60008 (formerly TSUS 807 and 806.30) American firms could operate subsidiary fabrication and assembly plants and return the output to their U.S. locations with only the value added by the the non-U.S. materials and the process of transformation in the Singapore plant being charged duty in the exchange.

Like Mexico, Singapore was a United Nations "recipient" country, so if the product contained 35 percent or more of Singapore content, chances are that it would qualify for import to the U.S. with no duty under the Generalized System of Preferences (G.S.P.).

Forms of business organization

Because of its small domestic market most projects in Singapore had to be export oriented.

Subcontract

Like in most other production sharing countries, enterprising natives of Singapore developed plants that provided a service for short-term assembly operations. Most of those companies kept offices or representatives in the major cities of developed countries to market their specialties to target industries. Contacts can still be made though Singapore embassies or its Economic Development Board.

Investment

Most business is carried on in the form of sole trader or partnership. An ordinary partnership is one where the partners share equally the gains and losses. A limited partnership is one in which one or more partners are only liable to the extent of their capital contributions. Of course a limited partnership must have one or more general partners without limit for the firm's debts. All sole traders and partnerships must be registered under the Singapore Business Registration Act of 1973.

Foreign corporations

The most common form of business entity in Singapore is the limited liability company which may be private or public.

Private company

A private company can

- restrict the right to transfer shares;
- limit its numbers to 50;
- prohibit public subscription to its shares;
- prohibit invitation of the public to deposit money with it;
- prevent shares being held directly or indirectly by a corporation.

Formation procedures of a private company

1 Obtain written approval from the Registrar of Companies to use the name.
2 If the proposed company has foreign participation, gain approval of the Trade Development Board in the case of a trading company, or the Economic Development Board and Monetary Authority in case of a manufacturing or finance company.
3 Two or more persons subscribe their names to the articles of association.
4 Submit an application with a copy of the company's memorandum and articles of association to the Registrar of Companies.
5 The company can commence business from the date the certificate of incorporation is issued.

Formation procedures of a public company

Although the procedures are almost exactly the same as that of a private company, a public company cannot begin business until it has filed a prospectus or statement in lieu of a prospectus.

Branches of foreign corporations

A branch of a foreign corporation must submit to the Registrar of Companies:

- a copy of its certificate of incorporation;
- a copy of its charter;
- a list of its directors;
- a memorandum of appointment stating the names and addresses of two agents in Singapore;
- a statutory declaration by the agents;
- a notice of the situation of its registered office in Singapore;
- a copy of annual accounts within two months after holding its annual meeting.

Singapore advantages

The Singapore dollar is generally stable at about half the value of the U.S. dollar and workers' salaries are very competitive. Table A1 shows typical salaries of various employment groups.

Working conditions

The Singapore Employment Act regulates the working conditions for those whose monthly salaries do not exceed S$1,250 or about U.S.$600.00. The working week is fixed at 44 hours.

Overtime

Payment at one and a half times the hourly rate of pay for overtime and two times the hourly rates for holidays and normal week days off. Overtime is limited to 72 hours a month.

Vacation

Under the Act, there are eleven paid public holidays, seven days' annual leave after one year's service and an additional one day's annual leave for every subsequent 12 months of continuous service with one employer. Sick leave, limited to 14 days, is paid after one year of service, but can be extended to as much as 60 days where hospitalization is involved. Retirement benefits may be payable after five years' service.

Table A1 Typical monthly salaries (Singapore)

Occupation	Average month basic wages (S$)
Basic unskilled labor	500–600
Officer clerk	750
Typist	750
Stenographic-typist	1,000
Steno-secretary	1,500
Sales, shop assistant	600
Production supervisor	1,500
Architect, engineer	2,600

Fringe benefits

Consideration of fair and reasonable modern benefits is a part of managing in Singapore. Such things as cafeterias, and day care are as much a part of business life in this country as in any throughout the world.

Social Security

The government social insurance program in this country is called the Central Provident Fund (CPF). All employees in the private sector are required to contribute and are augmented by their employers. The employer's contribution is 10 percent and the employee's is 25 percent, combining for the 35 percent of monthly wages subject to a ceiling of S$ 6,000 per month. Amounts may be withdrawn in a lump sum on reaching the statutory retirement age of 55 years or prematurely in the event of permanent disablement or migration. The board also allows funds to be withdrawn prior to retirement to purchase a home and for certain approved securities.

Another fund called the Skills Development Fund (SDF) requires employers to pay one percent on employees earning up to S$750 a month. This fund is used to pay grants to employers and promote the training skills necessary to carry out Singapore's restructuring efforts.

Medisave is Singapore's National Health Plan. It is designed to meet the basic needs of the average citizen. The income for the program comes from CPF. Six percent (three percent employer and three percent employee) is set aside to help pay hospitalization bills of the immediate family.

Ownership of land and buildings

Most industrial land is owned by the State and is governed by Ground Leases controlled and managed by the Jurong Town Corporation at reasonable rents. Jurong, the town immediately surrounding the port, has twenty-five industrial estates in which more than 3000 companies with 200,000 workers represent more than 70 percent of the nation's work force. Of this number, about 60 percent of the companies are foreign owned or joint ventures. Although there are other estates than those of Jurong in which many foreign companies are doing business, Jourong's popularity is its extensive infrastructure and support services including cargo handling at the Port and Marine Base.

Many industrialists prefer to buy or rent factories that are already built because they can begin production almost immediately. The various estates offer these standard factories at very competitive prices. Average rentals for upper floors are about S $065 per square foot per month and about S$0.95 per square foot for ground floor. Sale prices range from S$65 to S$175 per square foot.

Leases on industrial land with or without building, are granted for an initial period of 30 years with options for an additional 30 years.

Incentives

Singapore's list of incentives is rivaled by few nations in the production-sharing business. They are aggressive—Singapore wants your business. The country's incentives fall into two categories: economic expansion by income tax legislation and other non-fiscal expansion incentives.

Economic expansion by income tax relief

Economic expansion incentives are administered by the Economic Development Board which takes a very flexible approach to almost anything that has a job creative and technical transfer flavor.

Pioneer industries

Pioneer industries are those declared by the Minister of Finance to be in the economic interest of Singapore. These enterprises are exempt from company tax for five to ten years from the date they commence production.

Pioneer service companies

These are the following service-related industries that receive an incentive tax relief period for five years or more, but not to exceed ten years:

■ any engineering or technical services, including laboratory, consultancy and research and development activities;
■ computer-based information and other computer-related services;
■ development or production of any industrial design.

Expansion of established enterprise

A capital equipment expansion that exceeds S$10 million to improve an approved product may be granted an expansion certificate. This exempts the holder from tax on the increased income resulting from the expansion for a period of up to five years.

Expanding service companies

Companies that expand as a pioneer service company may apply for approval as an expanding service company. Once approved, the firm receives a tax exemption on the incremental profits made during a period not to exceed five years.

Export incentive

This incentive is designed to encourage manufactured exports. The normal period is five years, although it may be extended for up to fifteen years, if the fixed capital expenditure exceeds S$150 million and half of the paid-up capital is held by permanent residents of Singapore. During this period 90 percent of the company's qualifying export profits are to be exempt from tax. To qualify, at least 20 percent of the value of total sales must be exports, and must amount to more than S$100,000 per year.

Investment allowance

This incentive is an alternative to pioneer status and export incentives. It is particularly beneficial for projects which may not generate profits early enough to benefit from fixed period tax holiday schemes. Profits are tax-exempt at various percentages for different project and assets up to 50 percent of actual investment on factory buildings and new productive equipment for an approved project.

Liberalized investment allowance

This provides for a wider range of activities than the Investment Allowance scheme, and fixes the exempt rate on profits at 30 percent of the qualifying expenditure on machinery and equipment.

Warehousing and servicing incentives

The intent of this incentive is to encourage the establishment of warehouses for manufactured goods which are to be sold and exported. Half of the companies qualifying export profits are exempt from tax for five years.

International consultancy services incentive

Intended to encourage overseas projects in management, design engineering, plant fabrication and computer processing services, this incentive exempts half of the qualifying export profits for five years.

International trade incentive

Trading companies that export non-traditional Singapore products (other than coconut oil, tin, natural rubber, etc.) may be exempt from paying tax on half of their export profits for five years. The qualification is limited to companies that have a minimum of S$10 million per year Singapore manufactured or domestic produced, or at least S$20 million in non-traditional commodities.

Product development assistance

This scheme provides cash grants to encourage local design, development, and indigenous technical know-how. It is only available to companies that have at least 31 percent ownership by Singapore citizens of permanent residents. The maximum grant is limited to $5000, but can be applied to 50 percent of the cost feasibility studies as well as the costs of product development.

Tax exemption on interest on approved loans

The idea behind this incentive is to encourage foreign loans for capital investments. A tax exemption may be granted on interest withholding tax provided the consequence is a lower cost to the borrower.

Approved royalties, fees and development contributions

Application can be made for a reduced rate of tax or exemption altogether on payments of royalties, fees and development contributions.

New technology companies

This incentive scheme is to encourage ventures into new technology and applies to holding companies that are at least 50 percent owned by Singapore citizens or permanent residents. It provides tax allowances for losses made by a technology company.

Operational headquarters

To encourage multi-national corporations to set-up their headquarters in Singapore, a concessionary tax of only 10 percent on their service income is available for up to ten years.

Accelerated depreciation allowance

Singapore's Income Tax Act offers a normal depreciation of plant and machinery; however, an accelerated method allows most equipment to be written off over a period of three years, and computers, industrial robots and office automation in one year.

Research and development expenditure

In addition to investment and depreciation allowances, Singapore offers several other incentive schemes to stimulate quality industries and to promote research and development:

- double deduction of R&D expenditures, other than on buildings and equipment;
- extension of allowances on industrial buildings;
- a tax exempt reserve of 20 percent of their taxable income for R&D to be used within three years.

Shipping profits of Singapore ships

To encourage ship owners to register their ships in Singapore, profits of those that fly the country's flag are exempt from tax.

Other non-fiscal expansion incentives

These are an array of financing programs aimed at stimulating business development, particularly research and marketing for export.

Small industries finance scheme

This is a program that provides financial assistance in the form of low-interest loans to small local businesses (less than S$3 million in fixed productive assets). It is available to both manufacturing and service companies, including exporters.

Small Industries Technical Assistance Scheme (SITAS)

To encourage the use of external experts to upgrade business operations, the Economic Development Board will reimburse up to 90 percent of the cost of engaging a consultant.

Skills training grants

Assistance is available through this scheme to encourage existing operations to mechanize their operations. Training facilities and assistance is available to upgrade employee skills for the new equipment.

Interest grants for mechanization

This scheme is intended to reduce the cost of financing the cost of mechanization of existing manual operations.

Development consultancy

This scheme provides for grants paid to consultants to assist local Singapore businesses improve operations and training plans.

Small Enterprise Development Bureau

The Bureau acts as a one-stop assistance supermarket with six different programs available to stimulate the growth of small business.

Capital Assistance Scheme (CAS)

This is for investors who wish to apply for capital in the form of equity or fixed or floating rate loans which range from five to fifteen years.

Product Development Assistance Scheme (PDAS)

To encourage local company's product design and development, this scheme offers a grant equal to 50 percent of the approved development costs.

Initiatives in New Technology (INTECH)

This is an encouragement scheme for local manufacturers and service companies for investments and manpower development in the application of new technology. Grants are provided equal to 30–50 percent of approved costs of the project.

Market Development Assistance Scheme (MDAS)

Provides financial and other assistance to companies marketing Singapore-made goods and services overseas. Must be a Singapore registered company with at least 30 percent local equity.

Research and Development Assistance Scheme (RDAS)

This is an incentive which provides seed-money for industrial undertakings of R&D that a firm would not pursue because of insufficient resources of high risk.

Venture capital scheme

Under this scheme, an overseas investor is allowed to deduct from income up to 100 percent of the equity in an approved project which assists local companies to acquire or diversify into new technology industries.

Personal income tax

Income earned in Singapore is taxable whether or not the individual is a resident in Singapore for tax purposes. Personal income tax is charged on a sliding scale ranging from as little as 3.5 percent to 33 percent after deductions. A resident is one who is physically present in Singapore for 183 days or more in a year.

Non-resident income is not taxed if it does not exceed 60 days in a calendar year. Employment of greater than 60 days, but less than 183 days is taxed at 15 percent.

Appendix B
A glossary of international business terms

International business, like other specialized fields, has developed its own distinctive vocabulary which can mystify laymen. Many business people stumble over terms commonly used in trade and the acronyms that represent international organizations that guide, regulate, and facilitate trade. This lack of precision in the language impedes communication, causes misunderstandings, and delays transactions. Undoubtedly, it loses sales for global companies.

The source for this glossary of terms, frequently used in the global business system, was prepared by the U.S. Information Agency, which consulted experts in the U.S. Departments of Commerce, State, and Treasury, the U.S. International Trade Commission, the Office of the U.S. Trade Representative, and in the World Trade Organization and UNCTAD Secretariats in Geneva. It also includes other terms researched by the author and particularly applicable to the scope of this book.

Ad Valorem Tariff. A tariff calculated as percentage of the value of goods cleared through customs, e.g., 15 percent ad valorem means 15 percent of the value.

Adjustment Assistance. Financial, training and reemployment technical assistance to workers and technical assistance to firms and industries to help them cope with adjustment difficulties arising from increased import competition. The objective of the assistance is usually to help an industry become more competitive in the same line of production, or to move into other economic activities.

Agency for International Development (AID). The unit within the U.S. Government responsible for the administration of U.S. bilateral development assistance programs. AID also participates actively in the

the development of other U.S. policies and programs related to Third World economic development.

ATA Carnet. An international customs document that is recognized as an internationally valid guarantee and may be used in lieu of national customs documents and as security for import duties and taxes to cover the temporary admission of goods and sometimes the transit of goods. The ATA ("Admission Temporaire–Temporary Admission") Convention of 1961 authorized the ATA Carnet to replace the ECS ("Echantillons Commerciaux–Commercial Samples") Carnet that was created by a 1956 convention sponsored by the Customs Cooperation Council. ATA Carnets are issued by National Chambers of Commerce affiliated with the International Chamber of Commerce, which also guarantees payment of duties in the event of failure to re-export. A carnet does not replace an export license.

Balance of Payments. A tabulation of a country's credit and debit transactions with other countries and international institutions. These transactions are divided into two broad groups: Current Account and Capital Account. The Current Account includes exports and imports of goods, services (including investment income), and unilateral transfers. The Capital Account includes financial flows related to international direct investment, investment in government and private securities, international bank transactions, and changes in official gold holdings and foreign exchange reserves.

Balance of Trade. A component of the balance of payments, or the surplus or deficit that results from comparing a country's expenditures on merchandise imports and receipts derived from its merchandise exports.

Barriers. As used in this book, these are the laws, rules, and business practices imposed at and within the borders of one nation to *restrict* the success of businesses of another nation. Their intent is sometimes innocent, but more often are designed to keep global businesses out in order to protect domestic businesses.

Barter. The direct exchange of goods for other goods, without the use of money as a medium of exchange and without the involvement of a third party.

Beggar-Thy-Neighbor Policy. A course of action through which a country tries to reduce unemployment and increase domestic output by raising tariffs and instituting non-tariff barriers that impede imports, or by accomplishing the same objective through competitive devaluation. Countries that pursued such policies in the early 1930s found that other countries retaliated by raising their own barriers against imports, which, by reducing export markets, tended to worsen the economic difficulties that precipitated the initial protectionist action. The American Smoot-Hawley Tariff Act of 1930 is often cited as a conspicuous example of this approach.

Bilateral Trade Agreement. A formal or informal agreement involving commerce between two countries. Such agreements sometimes list the quantities of specific goods that may be exchanged between participating countries within a given period.

Bounties or Grants. Payments by governments to producers of goods, often to strengthen their competitive position.

Bonded (Customs) Warehouse. A bonded warehouse is a building or other secure area within the customs territory of a country where dutiable foreign merchandise may be placed for a controlled period without payment of duty. Generally, only cleaning, repacking and sorting may take place. The owner of the bonded warehouse incurs liability and must post a bond with the national customs service and abide by those regulations pertaining to control and declaration of tariffs for goods on departure. Liability is cancelled when the goods are removed and tariffs must be paid when the goods are entered for consumption.

Boycott. A refusal to deal commercially or otherwise with a person, firm or country.

Business. For purposes of this book the definition of business is: "make and/or sell goods or services for profit in a global context."

Codes of Conduct. International instruments that indicate standards of behavior by nation-states or multinational corporations deemed desirable by the international community. Several codes of conduct were negotiated during the Tokyo Round that liberalized and harmonized domestic measures that might impede trade, and these are considered legally binding for the countries that choose to adhere to them. Each of these codes is monitored by a special committee that meets under the auspices of GATT and encourages consultations and the settlement of disputes arising under the code. Countries that are not contracting parties to GATT may adhere to these codes. GATT Articles III and XXIII also contain commercial policy provisions that have been described as GATT's code of good conduct in trade matters. The United Nations has also encouraged the negotiation of several "voluntary" codes of conduct, including one that seeks to specify the rights and obligations of transnational corporations and of governments.

Commodity. Broadly defined, any article exchanged in trade, but most commonly used to refer to raw materials, including such minerals as tin, copper and manganese, and bulk-produced agricultural products such as coffee, tea and rubber.

Common External Tariff (CXT). A tariff rate uniformly applied by a common market or customs union, such as the European Community, to imports from countries outside the union. For example, the European Common Market is based on the principle of a free internal trade area with a common external tariff (sometimes referred to in French as the Tarif Exterieur Commun–TEC) applied to products imported from non-member countries. "Free trade areas" do not necessarily have common external tariffs.

Comparative Advantage. A central concept in international trade theory which holds that a country or a region should specialize in the production and export of those goods and services that it can produce relatively more efficiently than other goods and services, and import those goods and services in which it has a comparative disadvantage. This theory was first propounded by David Ricardo in 1817 as a basis for increasing the economic welfare of a population through international trade. The comparative advantage theory normally favors specialized production in a country based on intensive utilization of those factors of production in which the country is relatively well endowed (such as raw materials, fertile land or skilled labor), and perhaps also the accumulation of physical capital and the pace of research.

Countertrade. A reciprocal trading arrangement. Countertrade transactions include:

(a) **Counterpurchase** obligates the foreign supplier to purchase from the buyer goods and services unrelated to the goods and services sold, usually within a one- to five-year period.

(b) **Reverse countertrade** contracts require the importer (a U.S. buyer of machine tools from Eastern Europe, for example) to export goods equivalent in value to a specified percentage of the value of the imported goods—an obligation that can be sold to an exporter in a third country;

(c) **Buyback arrangements** obligate the foreign supplier of plant, machinery, or technology to buy from the importer a portion of the resultant production during a period of five to twenty-five years.

(d) **Clearing agreements** between two countries that agree to purchase specific amounts of each other's products over a specific period of time, using a designated "clearing currency" in the transactions.

(e) **"Switch"** arrangements that permit the sale of unpaid balance of a clearing account to be sold to a third party, usually at a discount, that may be used for producing goods in the country holding the balance.

(f) **"Swap"** schemes through which products from different locations are traded to save transportation costs (e.g. Soviet oil may be "swapped" for oil from a Latin American producer, so the Soviet oil is shipped to a country in South Asia, while the Latin American oil is shipped to Cuba).

(g) **Barter** arrangements are those through which two parties directly exchange goods deemed to be of approximately equivalent value without any flow of money taking place.

Coordinating Committee for Multilateral Export Controls (COCOM). A committee established in 1951 by NATO member countries to co-ordinate their policies relating to the restriction of exports of products and technical data of potential strategic value to the Soviet Union and certain other countries. To date, it consists of NATO countries plus Japan, but without Iceland.

Countervailing Duties. Special duties imposed on imports to offset the benefits of subsidies to producers or exports in the exporting country. GATT Article VI permits the use of such duties.

Current Account. That portion of a country's balance of payments that records current (as opposed to capital) transactions, including visible trade (exports and imports), invisible trade (income and expenditures for services), profits earned from foreign operations, interest and transfer payments.

Customs Classification. The particular category in a tariff nomenclature in which a product is classified for tariff purposes, or the procedure for determining the appropriate tariff category in a country's nomenclature system used for the classification, coding and description of internation-ally traded goods. Most important trading nations—except for the United States, Canada, and the Soviet Union—classify imported goods in conformity with the Customs Cooperation Council Nomenclature (CCCN), formerly known as the Brussels Tariff Nomenclature (BTN).

Customs Cooperation Council (CCC). An intergovernmental organiza-tion created in 1953 and headquartered in Brussels, through which customs officials of participating countries seek to simplify, standardize and conciliate customs procedures. The Council has sponsored a standardized product classification, a set of definitions of commodities for customs purposes, a standardized definition of value and a number of recommendations designed to facilitate customs procedures.

Customs Cooperation Council Nomenclature (CCCN). A system for classifying goods for customs purposes, formerly known as the Brussels Tariff Nomenclature (BTN).

Customs Harmonization. International efforts to increase the uniformity of customs nomenclatures and procedures in cooperating countries. The Customs Cooperation Council has been seeking since 1970 to develop an up-to-date and internationally accepted "Harmonized

Commodity Coding and Description System" for classifying goods for customs, statistical and other purposes. The Council hopes that most of the major trading countries will implement the system by 1987.

Devaluation. The lowering of the value of a national currency in terms of the currency of another nation. Devaluation tends to reduce domestic demand for imports in a country by raising their prices in terms of the devalued currency and to raise foreign demand for the country's exports by reducing their prices in terms of foreign currencies. Devaluation can therefore help to correct a balance of payments deficit and sometimes provide a short-term basis for economic adjustment of a national economy.

Developed Countries. A term used to distinguish the more industrialized nations—including all OECD member countries as well as the Soviet Union and most of the socialist countries of Eastern Europe—from "developing" or less developed countries. The developed countries are sometimes collectively designated as the "North," because most of them are in the Northern Hemisphere.

Developing Countries (see also LCDs). A broad range of countries that generally lack a high degree of industrialization, infrastructure and other capital investment, sophisticated technology, widespread literacy, and advanced living standards among their populations as a whole. The developing countries are sometimes collectively designated as the "South," because a large number of them are in the Southern Hemisphere. All of the countries of Africa (except South Africa), Asia and Oceania (except Australia, Japan and New Zealand), Latin America, and the Middle East are generally considered to be "developing countries," as are a few European countries (Cyprus, Malta, Turkey and Yugoslavia, for example). Some experts differentiate four sub-categories of developing countries as having different economic needs and interests:

1 A few relatively wealthy OPEC countries—sometimes referred to as oil exporting developing countries—share a particular interest in a financially sound international economy and open capital markets.
2 Newly industrializing countries (NICs) have a growing stake in an open international trading system.
3 A number of middle-income countries—principally commodity exporters—have shown a particular interest in commodity stabilization schemes.
4 More than 30 very poor countries ("least developed countries") are predominantly agricultural, have sharply limited development prospects during the near future, and tend to be heavily dependent on official development assistance.

Distortion. This is a significant bias in product sales for the businesses of one country over another that are not the result of the free-market competitive process.

Dispute Settlement. Resolution of conflict, usually through a compromise between opposing claims, sometimes facilitated through the efforts of an intermediary. GATT Articles XXII and XXIII set out consultation procedures a contracting party may follow to obtain legal redress if it believes its benefits under GATT are impaired.

Dumping. The sale of an imported commodity at "less than fair value," usually considered to be a price lower than that at which it is sold within the exporting country or to third countries. "Fair value" can also be the constructed value of the merchandise, which includes a mandatory eight percent profit margin, plus cost of production. Dumping is generally recognized as an unfair trade practice that can disrupt markets and injure producers of competitive products in the importing country. Article VI of GATT permits the imposition of special Anti-Dumping Duties against "dumped" goods equal to the difference between their export price and their normal value in the exporting country.

Economic Denationalization. These are companies that have adopted the concept that their operations become country neutral in terms of personnel and headquarters.

Economic Development. Some use the term economic development only in the sense of the struggle of those nations that are less developed in terms of relative personal living standards. But, development is the primary worry of every national government and is the summation of those complex factors of infrastructure, human health and education, as well as capital to allow people to achieve a higher living standard.

Economic Growth. This is the way economic development is measured. It tends to be measured in terms of nation-states, but can be measured in terms of global growth. Growth is typically measured as a percentage of improvement of gross domestic product over historical norms, but is more and more being measured as gross global product, including the benefits of cross-border trade.

Embargo. A prohibition upon exports or imports, either with respect to specific products or specific countries. Historically, embargoes have been ordered most frequently in time of war, but they may also be applied for political, economic or sanitary purposes. Embargoes imposed against an individual country by the United Nations—or a group of nations—in an effort to influence its conduct or its policies are sometimes called "sanctions."

Escape Clause. A provision in a bilateral or multilateral commercial agreement permitting a signatory nation to suspend tariff or other concessions when imports threaten serious harm to the producers of competitive domestic goods. GATT Article XIX sanctions such "safeguard" provisions to help firms and workers adversely affected by a relatively sudden surge of imports adjust to the rising level of import competition.

European Union (EU). A term for the political union of the European Communities (EC) that resulted from the 1992 Maastric Treaty and the 1967 "Treaty of Fusion" that merged the secretariat (the "Commission") and the intergovernmental executive body (the "Council") of the older European Economic Community (EEC) with those of the European Coal and Steel Community (ECSC) and the European Atomic Energy Community ("EURATOM"), which was established to develop nuclear fuel and power for civilian purposes. The EEC first came into operation on January 1 1958, based on the Treaty of Rome, with six participating member states—France, Italy, the Federal Republic of Germany, Belgium, the Netherlands and Luxembourg). From the beginning, a principal objective of the Community was the establishment of a customs union, other forms of economic integration, and political cooperation among member countries. The Treaty of Rome provided for the gradual elimination of customs duties and other internal trade barriers, the establishment of a common external tariff, and guarantees of free movement of labor and capital within the Community. The United Kingdom, Denmark and Ireland joined the Community in 1973, Greece in 1981, and Spain and Portugal in 1986. The Community is headquartered in Brussels. The Council meets several times a year at Foreign Minister level, and occasionally at Heads of State level. Technical experts from Community capitals meet regularly to deal with specialized issues in such areas as agriculture, transportation or trade policy.

European Free Trade Association (EFTA). A regional grouping established in 1960 by the Stockholm Convention, headquartered in Geneva, now comprising Austria, Iceland, Norway, Sweden, and Switzerland. Finland is an Associate Member. Denmark and the United Kingdom were formerly members, but they withdrew from EFTA when they joined the European Community in 1973. Portugal, also a former member, withdrew from EFTA in 1986 when it joined the EC. EFTA member countries have gradually eliminated tariffs on manufactured goods originating and traded within EFTA. Agricultural products, for the most part, are not included on the EFTA schedule for internal tariff reductions. Each member country maintains its own external tariff schedule and each has concluded a trade agreement with the European Community that provides for the mutual elimination of tariffs for most manufactured goods except for a few sensitive products. As a result, the European Community and EFTA form a de facto free trade area.

Exchange Controls. The rationing of foreign currencies, bank drafts, and other instruments for settling international financial obligations by countries seeking to ameliorate acute balance of payments difficulties. When such measures are imposed, importers must apply for prior authorization from the government to obtain the foreign currency required to bring in designated amounts and types of goods. Since such measures have the effect of restricting imports, they are considered non-tariff barriers to trade.

Exchange Rate. The price (or rate) at which one currency is exchanged for another currency, for gold, or for Special Drawing Rights (SDRs).

Excise Tax. A selective tax—sometimes called a consumption tax—on certain goods produced within or imported into a country.

Export-Import Bank (Eximbank). A public corporation created to make guarantees and insure loans to help finance exports, particularly for equipment to be used in capital improvement projects. EXIM banks also provide short-term insurance for both commercial and political risks, either directly or in cooperation with commercial banks.

Export Quotas. Specific restrictions or ceilings imposed by an exporting country on the value or volume of certain imports, designated to protect domestic producers and consumers from temporary shortages of the goods affected or to bolster their prices in world markets. Some international commodity agreements explicitly indicate when producers should apply such restraints. Export quotas are also often applied in orderly marketing agreements and voluntary restraint agreements, to promote domestic processing of raw materials in countries that produce them.

Export Restraints. Quantitative restrictions imposed by exporting countries to limit exports to specified foreign markets, usually pursuant to a formal or informal agreement concluded at the request of the importing countries.

Export Subsidies. Government payments or other financially quantifiable benefits provided to domestic producers or exporters contingent on the export of their goods or services. GATT Article XVI recognizes that subsidies in general, and especially export subsidies, distort normal commercial activities and hinder the achievement of GATT objectives. An Agreement on Subsidies and Countervailing Duties negotiated during the Tokyo Round strengthened the GATT rules on export subsidies and provided for an outright prohibition of export subsidies by developed countries for manufactured and semi-manufactured products. The Agreement also established a special committee, serviced by signatories. Under certain conditions, the Agreement allows developing countries to use export subsidies on manufactured and semi-manufactured products, and on primary products as well, provided that the subsidies do not result in more than an equitable share of world exports of the product for the country.

Export Trading Company. A corporation or other business unit organized and operated principally for the purpose of exporting goods and services, or of providing export-related services to other companies. The Export Trading Company Act of 1982 exempts authorized trading companies from certain provisions of U.S. anti-trust laws.

Fair Trade. Fair trade has two definitions. The first is the concept that all nations should operate under the same set of international trade and investment rules; i.e. a common commercial code. The second definition occurs when one nation unilaterally imposes or threatens reciprocal action on the businesses of another nation which have caused a distortion of the international trade and investment markets with whom the first nation could not get agreement. The unilateral implications of "fair trade" actions are protectionist and are often said to "level the playing field."

Free Trade. This is a theoretical concept that assumes international trade should be guided by the "invisible hand" of the market, unhampered by government measures such as tariffs or non-tariff barriers. Often attributed to Adam Smith, an eighteenth-century economist, this utopian idea implies no regulation by governments. Those who espouse it believe that market forces by themselves determine the outcome of business success. Most practical business managers view the term "free trade" simply as a goal.

Realistic thinkers understand that pure *laissez faire* cross-border business activity is unattainable. They see the objective of trade liberalization to achieve "freer trade" because it is generally recognized among trade policy officials that some restrictions on trade are likely to remain in effect for the foreseeable future.

Free Trade Area. A group of two or more countries that have eliminated tariff and most non-tariff barriers affecting trade among themselves, while each participating country applies its own independent schedule of tariffs to imports from countries that are not members. The best-known example is the European Free Trade Association (EFTA)—and the free trade area for manufactured goods that has been created through the trade agreements that have been concluded between the European Community and the individual EFTA countries. GATT Article XXIV spells out the meaning of a free trade area in GATT and specifies the applicability of other GATT provisions to free trade areas.

Free Zone. An area within a country (a seaport, airport, warehouse or any designated area) regarded as being outside its customs territory. Importers may, therefore, bring goods of foreign origin into such an area without paying customs duties and taxes, pending their eventual processing, transhipment or re-exportation. Free zones were numerous and prosperous during an earlier period when tariffs were high. Some still exist in capital cities, transport junctions and major seaports, but their number and prominence have declined as tariffs have fallen in recent years. Free zones may also be known as "free ports," "free warehouses," and "foreign trade zones."

General Agreement on Tariffs and Trade (GATT). A multilateral trade agreement aimed at expanding international trade as a means of raising world welfare. GATT rules reduce uncertainty in connection with commercial transactions across national borders. Ninety-two countries accounting for approximately 80 percent of world trade are Contracting Parties to GATT, and some 30 additional countries associated with it benefit from the application of its provisions to their trade. The designation "GATT" also refers to the organization headquartered in Geneva through which the General Agreement is enforced. This organization provides a framework within which international negotiations—known as "rounds"–are conducted to lower tariffs and other barriers to trade, and a consultative mechanism that may be invoked by governments seeking to protect their trade interests. The GATT was signed in 1947, as an interim agreement. It has been internationally recognized as the key international institution concerned with international trade negotiations since it became clear that the U.S. would not ratify the Havana Charter of 1948, which would have created an International Trade Organization (ITO) as a specialized agency of the United Nations system, similar to the International Monetary Fund and the World Bank. The Interim Commission of the ITO (ICITO), which was established to facilitate the creation of the ITO, subsequently became the GATT Secretariat. The cornerstone of the GATT is the Most-Favored-Nation clause (Article I of the General Agreement). For the United States, the GATT came into existence as an executive agreement, which, under the U.S. Constitution, does not require Senate ratification. Part Four of the General Agreement (Articles XXXVI, XXXVII, and XXXVIII), adopted in 1965, contains explicit commitments to ensure appropriate recognition of the development needs of developing country contracting parties.

Generalized System of Preferences (GSP). A concept developed within UNCTAD to encourage the expansion of manufactured and semi-manufactured exports from developing countries by making goods more competitive in developed-country markets through tariff preferences. The GSP reflects international agreement, negotiated at

UNCTAD-II in New Delhi in 1968, that a temporary and non-reciprocal grant of preferences by developed countries to developing countries would be equitable and, in the long term, mutually beneficial.

Global Business. This is a private for profit organization that has a worldwide point of view and makes no distinction between domestic and international business. In practical terms it may favor one market region over another, but that is probably a result of early growth— emerging from the imprint of its founding country or more probably because of some tax or investment advantage. A global viewpoint eventually invades every business decision that affects the bottom line. Leaders are selected for the organization because of their internationalization and experience. Products and raw materials are marketed and sourced on a worldwide basis and staff have global responsibilities.

Global Business System. This is the overarching support system that harmonizes business methods, rules, and processes which permit greater flows of wealth across borders. It is a growing movement toward a linkage of the economies of one nation to that of others. This system overlays nation-states and their national economies. National borders do not always coincide with economic borders.

All nations have interstate controls; however, the laws, regulations, procedures and practices vary among the states, often making it difficult for businesses to operate on a global basis. Interstate controls cause conflict when they restrain free trade and investment to the extent that there are major distortions. This leads toward protectionism, depression, and war.

Globalism. Globalism has many meanings. First, it is used in the sense of a movement or a trend, something in motion. Some say "the world is getting smaller." Another use of the term has to do with businesses that view their market in a global context as opposed to a national or domestic sense. Finally, there is its use as it relates to commonality or standardization of production practices, products, and services across many different countries.

Government Procurement Policies and Practices. The means and mechanisms through which official government agencies purchase goods and services. Government procurement policies and practices are non-tariff barriers to trade, if they discriminate in favor of domestic suppliers when competitive imported goods are cheaper or of better quality. Most governments traditionally award such contracts on the basis of bids solicited from selected domestic suppliers, or through private negotiations with suppliers that involve little, if any, competition. Other countries, including the United States, gave domestic suppliers a specified preferential margin, as compared with foreign suppliers. The Government Procurement Code negotiated during the

Tokyo Round sought to reduce, if not eliminate, the "buy national" bias underlying such practices by improving transparency and equity in national procurement practices and by ensuring effective recourse to dispute settlement procedures. The Code became effective January 1 1981.

Graduation. The presumption that individual developing countries are capable of assuming greater responsibilities and obligations in the international community—within GATT or the World Bank, for example—as their economics advance, through industrialization, export development, and rising living standards. In this sense, graduation implies that donor countries may remove the more advanced developing countries from eligibility for all or some products under the generalized system of preferences. Within the World Bank, graduation moves a country from dependence on concessional grants to non-concessional loans from international financial institutions and private banks.

Harmonization. This is the process of defining in peaceful, cooperative negotiations a common set of rules and procedures so that international trade and investment can be progressive and without conflict.

Import Substitution. An attempt by a country to reduce imports (and hence foreign exchange expenditures) by encouraging the development of domestic industries.

Incentives. For purposes of explanation, incentives are the various laws and rules, exceptions to laws and rules, and financial "carrots" offered by governments to stimulate or create global business and trade. These schemes are designed to encourage foreign businesses to operate in a given country for purposes of economic development and growth.

Industrial Policy. Encompasses traditional government policies intended to provide a favorable economic climate for the development of industry in general or specific industrial sectors. Instruments of industrial policy may include tax incentives to promote investments or exports, direct or indirect subsidies, special financing arrangements, protection against foreign competition, worker training programs, regional development programs, assistance for research and development, and measures to help small business firms. Historically, the term industrial policy has been associated with at least some degree of centralized economic planning or indicative planning, but this connotation is not always intended by its contemporary advocates.

Infant Industry Argument. This is the view that "temporary protection" for a new industry or firm in a particular country through tariff and non-tariff barriers to imports can help it to become established and eventually competitive in world markets. Historically, new industries that are soundly based and efficiently operated have experienced declining costs as output expands and production experience is acquired. However, industries that have been established and operated with heavy dependence on direct or indirect government subsidies have sometimes found it difficult to relinquish that support. The rationale underlying the generalized system of preferences is comparable to that of the infant industry argument.

Intellectual Property. Ownership conferring the right to possess, use, or dispose of products created by human ingenuity, including patents, trademarks and copyrights.

Interdependence. This is the notion that individual businesses, products, and national economies are no longer independent in their operations but are reliant to some extent on the commingling of the economies, business and products of other nations.

International Monetary Fund (IMF). An international financial institution proposed at the 1944 Bretton Woods Conference and established in 1946 that seeks to stabilize the international monetary system as a sound basis for the orderly expansion of international trade. Specifically, among other things, the Fund monitors exchange rate policies of member countries, lends them foreign exchange resources to support their adjustment policies when they experience balance of payments difficulties, and provides them financial assistance through a special "compensatory financing facility" when they experience temporary shortfalls in commodity export earnings.

International Trade Administration (ITA). The trade unit of the U.S. Department of Commerce, ITA carries out the U.S. Government's non-agricultural foreign trade activities. It encourages and promotes U.S. exports of manufactured goods, administers U.S. statutes and agreements dealing with foreign trade, and advises on U.S. international trade and commercial policy.

Interstate Controls. These are the laws, regulations, procedures, and practices *between* nations or economic unions of nations that inhibit or stimulate "free trade". Some controls are *barriers* which cause significant distortions to free trade while at the same time others are stimulants in the form of *incentives*. Thus controls may be visualized as driving economic growth. All sovereign nations, to some extent, control the flow of goods, thought, services, funds, freedom of movement, etc. across their borders. Not all barriers are bad; not all stimulants are good. For instance public health conditions in one nation may dictate certain barriers to free trade that may differ from another.

Investment Performance Requirements. Special conditions imposed on direct foreign investment by recipient governments, sometimes requiring commitments to export a certain percentage of the output, to purchase given supplies locally, or to ensure the employment of a specified percentage of local labor and management.

Joint Venture. A form of business partnership involving joint management and the sharing of risks and profits, as between enterprises based in different countries. If joint ownership of capital is involved the partnership is known as an equity joint venture.

Least-Developed Countries (LDCs). Some 36 of the world's poorest countries, considered by the United Nations to be the least developed of the less-developed countries. Most of them are small in terms of area and population, and some are land-locked or small island countries. They are generally characterized by low percapita incomes, literacy levels, and medical standards; subsistence agriculture; and a lack of exploitable minerals and competitive industries. Many suffer from aridity, floods, hurricanes, and excessive animal and plant pests, and most are situated in the zone 10 to 30 degrees north latitude. These countries have little prospect of rapid economic development in the foreseeable future and are likely to remain heavily dependent upon official development assistance for many years. Most are in Africa, but a few, such as Bangladesh, Afghanistan, Laos, and Nepal, are in Asia. Haiti is the only country in the Western Hemisphere classified by the United Nations as "least developed." See "developing countries."

Liberal. When referring to trade policy, "liberal" usually means relatively free of import controls or restraints and/or a preference for reducing existing barriers to trade, often contrasted with the protectionist preference for retaining or raising selected barries to imports.

Mixed Credits. Exceptionally liberal financing terms for an export sale, ostensibly provided for a foreign aid purpose.

Mercantilism. A prominent economic philosophy in the sixteenth and seventeenth centuries that equated the accumulation and possession of gold and other international monetary assets, such as foreign currency reserves, with national wealth. Although this point of view is generally discredited among twentieth-century economists and trade policy experts, some contemporary politicians still favor policies designated to create trade "surpluses," such as import substitution and tariff protection for domestic industries, as essential to national economic strength.

Most favored nation Treatment (MFN). The policy of non-discrimination in trade policy that provides to all trading partners the same customs and tariff treatment given to the so-called "most-favored-nation." This fundamental principle was a feature of U.S. trade policy as early as 1778. Since 1923 the United States has incorporated an "unconditional" most-favored-nation clause in its trade agreements, binding the contracting governments to confer upon each other all the most favorable trade concessions that either may grant to any other country subsequent to the signing of the agreement. The United States now applies this provision to its trade with all of its trading partners except for those specifically excluded by law. The MFN principle has also provided the foundation of the world trading system since the end of World War II. All contracting parties to GATT apply MFN treatment to one another under Article I of GATT.

Multi-Fiber Arrangement Regarding International Trade in Textiles (MFA). An international compact under GATT that allows and importing signatory country to apply quantitative restrictions on textiles imports when it considers them necessary to prevent market disruption. The MFA provides a framework for regulating international trade in textiles and apparel with the objectives of achieving "orderly marketing" of such products, and of avoiding "market disruption" in importing countries. It provides a basis on which major importers, such as the United States and the European Community, may negotiate bilateral agreements or, if necessary, impose restraints on imports from low-wage producing countries. It provides, among other things, standards for determining market disruption, minimum levels of import restraints, and equal growth of imports. Since an importing country may impose such quotas unilaterally to restrict rapidly rising textiles imports, many important textiles-exporting countries consider it advantageous to enter into bilateral agreements with the principal textile-importing countries. The MFA went into effect on January 1 1974, was renewed in December 1977, in December 1981, and again in July 1986, for five years. It succeeded the Long-term Agreement on International Trade in Cotton Textiles ("The LTA"), which had been in effect since 1962. Whereas the LTA applied only to cotton textiles, the MFA now applies to wool, man-made (synthetic) fiber, silk blend and other vegetable fiber textiles and apparel.

Multilateral Agreement. An international contract involving three or more parties. For example, GATT has been, since its establishment in 1947, seeking to promote trade liberalization through multilateral negotiations.

Multilateral Trade Negotiations (MTN). Seven rounds of "Multilateral Trade Negotiations" have been held under the auspices of GATT since 1947. Each round represented a discrete and lengthy series of interacting bargaining sessions among the participating contracting parties in search of mutually beneficial agreements for the reduction of barriers to world trade. The agreements ultimately reached at the conclusion of each round became new GATT commitments and thus amounted to an important step in the evolution of the world trading system.

Nationalism. The emotions of nationalism conflict with business profits at the borders of nation-states. In order to influence the economic destiny of their state, governments develop interstate controls that give and take away as conditions change.

National Economy. The national economy is that which is measured within the boundaries of a sovereign nation.

Nations. These are clusters of people gathered within a frontier. States are also nations. A nation is an ethnic or social entity.

Nation-states. When nations are combined they are called nation-states and are basically the people within a sovereign government of a territory and economy. Sovereignty is the essential ingredient of *statehood*.

Nationalism. This is the emotionalism that bonds people to the territory called the nation. Nationalism is also a cultural phenomena exalting loyalty, devotion, and duty to ethnic and tribal groups as well as territory. In the words of Jan Pen, noted Dutch economist, "nationalism at best is poetic nonsense and at worst an invitation to murder. Nationalism leads to protectionism, the choking off of imports." Of course, not all nations are equal; therefore, welfare or economic development is an implied reason for interstate control of business activity.

Newly Industrializing Countries (NICs). Relatively advanced developing countries whose industrial production and exports have grown rapidly in recent years. Examples include Brazil, Hong Kong, Korea, Mexico, Singapore and Taiwan.

Non-Market Economy (NME). A national economy or a country in which the government seeks to determine economic activity largely through a mechanism of central planning, as in the Soviet Union, in contrast to a market economy that depends heavily upon market forces to allocate productive resources. In a "non-market" economy, production targets, prices, costs, investment allocations, raw materials, labor, international trade, and most other economic aggregates are manipulated within a national economic plan drawn up by a central planning authority, and hence the public sector makes the major decisions affecting demand and supply within the national economy.

Non-Tariff Barriers (NTBs). Government measures other than tariffs that restrict imports. Such measures have become relatively more conspicuous impediments to trade as tariffs have been reduced during the period since World War II.

Orderly Marketing Agreements (OMAs). International agreements negotiated between two or more governments, in which the trading partners agree to restrain the growth of trade in specified "sensitive" products, usually through the imposition of import quotas. Orderly

Marketing Agreements are intended to ensure that future trade increases will not disrupt, threaten or impair competitive industries or their workers in importing countries.

Organization for Economic Cooperation and Development (OECD). An organization based in Paris with a membership of the 24 developed countries. Their basic aims are: to achieve the highest sustainable economic growth and employment while maintaining financial stability; and to contribute to sound economic expansion worldwide and to the expansion of world trade on a multilateral, non-discriminatory basis. The OECD succeeded the Organization for European Economic Corporation (OEEC) in 1961, after the post-World War II economic reconstruction of Europe had been largely accomplished.

Organization of Petroleum Exporting Countries (OPEC). A cartel comprising 13 leading oil producing countries that seek to coordinate oil production and pricing policies.

Paris Club. A popular designation for meetings between representatives of a developing country that wishes to renegotiate its "official" debt (normally excluding debts owned by and to the private sector without official guarantees) and representatives of the relevant creditor governments and international institutions. Such meetings normally take place at the initiative of a debtor country that wishes to consolidate all or part of its debt-service payments falling due over a specified period. The meetings are traditionally chaired by a senior official of the French Treasury Department. Comparable meetings occasionally take place in London and in New York for countries that wish to renegotiate repayment terms for their debts to private banks. Such meetings are sometimes called "creditors clubs."

Par Value. The official fixed exchange rate between two currencies or between a currency and a specific weight of gold or a basket of currencies.

Peril Point. A hypothetical limit beyond which a reduction in tariff protection would cause injury to a domestic industry.

Protectionism. The deliberate use or encouragement of restrictions on imports to enable inefficient domestic producers to compete successfully with foreign producers.

Quantitative Restrictions (QRs). Explicit limits, or quotas, on the physical amounts of particular commodities that can be imported or exported during a specific time period, usually measured by volume but sometimes by value. The quota may be applied on a "selective" basis, with varying limits set according to the country of origin, or on a quantitative global basis that only specifies the total limit and thus tends to benefit more efficient suppliers. Quotas are frequently administered through a system of licensing. GATT Article XI generally prohibits the use of quantitative restrictions, except under conditions specified by other GATT articles; Article XIX permits quotas to safeguard certain industries from damage by rapidly rising imports; Articles XII and XVIII provide that quotas may be imposed for balance of payments reasons under circumstances laid out in Article XV; Article XX permits special measures to apply to public health, gold stocks, items of archaeological or historic interest, and several other categories of goods; and Article XXI recognizes the overriding importance of national security. Article XII provides that quantitative restrictions, whenever applied, should be non-discriminatory.

Reciprocity. The practice by which governments extend similar concessions to each other, as when one government lowers its tariffs or other barriers impeding its imports in exchange for equivalent concessions from a trading partner on barriers affecting its exports (a "balance of concessions"). Reciprocity has traditionally been a principal objective of negotiators in GATT "rounds." Reciprocity is also defined as "mutuality of benefits," "quid pro quo," and "equivalence" of advantages. GATT Part IV (especially GATT Article XXXVI) and the "Enabling Clause" of the Tokyo Round "Framework Agreement" exempt developing countries from the rigorous application of reciprocity in their negotiations with developed countries.

Retaliation. Action taken by a country to restrain its imports from a country that has increased a tariff or imposed other measures that adversely affects its exports in a manner inconsistent with GATT. The GATT, in certain circumstances, permits such reprisal, although this has very rarely been practiced. The value of trade affected by such retaliatory measures should, in theory, approximately equal the value affected by the initial import restriction.

Round of Trade Negotiations. A cycle of multilateral trade negotiations under the aegis of GATT, culminating in simultaneous trade agreements among participating countries to reduce tariff and non-tariff barriers to trade. Seven "rounds" have been completed thus far: Geneva, 1947–48; Annecy, France, 1949; Torquay, England, 1950–51; Geneva, 1956; Geneva, 1960–62 (the Dillon Round); Geneva, 1963–67 (the Kennedy Round); Geneva, 1973–79 (the Tokyo Round), and Uruguay Round 1986–1993.

Services. Economic activities—such as transportation, banking, insurance, tourism, space launching telecommunications, advertising, entertainment, data processing, consulting and the licensing of intellectual property–that are usually of an intangible character and often consumed as they are produced. Service industries have become increasingly important since the 1920s. Services now account for more than two-thirds of the economic activity of the United States and about 25 percent of world trade. Traditional GATT rules have not applied to trade in services.

Sovereignty. This is the notion of freedom from external control and that governing is accomplished within small pieces of specific territories of earth called *states*. The characteristics of states vary. Some are kingdoms, some are religion specific, all have politics and boundaries, but their economics seem to vary widely. The political borders of these states may serve as barriers to the free movement of people, goods, services, and capital.

Special Drawing Rights (SDRs). Created in 1969 by the International Monetary Fund as a supplemental international monetary reserve asset. SDRs are available to governments through the Fund and may be used in transactions between the Fund and member governments. IMF member countries have agreed to regard SDRs as complementary to gold and reserve currencies in settling their international accounts. The unit value of an SDR reflects the foreign exchange value of a "basket" of currencies of several major trading countries (the U.S. dollar, the German mark, the French franc, the Japanese yen, and the British pound). The SDR has become the unit of account used by the Fund and several national currencies are pegged to it. Some commercial banks accept deposits denominated in SDRs (although they are unofficial and not the same units transacted among governments and the fund).

State Trading Nations. Countries such as the Soviet Union, the People's Republic of China, and nations of Eastern Europe that rely heavily on government entities, instead of the private sector, to conduct trade with other countries. Some of these countries, (e.g. Czechoslovakia and Cuba) have long been contracting parties to GATT, whereas others (e.g., Poland, Hungary and Romania) became contracting parties later under special Protocols of Accession. The different terms and conditions under which these countries acceded to GATT were designed in each case to ensure steady expansion of the countries' trade with other GATT countries, taking into account the relative insignificance of tariffs on imports into state trading nations.

Subsidy. An economic benefit granted by a government to producers of goods, often to strength their competitive position. The subsidy may be direct (a cash grant) or indirect (low-interest export credits guaranteed by a government agency, for example).

Tariff. A duty (or tax) levied upon goods transported from one customs area to another. Tariffs raise the prices of imported goods, thus making them less competitive within the market of the importing country.

After seven "rounds" of GATT trade negotiations that focused heavily on tariff reductions, tariffs are less important measures of protection than they used to be. The term "tariff" often refers to a comprehensive list or "schedule" of merchandise with the rate of duty to be paid to the government for importing products listed.

Terms of Trade. The volume of exports that can be traded for a given volume of imports. Changes in the terms of trade are generally measured by comparing changes in the ratio of export prices to import prices. The terms of trade are considered to have improved when a given volume of exports can be exchanged for a larger volume of imports. Some economists have discerned an overall deteriorating trend in this ratio for developing countries as a whole. Other economists maintain that whereas the terms of trade may have become less favorable for certain countries during certain periods–and even for all developing countries during some periods–the same terms of trade have improved for other developing countries in the same periods and perhaps for most developing countries during other periods.

Tied Loan. A loan made by a government agency that requires a foreign borrower to spend the proceeds in the lender's country.

Trade Policy Committee (TPC). A senior inter-agency committee of the U.S. Government, chaired by the U.S. Trade Representative, that provides broad guidance to the President on trade policy issues. Members include the Secretaries of Commerce, State, Treasury, Agriculture, and Labor.

Trade Representatives. A cabinet-level official with the rank of Ambassador who is the principal adviser to the government on international trade policy. Trade representatives are concerned with the expansion of exports, participation in GATT, commodity issues, East-West and North-South trade, and direct investment related to trade.

Transfer of Technology. The movement of modern or scientific methods of production or distribution from one enterprise, institution or country to another, as through foreign investment, international trade licensing of patent rights, technical assistance or training.

Transparency. Visibility and clarity of laws and regulations. Some of the codes of conduct negotiated during the Tokyo Round sought to increase the transparency of non-tariff barriers that impede trade.

Trigger Price Mechanism (TPM). A system for monitoring imported goods to identify imports that are possibly being "dumped" in a country or subsidized by the governments of exporting countries. The minimum price under this system is based on the estimated landed cost at a port of entry of steel produced by the world's most efficient producers.

Imported steel entering below that price may "trigger" formal anti-dumping investigations by the government.

Turnkey Contract. A contract under which the contractor assumes responsibility to the client for constructing productive instalations and ensuring that they operate effectively before turning them over to the client. By centering responsibility for the contributions of all participants in the project in his own hands, the contractor is often able to arrange more favorable financing terms than the client could. The responsibility of the contractor ends when the completed installation is handed over to the client.

Unfair Trade Practices. Unusual government support to firms—such as export subsidies—or certain anti-competitive practices by firms themselves—such as dumping, boycotts or discriminatory shipping arrangements—that result in competitive advantages for the benefiting firms in international trade.

United Nations Conference on Trade and Development (UNCTAD). A subsidiary organ of the United States General Assembly that seeks to focus international attention on economic measures that might accelerate Third World development. The Conference was first convened (UNCTAD-I) in Geneva in 1964.

Valuation. The appraisal of the worth of imported goods by customs officials for the purpose of determining the amount of duty payable in the importing country. The GATT Customs Valuation Code obligates governments that sign it to use the "transaction value" of imported goods—or the price actually paid or payable for them—as the principal basis for valuing the goods for customs purposes.

Value-Added Tax (VAT). An indirect tax on consumption that is levied at each discrete point in the chain of production and distribution, from the raw material stage to final consumption. Each processor or merchant pays a tax proportional to the amount by which he increases the value of the goods he purchases for resale after making his own contribution. The value-added tax is imposed throughout the European Community and EFTA countries, but the tax rates have not been harmonized among those countries.

Voluntary Restraint Agreements (VRAs). Informal arrangements through which exporters voluntarily restrain certain exports, usually through export quotas, to avoid economic dislocation in an importing country, and to avert the possible imposition of mandatory import restrictions. Such arrangements do not normally entail "compensation" for the exporting country.

World Bank. The International Bank for Reconstruction and Development (IBRD), commonly referred to as the World Bank, is an intergovernmental financial institution located in Washington, D.C. Its objectives are to help raise productivity and incomes and reduce poverty in developing countries. It was established in December 1945 on the basis of a plan developed at the Bretton Woods Conference of 1944. The Bank loans financial resources to creditworthy developing countries. It raises most of its funds by selling bonds in the world's major capital markets. Its bonds have, over the years, earned a quality rating enjoyed only by sound governments and leading corporations. Projects supported by the World Bank normally receive high priority within recipient governments and are usually well planned and supervised. The World Bank earns a profit, which is plowed back into its capital.

World Intellectual Property Organization (WIPO). A specialized agency of the United Nations system that seeks to promote international co-operation in the protection of intellectual property. WIPO administers the International Union for the Protection of Industrial Property (the "Paris Union"), which was founded in 1883 to reduce discrimination in national patent practices, the International Union for the Protection of Literary and Artistic Works (the "Bern Union"), which was founded in 1886 to provide analogous functions with respect to copyrights, and other treaties, conventions and agreements concerned with intellectual property.

World Trade Organization (WTO). The WTO supersedes the General Agreement on Tariffs and Trade (GATT) but is expanded to include bodies governing new issue areas such as intellectual property and trade in services. The objective of the WTO is to promote the use of agreed multilateral rules and disciplines and limit the resort to unilateral measures for resolution of trade conflicts. The supreme body is a Ministeria Conference which meets at least every two years. The General Council implements ministerial directives and oversees the running of the dispute settlement body and the trade policy review mechanism, which periodically examines the policies of individual contracting parties.

Appendix C
Notes for Chapter One

Technical note

The study uses four types of conversion rates: market exchange rates (MERS) as published by the International Monetary Fund, purchasing power parity (PPPs) estimates from Penn World Tables, World Bank Atlas (WA) conversion rates used by the World Bank, and price adjusted rates of exchange (PAREs) developed by the Statistical Division of the United Nations Secretariat.

Alternative measures of gross world product and its distribution

Among the most important indicators of global development trends are those relating to the growth of gross world product (GWP) and its distribution among countries and regions. Their central importance lies in the fact that they form the basis on which assessments of recent world economic performance are made, and consequently they affect discussions on the current economic situation and the immediate out-look for economic growth in all countries and regions. In influencing expectations about the likely course of world and national economic activity, these indicators are key inputs into discussions of important macroeconomic problems, such as inflation, unemployment and balance of payments positions. Estimates of gross world product and its distribution by country, and estimates of percapita income, also underlie the distribution of concessional assistance and the implemen-tation of measures undertaken to promote development in the world's poorest countries. Finally, these estimates are used to evaluate the probable impact of alternative national and international policy mea-sures on the short-, medium- and long-term possibilities for world growth and distribution and hence affect the debate about appropriate policies for overcoming present world economic problems and fostering more balanced and equitable world economic development.

For these reasons the question of the meaning and reliability of indicators of world economic activity and country contributions to it is a particularly important one. This note presents some alternative estimates of gross world product and its distribution by country for the period 1970–1991 based on a recent study by the United Nations Statistical Division. That study assessed changes in the level and distribution of gross domestic product (GDP) of 178 countries during the period 1970–1989 with the use of alternative conversion factors when weighting each country's domestic economic activity as it is entered into a composite world total.

The present note updates the previous study by incorporating more recent data for 183 countries. Given the diversity and complexity of economic activity carried out at the national level, and given known areas of statistical weakness, summary measurements of domestic economic activity are not perfect and are subject to revision over the course of time. Notwithstanding these deficiencies it is generally recognized that for most countries the reporting system for the national accounts, which is based on the standard concepts of the System of National Accounts, is sufficiently accurate when dealing with distribution and changes over time. While perhaps less accurate when measuring levels, the picture presented of the national economic landscape and changes in its profile over time do reflect actual changes taking place in the country.

Alternative methods of converting local currency data to a common currency

One limitation in presenting estimates of the distribution and level of gross world product is that market exchange rates used to translate national currency data into any one common currency do not provide reliable and stable estimates of the relative purchasing power of national currencies. Even when determined directly by the market, exchange rates reflect only the recent prices of internationally traded products and services and are frequently affected. The other kinds of international transactions, such as foreign investment and loans, transfers of incomes and remittances, interest rate movements, expectations in financial markets and other factors, may also cause large short-term fluctuations in exchange rates, even when no real underlying change in economic circumstances has occurred. Significant short-term drain on market exchange rates from long-term averages and large fluctuations in their relative values in the short term reduce their usefulness as conversion factors when estimating levels of world output and its distribution. This is due to marked year-to-year variations in exchange rate relationships leading to correspondingly large variations in the distribution and estimated value of gross world product.

Moreover, when comparing gross product between countries, market exchange rate conversions of country GDPs to a common currency, such as the United States dollar, may understate the dollar value of output produced in low-income economies relative to that produced in high-income economies because of differences in the size of the tradable and non-tradable sectors. As a result, they might misrepresent the actual value of output produced when aggregating individual country estimates of domestic product into regional and world totals. Studies undertaken as part of the United Nations International Comparison Project (ICP) have shown that in low percapita GDP countries, the market exchange rate may understate purchasing power parity by a factor of three or more. As such, there is a tendency for the volume of goods and services produced in developing countries to be understated relative to that produced in economically more developed countries, and for the share of the developing countries in the world total to be correspondingly underestimated. Consequently, estimates of world economic growth are affected because the time-series for the growth of GDP in the developing countries enters with a smaller weight in the composite world series when using market exchange rates.

In response to the need for factory comparisons of output level products in different countries, the present analysis makes use of a comprehensive national accounts database for 183 individual countries and areas which has been compiled on the basis of submissions by national statistical offices to the annual questionnaire on national accounts issued jointly by the United Nations and the Organization for Economic Cooperation and Development.

For such comparison conversion rates have been used to translate the national currency estimates of GDP into a common currency: market exchange rates (MERs), published by the International Monetary fund; price-adjusted rates of exchange (PAREs) developed by the United Nations Statistical Division; World Bank Atlas (WA) conversion rates, used by the World Bank; and purchasing power parity (PPP) estimates from the Penn World Tables data bank, developed by the University of Pennsylvania. These alternative methods of weighting individual country GDPs yield alternative estimates of gross world product.

Market Exchange Rates

MERs are the conversion factors most frequently used to translate national currency estimates of gross domestic product to a common unit of account. "The rates used in the study are annual averages communicated to the International Monetary Fund by the monetary authority of each member country and agreed to by the Fund." As used by the IMF, the term "market rate" refers to the principal exchange rate used for the majority of current transactions. Where market rates were not available from the IMF conversion factors, use was made of the averages of United Nations operational rates of exchange, which were primarily established for accounting purposes and which are applied to all official transactions of the United Nations with those countries. The rates may take the form of official, commercial or tourist rates of exchange. Applying the annual market exchange rates for each country to its corresponding annual current price national currency estimates for GDP, yields 183 country time-series of nominal United States dollar GDP, which are then aggregated into world and regional totals for the period 1970–1991. This estimate for gross world product corresponds broadly to the level of world output measured at market prices and exchange rates.

Price Adjusted Rates of Exchange

The purpose of the PARE method is to derive a conversion rate for analytical use which reflect with sufficient accuracy the relative price changes over time. The Statistical Division developed the PARE methodology principally for administrative application by United Nations organs on an *ad hoc* basis, with the original intention of applying exchange rate adjustments to a limited number of countries beset by severe inflation and changes in domestic prices that diverge considerably from exchange rate movements. PARE rates are obtained by extrapolating the average exchange rate of a fixed "representative" base year or base period by price movements based on GDP-implicit price deflators.

The application of the PARE methodology eliminates most of the distorting effects mentioned when discussing market exchange rates and other conversion rates. PARE rates are likewise applicable to a larger number of transactions as its use of GDP-implicit price deflators reflects not only internationally tradable goods and services, as do MERs, but also all goods and services produced in the economy.

Two types of price-adjusted exchange rates have been developed by the Statistical Division. Absolute PARE rates are derived by extrapolating the average exchange rates computed over a base period with the use of price indices for each conversion series for each country's gross national product. Prices and period-average aggregating all country data yields a time-series in constant United States dollars which reflects the real increase in world production over time.

Relative PARE rates, on the other hand, adjust the absolute PARE rates for the rate of inflation in the United States. The use of relative PARE rates provides a nominal estimate of a country's output for aggregation into a total for gross world product as it simulates exchange rates that should reflect changes in relative price levels. Using this method, there is no difference between absolute and relative PAREs when computing the distribution of gross world product in any one year. However, only relative PAREs—which reflect nominal GDP levels—will be included in later discussion of total distribution of total and percapita gross world product.

World bank atlas conversion rates

Each annual WA conversion rate is based on a moving average of three conversion rates, each linked to a different year. For any year, the WA rate is calculated as a simple average of the exchange rate of the present year, a PARE rate for the present year using the previous year as a base and a PARE rate for the present year using the exchange rate of two years ago as a base. The method assumes that exchange rates largely adjust themselves to price changes within a period of three years. In cases where the basic methodology yields shifts that do not reflect underlying economic conditions, the World Bank applies different variants of its conversion method. These variants adjust for differences in fiscal years, multiple exchange rates and unrealistic United States dollar conversion factors.

Purchasing power parities

The United Nations International Comparison Project has developed a methodology to enable conversion of national currency output levels into a common unit of measurement. This approach is keyed on purchasing power parity coefficients instead of a set of common prices. The average PPPs applied to the GDP for each country are obtained as weighted averages of weighted price relative to individual baskets of goods and services, using as weights the total expenditures on those goods and services in GDP. Unlike the PARE and Atlas rates, PPPs are not derived from actual exchange rates; they are obtained independent measures based on information from price surveys and represent a common set of international prices reflecting purchasing power parity in the year. This approach provides estimates of gross world product measured in "international dollars" rather than the conventional United States dollars of the exchange rate methods.

The methodology of the ICP has been applied to detailed data for a sample of countries for the years 1970 (16 countries), 1975 (34 countries), 1980 (60 countries) and 1985 (64 countries). Because the number of direct estimates of PPPs is limited in terms of countries and years, the Penn World Tables data bank developed at the University of Pennsylvania has supplemented these direct estimates with information based on less comprehensive price and expenditure surveys, which allow for extending ICP results to other countries. Annual inter-temporal interpolations and extensions to non-benchmark years were performed on the basis of price indices for GDP components of individual countries relative to the corresponding price indices of the United States. Since no information later than the 1990 PPPs was available and coverage of years for some countries was uneven, PPP rates for missing years and 1991 were derived by applying the trend of relative PARE rates based on 1970–1991 to the available levels of PPPs. Application of the annual PPP conversion factors to the current price national currency estimates of GDP for the 149 counties for which relevant data have been estimated and their aggregation provides nominal estimates of gross world product measured at PPPs for each year.

Bibliography

Chapter one

Council for Economic Planning and Development (CEPD) (1990) *World Development Report 1990*; World Bank, Taiwan Statistical Data Book.

Krueger, Anne O. (1983) "The Effects of Trade Strategies on Growth," *Finance and Development*, June, p. 7.

Ohmae, Kenichi (1990), *The Borderless World: Power and Strategy in the Interlinked Economy*, Harper Business, NY.

Trends in International Distribution of Gross World Product, (1993) Special Issue National Accounts Statistics, Serial, No. 18, Department for Economic and Social Information and Policy Analysis, Statistical Division, United Nations, NY.

United Nations (1994) *Handbook of International Trade and Development Strategies, 1976, 1983, 1984 and 1985.*

Chapter three

Nelson, Carl A. (1990), "Educating for Global Business: A Building Block Approach," *Association for Global Business Proceedings*, Vol. 1, p. 121.

Nelson, Carl A. (1990), *Import/Export: How to Get Started in International Trade*, TAB Books, Inc.

Thurow, Lester C. (1990), Speech given at the U.S. Grant Hotel in San Diego, California, Tuesday, November 27.

Chapter four

Arnolds, H. (1996), *Materialwirtschaft und Einkauf*, Vol. 9, p. 32, Wiesbaden.

Bedacht, F. (1995), *Global Sourcing*, Wiesbaden.

Dicken, P. (1986), *Global Shift: Industrial Change in a Turbulent World*, Guilford Press, London.

Dyer, J.H.I. and Ouchi, W.C. (1993), "Japanese-Style Partnerships: Giving Companies a Competitive Edge," Fall, *Sloan Management Review*, p. 35.

Juran, Dr. Joseph M. (1985), *Juaran on Quality Improvement*, Juran Enterprises, Inc., New York, NY.

Menzl, A. (1994), "Global Sourcing," *Thexis*, Vol. 11, p. 22.

Ohno, T. (1993), *The Toyota Production System*, Prod. Press, New York.

Porter, Michael E. (1992), *Competitive Advantage*, Harvard Business School.

Porter, Michael E. (1989), *Global Competition*, Harvard Business School, Boston.

Raia, Ernest (1989), "Better Value, Bigger Profits", *Purchasing*, June 8, p. 18.

Richardson, J. (1993), "Parallel Sourcing and Supplier Performance in the Japanese Automobile Industry," *Strategic Management Journal*, Vol. 141, p. 28.

Rugnetta, Frank (1989), Personal interview with Dr. Carl A. Nelson, Solar Turbines, Inc., Subsidiary of Caterpillar, Inc., May 10.

Suzaki, Kiyoshi (1987), *The New Manufacturing Challenge: Techniques for Continuous Improvement*, The Free Press, NY.

Wildemann, H. (1992), "Entwicklungsstrategien fur Zulieferunternehmen," *ZfB*, Vol. 41, Berlin.

Wildemann, H. (1997), "Produktions- und Zuliefernetzwerke," *Leitfaden zur Einführung europäischer Keiretsu-Systeme*, Vol. 2, Munich.

Wolters, H. (1995), *Modul- und Systembeschaffung in der Automobilindustrie*, Wiesbaden.

Chapter five

Acuff, Frank L. (1993), *How to Negotiate Anything with Anyone Anywhere Around the World*, AMACOM, NY.

Axtell, Roger E. (1985), Editor and Compiler, *Do's and Tabos Around the World: A Guide to International Behavior*, The Parket Pen Company, NY.

Chung, Dr. Sunny (1989), "Here's Help in Understanding International Culture Shock", *Currents*, the Newsletter of United States International University, Vol. 1, San Diego.

Harris, Phillip and Moran, Robert (1982), *Managing Cultural Differences*, Intercultural Press, Inc, Yarmouth, ME.

Jang, Song-Hyon (1985), "The Ten Commandments for doing Business in Korea", *Business Korea*, January, p. 16.

Lowe, Janet (1985), "It's Just a Matter of Manners", *The San Diego Tribune*, June 15, p. c–1.

Nelson, Carl A., Commander U. S. Navy (1971), "Student notes for Cross-cultural Survival", U. S. Navy, Pre-Vietnam duty.

Nelson, Carl A. (1995), *Import/Export: How to Get Started in International Trade*, 2nd Edition, McGraw-Hill, New Yord.

Nelson, Carl A. (1988), *Proctocol for Profit: A Manager's Guide to Competing Worldwide*, International Thomson Business Press, London.

Oberg, Dr. Kalervo (1955), "Culture Shock", *Anthropologist*, Health, Welfare and Housing Division, U.S. A.I.D./Brazil, Vol. 1, p. 38.

San Diego Union (1989), ed., "Time can Reap Japanese Sales", January 21.

Seligman, Scott D. (1983), "A Shirt-sleeve Guide to Chinese Corporate Etiquette", *The Chinese Business Review*, January-February, p. 15.

Chapter six

Mill, John Stuart (1920), *Principles of Political Economy*, (1848) London: Longmans, Green and Co., Book III.

Mum, Thomas (1949), *England's Treasure by Forraign Trade*, Oxford, England: Basil Blackwell & Mott.

Ohlin, Bertil (1952), *Interregional and International Trade*, Cambridge: Harvard University Press.

Rabushka, Alvin (1985), *From Adam Smith to the Wealth of America*, 2nd edition, New Brunswick (USA) and Oxford (UK).

Ricardo, David (1948), *On the Principals of Political Economy and Taxation*, 1817, New York: E.P. Dutton & Co.

Smith, Adam (1937), *An Inquiry into the Nature and Causes of the Wealth of Nations*, 1776, New York: Random House.

Vernon, Raymond (1966), "International Investment and International Trade in the Product Cycle." *Quarterly Journal of Economics* 80, no. 2 (May).

Chapter seven

Committee on the Development of Trade (1985) *Marketing Managment in East-West Trade*, United Nations Economic Commission for Europe, Geneva.

Department of International Economic and Social Affairs (1984), *Crisis or Reform: Breaking the Barriers to Development* (Views and Recommendations of the Committee for Development Planning), United Nations, New York.

Department of International Economic and Social Affairs (1987) *Development Under Siege: Constraints and Opportunities in a Changing Global Economy* (Views and Recommendations of the Committee for Development Planning), United Nations, New York.

Department of International Economic and Social Affairs (1988) *Modelling of World Economic Development*, United Nations, New York.

Domar, E.D. (1947) "Expansion and Employment," *American Economic Review*, XXXVII (March) pp. 34–5.

Harrod, R.F. (1949), *Towards a Dynamic Economics*, London: The Macmillan, Co.

Marx, Karl Heinrich, *Das Kapital*, as explained in A. Giddens (1971), *Capitalism and Modern Social Theory*, Cambridge University Press, London.

Smith, Adam (1937), *An Inquiry into the Nature and Causes of the Wealth of Nations*, 1776, New York: Random House.

Todaro, Michael P. (1998) *Economic Development in the Third World*, 4th Edition, NY: Longman, Inc.

Transforming the World-Economy? (1984) Nine Critical Essays on the New International Economic Order, Ed., The United Nations University, Tokyo.

Uncitral Secretariat (1986) *Uncitral: The United Nations Commission on International Trade Law*, United Nations, New York.

United Nations "Economic Growth Trends and Effect on Government Policies", *United Nations Annual Report*, 1960s-90, 1983, 1984, 1985, 1986, 1987, 1988, 1989.

United Nations (1988) *USSR: New management mechanism in foreign economic relations*, United Nations conference on Trade and Development, New York.

Chapter eight

Ohmae, Kenichi (1990) *The Borderless World: Power and Strategy in the Interlinked Economy*, Harper Business, NY.

Chapter nine

Allende-Vera, Baltasar (1990), *Political Risk Analysis: Review, Issues, and Assessment*, Houston: University of Houston-Downtown.

Boyer, Edward (1983), "How Japan Manages Declining Industries", (Feb. 10), *Fortune Magazine*, NY, p. 118.

The Economist (1978) "The State in the Market," December, London.

Fortune (1991) "The History of an Unlikely Buzzword," September 23, p. 140.

Johnson, Chalmers (1982), *MITI and the Japanese Miracle: The Growth of Industrial Policy*, Stanford: Stanford University Press.

Johnson, Chalmers (1985), "The Institutional Foundations of Japanese Industrial Policy", *California Management Review* 27 (4) (Summer)

Kotobe, Masaaki (1985), "The Roles of Japanese Industrial Policy for Export Success: A Theoretical Perspective", *The Columbia Journal of World Business*, 20 (3) (Fall), New York.

Nelson, Carl A. (1990), "In Search of a New Global Trade Theory", *Association for Global Business Proceedings*, Harrisonburg, Virginia, p. 352.

Nelson, Carl A. (1997), "Economic Development and Political Reality," *The World & I*, June, p. 331.

Neilsen, Richard P. (1982), "Government-Owned Businesses: Market Presence, Advantages, Rationales", *The American Journal of Economics and Sociology*, 41 (1), January.

Neilsen, R.P. (1984) "Industrial Policy: The Case for National Strategies for World Markets", *Long Range Planning*, 17 (5) October.

Neilsen, R.P. (1983), "Should a Country Move Toward International Strategic market Planning?" *California Management Review*, 25 (2) January.

Perkins, Edwin J. (1983), *The World Economy in the Twentieth Century*, Cambridge, Mass: Schenkman Publishing Co.

Rabushka, Alvin (1985), *From Adam Smith to the Wealth of America*, 2nd edition, New Brunswick (USA) and Oxford (UK) Transaction Press.

Tsurumi, Yoshi (1982), "Japan's Challenge to the U.S.: Industrial Policy and Corporate Strategies", (Summer) *Columbia Journal of World Business*, (Summer) p. 33.

Tsurumi, Yoshi (1978), "The Case of Japan: Price Bargaining and Controls on Oil Products", *Journal of Comparative Economics*, Vol. 2, p. 61.

United Nations (1993) *Trends in International Distribution of Gross World Product*, special issue National Accounts Statistics, Series X, No 18, Department for Economic and Social Information and Policy Analysis Statistical Division.

Chapter ten

Abrams, E. and Abrams, F.S. (1975), "Immigration Policy—Who Gets in and Why?" *The Public Interest*, Vol. 38, pp. 3–29.

Bernard, W.S. (1953), Economic effects of immigration, *in: Immigration: An American Dilemma*, edited by Iegier, B.M., Liberty Press, NY, pp. 570.

Business Week (1997) "Job Mobility, American Style," January 27, p. 20.

California State World Trade Commission and the California European Trade and Investment Office (1989) *Europe: 1992, Implications for California Businesses, A Guidebook*, Office of the Government,State of California

Chiswick, B.R. (1988), "Illegal Immigration and Immigration Control," *Journal of Economic Perspectives*, Vol. 1, pp. 101–15.

Commission of the European Communities (1991) "Immigration of Citizens from Third Countries into the Southern Member States of the EEC.

Djajic, S. (1997), "Illegal immigration And Resource Allocation," *International Economic Review*, Vol. 38, No. 1, February, pp. 97–118.

Flagstaff Institute (1990) " Mexico's In-bond Processing Industry, the Maquiladoras", P.O. Box 986, Flagstaff AZ.

French, W.L. (1994), *Human Resources Management*, HM Press, Boston.

Greenhalgh, C. and Mavrotas, J. (1996), "Job Training, New Technology and Labour Turnover," *British Journal of Industrial Relations*, March, pp. 131–51.

Greenwood, M.J. and McDowell, C. (1986), "The Factor Market Consequences of U.S immigration," *Journal of Economic Literature*, Vol. 1, pp. 1738–72.

Harrison, L.E. (1992), "Those Huddled, Unskilled Masses: is Our Immigration Policy Contributing to Our Economic Undoing," *The Washington Post*, June 16.

Horowitz, Rose A (1989) "Soviets Design Incentives for New 'Free Zones'", *The Journal of Commerce*, July 26, p. 36.

International Management (1991) "Mobile Workers May Stay Put," May, pp. 18–19.

Magee, John F., "1992: Moves Americans Must make", *Harvard Business Review*, May–June 1989, p. 41.

Mukherjee, N. (1995), *Gatt-Uruguay Round, Trade in Services and Developing Countries*, Delhi.

Nelson, Carl A. (1985), "Manufacturing in Mexico Using a Maquiladora," *American Import/Export Manager*, September, p. 85.

Training (1997) "The New Job Mobility," pp. 12–13

United States International Trade Commission (1986), *The Impact of Increased United States-Mexico Trade Southwest Border Development*, Report to the Senate Committee on finance on Investigation No. 332–223, November, Under Section 332 of the Tariff Act of 1930, USITC Publication 1915, Washington DC.

United States International Trade Commission (1988) *The Use and Economic Impact of TSUS Items 806.30 and 807*, Report to the Subcommittee on Trade, Committee on Ways and means, U.S. House of Representatives, on Investigation No. 332–244 under section 332 (b) of the Tariff Act of 1930, USITC Publication 2053, January, United States International Trade Commission, Washington DC.

Waldinger, R. and Bailey. T. (1994), "The New Immigrants," in The Changing U.S. Labor Market, (Glnzberg, E. ed.), Russell, Sage, Colorado, p. 144.

The Wall Street Journal (1998) "In India, a Brave New World," March 25.

Chapter eleven

Ballassa, Bela (1979), "The Changing Pattern of Comparative Advantage in Manufacturing Goods," *Review of Economics and Statistics*, May, pp. 259–66.

Chenery, Hollis (1979), *Structural Changes and Development Policy*, Baltimore: Johns Hopkins University Press.

Council for Economic Planning and Development, (1990), *World Development Report 1990; World Bank, Taiwan Statistical Data Book*.

Domar, E.D. (1947), "Expansion and Employment," *American Economic Review*, XXXVII, March, pp. 34–5.

Fortune (1991), "The History of an Unlikely Buzzword," September 23, p. 140.

Friedman, Milton (1968), "The Role of Monetary Policy," *American Economic Review*, March, Vol. 2, p. 32.

Harrod, R.F. (1949), *Towards a Dynamic Economics*, London: The Macmillan, Co.

Heckscher, Eli F. (1919), "Thought of Foreign Trade on the Distribution of Income," *Economisk Ticlskrift*, XXI, p. 63.

Holmes, Kim R., Johnson, Bryan T., and Kirkpatric, Melanie (eds) (1997), *1997 Index of Economic Freedom*, The Heritage Foundation, the Wall Street Journal, Dow Jones & Co., Inc.

Johnson, Chalmers (1982), *MITI and the Japanese Miracle: The Growth of industrial Policy*, Stanford: Stanford University Press.

Johnson, Chalmbers (1985), "The Institutional Foundations of Japanese Industrial Policy", *California Management Review* 27 (4), Summer.

Keynes, John Maynard (1936), *The General Theory of Employment, Interest and Money*, New York: Harcourt, Brace.

Korten, David C. (1995), *When Corporations Rule the World*, Kumarian Press, Hartford, CT.

Kotobe, Masaaki (1985), "The Roles of Japanese Industrial Policy for Export Success: A Theoretical Perspective", the *Columbia Journal of World Business*, 20 (3), Fall, p. 52.

Krueger, Anne O. (1983), "The Effects of Trade Strategies on Growth," *Finance and Development*, June p. 7.

Leone, Robert A. and Bradley, Stephen P. (1981), "Toward an Effective Industrial Policy", *Harvard Business Review*, 59 (6) November/December.

Lindblom,Charles E. (1977), *Politics and Markets: The World's Political-Economic Systems*, New York: Basic Books.

Mill, John S. (1920) *Principles of Political Economy*. London: Longmans, Green and Co., (Originally published in 1848).

Mum, Thomas (1949), *England's Treasure by Forraign Trade*, Oxford, England: Basil Blackwell & Mott.

Neilsen, R.P. (1983), "Should a Country Move Toward International Strategic market Planning?" *California Management Review*, January, 25 (2).

Nelson, Carl A. (1994), *Managing Globally: A Complete Guide to Competing Worldwide*, Irwin, Burr Ridge.

Office of the United States Trade Representative (1987) *The 1987 National Trade Estimate Report on Foreign Trade Barriers*, Department of Agriculture, and Department of Commerce, Washington, DC.

Ohlin, Bertil (1952), *Interregional and International Trade*, Cambridge: Harvard University Press.

Ohmae, Kenichi (1990), *The Borderless World: Power and Strategy in the Interlinked Economy*, Harper Business, NY.

Perkins, Edwin J. (1983), *The World Economy in the Twentieth Century*, Cambridge, Mass: Schenkman Publishing Co.

Rabushka, Alvin (1985), *From Adam Smith to the Wealth of America*, 2nd edition, Transaction Press, New Brunswick (USA) and Oxford (UK).

Ricardo, David (1948), *On the Principles of Political Economy and Taxation*, 1817, New York: E.P. Dutton & Co.

Rostow, W.W. (1960), *The Stages of Economic Growth, A Non-Communist Manifesto*, London: Cambridge University Press.

Smith, Adam (1937), *An Inquiry into the Nature and Causes of the Wealth of Nations*, 1776, New York: Random House.

Superintendent of Documents (1987) *Foreign Trade Barriers*, U.S. Government Printing Office, U.S. Government Printing Office, Washington, DC.

Sweeney, Paul and Dierks, Carsten (1988) *Europe 1992: The Removal of Trade barriers in the Common market in 1992 and the Implications for American Businesses*, a research paper by Texas A&M University, Department of Marketing, College of Business Administration.

Thurow, Lester (1992), *Head to Head: The Coming Economic Battle Among Japan, Europe, and America*, Morrow.

Tsurumi, Yoshi (1982), "Japan's Challenge to the U.S.: Industrial Policy and Corporate Strategies", *Columbia Journal of World Business*, Summer, Vol. 1, p. 99.

Uncitral Secretariat (1986), *Uncitral: The United Nations Commission on International Trade Law*, New York: United Nations.

United Nations (1984), *Handbook of International Trade and Development Statistics*, 1976, 1983, 1984, and 1985; and *Council of Economic Planning and Development, Republic of China, Taiwan Statistical Data Book.*

United Nations Annual Reports (1960–89), "Economic Growth Trends and Effect on Government Policies", 1960s-90, 1983, 1984, 1985, 1986, 1987, 1988, 1989.

United Nations University (1984), *Transforming the World-Economy?* Nine Critical Essays on the New International Economic Order, Ed., The United Nations University, Tokyo.

United Nations Conference on Trade and Development (1988), *USSR: New Management Mechanism in Foreign Economic Relations*, United Nations Conference on Trade and Development, New York.

U.S. Department of Commerce, International Trade Administration, *Foreign Business Practices: Materials on practical aspects of exporting, international licensing and investing*, Superintendent of Documents, GPO, April 1985

Vernon, Raymond (1966), "International Investment and International Trade in the Product Cycle." *Quarterly Journal of Economics* 80, no. 2 (May).

Chapter twelve

Levi, Maurice (1983), *International Finance: Financial Management and the International Economy*, McGraw-Hill, NY.

Nelson, Carl A. (1984), "Countertrade in the PRC", *American Import/Export Manager*, September, p. 26.

Nelson, Carl A. (1984), "Guidelines For Using Countertrade", *American Import/Export Manager*, September, p. 34.

Nelson, Carl A. (1986), "Hot Corner U.S.A., *Chula Vista Chamber of Commerce Perspectives*, July, Vol. 1, 7, p. 1.

United States International Trade Commission (1985) "Assessment of the Effects of Barter and Countertrade Transactions on U.S. Industries", USITC Publication 1766, Washington, DC, October 1985.

Verzariu, Pompiliu, *International Countertrade: A Guide for Managers and Executives*, U.S. Department of Commerce, ITA, Washington, DC, November 1984.

Chapter thirteen

Customs Cooperation Council (1988) *Brief Guide to the Customs Valuation Code*, 2nd edition, Brussels.

Curzon, Gerald (1965), *Multilateral Commercial Policy*, London.

Customs Convention on Containers, (1972), UN/IMCO, NY.

Customs Co-operation Council (1988), In Brief, Brussels.

Customs Cooperation Council (1989) *Introducing The Kyoto Convention: Simplification and Harmonizatio of Customs Procedures Background, Benefits and Procedure for Accession*, Customs Co-operation Council, Brussels.

Customs Tomorrow (1989), Final CCC Report, November, Department of the Treasury, Wash. DC.

General Agreement on Tariffs and Trade (1969), Basic Instruments and Selected Documents, Wash. DC.

Mauer, Jennifer Fron and Smith, Craig S. (1998), "Prozac's maker Confronts China Over Knockoffs," *The Wall Street Journal*, April 15.

Morrison, Ann V. and Layton, Robin (1986), "GATT . . . A Look Back As the Ministerial Meeting Approaches," *Business America*, June 23.

Morrison, Ann V. (1986), "GATT's Seven Rounds of Trade Talks Span More Than Thirty Years," *Business America*, June 23.

Morrison, Ann V. (1986), "Tokyo Round Agreements Set Rules for Nontariff Measures," *Business America*, July 7.

Pen, Jan (1967), *A Primer on International Trade*, New York: Random House.

Searing, Marjory E. (1989), "The Uruguay Round–Up and Running," *Business America*, May 8.

Sek, Lenore (1988), "Trade Negotiations: The Uruguay Round," December 20, CRS Issue Brief, DC.

Sheth, Jagdish and Eshghi, Abdolreza (eds) (1990) *Global Macroeconomic Perspectives*, Southwestern, Texas.

United Nations (1989) *Uruguay Round: Papers on Selected Issues*, United Nations Conference on Trade and Development, United Nations, NY.

U.S. Department of Commerce (1980) *Subsidies and Countervailing Measures*, The Tokyo Round Agreements, Vol. 1, May, U.S. Department of Commerce, Washington DC.

U.S. Department of Commerce (1981) *Government Procurement*, The Tokyo Round Agreements, Vol. 2, July, U.S. Department of Commerce, Washington DC.

U.S. Department of Commerce (1981) *Technical Barriers to Trade*, The Tokyo Round Agreements, Vol. 4, September, U.S. Department of Commerce, Washington DC.

U.S. Department of Commerce (1981) *Trade in civil Aircraft*, The Tokyo Round Agreements, Vol. 3,, August U.S. Department of Commerce, Washington DC.

U.S. Department of Commerce (1982) Anti-dumping Duties, The Tokyo Round Agreements, Vol. 5, December, U.S. Department of Commerce, Washington DC.

U.S. Department of Commerce (1982) Agreement on Import Licensing Procedures, The Tokyo Round Agreements, Vol. 6, November, U.S. Department of Commerce, Washington DC.

U.S. Department of Commerce (1983) Customs Valuation, The Tokyo Round Agreements, Vol. 7, U.S., November, U.S. Department of Commerce, Washington DC.

U.S. Department of Commerce (1988) *Uruguay Round Update*, February, U.S. Department of Commerce, Washington DC.

U.S. Department of Commerce (1988) *Uruguay Round Update*, May, U.S. Department of Commerce, Washington DC.

U.S. Department of Commerce (1988) *Uruguay Round Update*, September, U.S. Department of Commerce, Washington DC.

U.S. Department of Commcerce (1989) *Uruguay Round Update*, January, U.S. Department of Commerce, Washington DC.

U.S. Department of Commerce (1989) *Uruguay Round Update*, May, U.S. Department of Commerce, Washington DC.

U.S. Department of Commerce (1989) *Uruguay Round Update*, September, U.S. Department of Commerce, Washington DC.

U.S. Department of Commerce (1990) *Uruguay Round Update*, February, U.S. Department of Commerce, Washington DC.

U.S. Department of Commerce (1991) *Uruguay Round Update*, February, U.S. Department of Commerce, Washington DC.

Chapter fourteen

Balassa, Bela (1961), *The Theory of Economic Integration*, Richard D. Irwin, Inc., Burr Ridge, Illinois.

Behbehani, Mustafa (1989), "The Gulf Cooperation Council's Intratrade: A Regional Integration Perspective", San Diego: United States International University.

Bureau of Public Affairs (1990) *U.S. Foreign Economic Policies*, September, U.S. Department of State.

Business Amcerica (1993) "EC Single Market Opens to Business," March 8.

Caldwell, Robert J. (1998) "Talking Trade," *The San Diego Union-Tribune*, April 19.

California Chamber of Commerce and California Trade and Commerce Agency (1993) *European Community and Europe: A Legal Guide to Business Development*, California Chamber of Commerce and California Trade and Commerce Agency, Sacremento.

Commission of the European Communities (1992) *A Single Market for Goods*, Commission of the European Communities, Luxembourg.

Commission of The European Communities (1992) *Europe in Ten Lessons*, Commission of the European Communities, Luxembourg.

Commission of the European Communities (1992) *European Union*, Commission of the European Communities, Luxembourg.

Commission of the European Communities (1992) *The European Community 1992 and Beyond*, Commission of the European Communities, Luxembourg.

Commission of the European Communities (1992) *The European Financial Common Market*, Commission of the European Communities, Luxembourg.

Commission of the European Communities (1992) *From Single market to European Union*, Commission of the European Communities, Luxembourg.

Commission of the European Communities (1992) *The Single Market in Action*, Commission of the European Communities, Luxembourg.

Davis, Bob (1998), "Barshefsky and EU Trade Chief Revive Idea of Trans-Atlantic Free-Trade pact," *The Wall Street Journal*, April 20.

Department of Public Information (1986) *Everyone's United Nations*, 10th edition, United Nations, New York.

Department of Public Information (1987) *Basic Facts: about the United Nations*, New York: United Nations.

Department of Public Information (1989) *Charter of the United Nations and Statute of the International Court of Justice*, New York: United Nations.

Garcia, Linda (1992) "Global Standards: Building Blocks for the Future," report for the Office of Technology Assessment, U.S. Congress, Washington DC.

Goldsborough, James O. (1998), "The Value of Free Trade for the Americas, *The San Diego Union-Tribune*, April 20.

Hagigh, Sara E. and Saunders, Mary (1992), "Europe 1992: Preparing for the Europe of Tomorrow," *Business America*, February 24, pp. 6–8 and pp. 30–33.

Marotta, George (1989), "Europe, Inc.", *San Diego Union*, August 20.

Nelson, Carl A. (1985), "Foreign Trade Zones Save For Some", *San Diego Daily Transcript*, July 16, p. 4A.

Office for Official Publications of the European Communities (1992) *The ABC of Community Law*, Office for Official Publications of the European Communities, Luxembourg.

Office for Official Publications of the European Communities (1992) *The European Community as a Publisher, 1992–93*, Office for Official Publications of the European Communities, Luxembourg.

Root, Franklin R. (1990), *International Trade & Investment*, 6th edition, Texas:South-Western Publishing Co.

Roson, Peter, (1980) *The Economics of International Integration*, London: Allen and Unwin.

Saunders, Mary (1993),"Obtaining EC-Wide Certification for Industrial Products," *Business America*, March 8, pp. 28–31.

The Journal of Commerce (1990) "IDB Approves $3.8 Billion for Latin America, Caribbean," Friday December 28.

The San Diego Union (1991) "Bank to Pump Loans into E. Europe," Tuesday, April 16.

Tinbergen, Jan (1965), *International Economic Integration*, Verso Amsterdam, London, New York.

United Nations (1985) *Export Processing Free Zones in Developing Countries: Implications for Trade and Industrialization Policies*, United Nations Conference on Trade and Development, New York.

U.S. Department of Commerce (1989) EC 1992: A commerce Department Analysis of European Community Directives, volume 1, May, International Trade Administration, Washington DC.

U.S. Department of Commcerce (1989) EC 1992: A commerce Department Analysis of European Community Directives, Volume 2, September, International Trade Administration, Washington DC.

U.S. Department of Commerce (1990) EC 1992: A commerce Department Analysis of European Community Directives, Volume 3, March, International Trade Administration, Washington DC.

U.S. Department of Commcerce (1991) "Chemicals and European Community Directives," ITA Document, October 1, U.S. Department of Commerce, Washington DC.

U.S. Department of Commerce (1991) "EC Labor Policy—An Integral Part of 1992," ITA Document, October 1, U.S. Department of Commerce, Washington DC.

U.S. Department of Commerce (1991) "The European Community and Environmental Policy and Regulations," ITA Document, April 1, U.S. Department of Commerce, Washington DC.

U.S. Department of Commerce (1993) "EC Product Standards Under the Internal Market Program," ITA Document, February 10, U.S. Department of Commerce, Washington DC.

Index